# THE BETTER ADMINISTRATION OF
# THE POOR LAW

*CHARITY ORGANISATION SERIES.*

# THE BETTER ADMINISTRATION

## OF

# THE POOR LAW

BY

W. CHANCE

M.A. TRIN. COLL., CAMB.

*Barrister-at-Law, Hon. Sec. Central Poor Law Conferences, and a Guardian of the Poor (Farnham Union)*

"Video meliora proboque:
Deteriora sequor."

Ovid. *Met.* vii. 20.

LONDON
SWAN SONNENSCHEIN & CO.
PATERNOSTER SQUARE
1895

# PREFACE.

This work has been compiled in the hope that it may serve as a guide to those who are called upon to administer the Poor Law. Many Guardians coming new to the work are anxious to learn their duties, but there are few books which are of much assistance in showing them what are the true principles upon which Poor Law relief should be administered. The great report of 1834 (which should be read and digested by every Guardian) deals after all with a state of society and things which does not exist now; and, because this is so, many persons are apt to consider it out of date and of no use for present purposes. This is an error. The principles underlying the grant of poor relief which it lays down are good for all time. Had the Poor Law been administered, since 1834, strictly on these principles in every Union, as was done in Atcham, pauperism would probably have been reduced to a negligeable quantity. Even, however, with defective and faulty administration, pauperism has diminished in an extraordinary degree, and it is well to remember this fact when the pauperism of to-day is considered; sad it is, indeed, to think that in 1894 the mean number of our paupers should have been 787,933, or 26·5 per 1000 of the whole population of England and Wales; but in 1849 the number was 1,088,659, or 62·7 per 1000 of the population. So, too, in 1894, our able-bodied paupers (excluding vagrants) amounted to 3·5 per 1000 of the population, while in 1849 they were 13·2 per 1000. But the most significant figures are those for 1871. Then the mean number of our paupers was 1,037,360, or 46·1 per 1000, and the mean number of adult able-bodied paupers 172,460, or

7·7 per 1000. In other words, we have only half the pauperism to-day that we had 22 years ago. Now it is a curious fact that it was about 1869 that attention was drawn to our increasing pauperism. The celebrated circular of Mr. Goschen appeared about this time, and inspectors were sent into the country to report on the administration of the Poor Law in typical Unions. There was a general stir in Poor Law matters, and there is not the least doubt that the result was a change in the then existing system of administration. A few Unions boldly adopted a policy of in-door relief only, with the most encouraging results. These were exceptional cases. Other Unions, however, began either then or shortly afterwards to administer out-door relief more strictly. It is impossible not to trace the extraordinary reduction in our pauperism since 1870 mainly to this cause, and therefore the Reports of the Local Government Board which cover the period are of great value, and especially the reports of the Poor Law Inspectors which will be found there. Now many people are inclined to regard our Poor Law Inspectors as mere theorists with no practical knowledge of Poor Law Administration. This is a great mistake. Not only have these very able men an intimate acquaintance with the history of our Poor Law, but it is part of their duty to be present from time to time at the meetings of Boards of Guardians within their districts. Many of them have had as many years' experience of the Poor Law as their critics have had days. Their roving commission enables them to compare the administration of the Poor Law in one Union with that in another. If they find pauperism rampant in one Union, and almost non-existent in another (with no ascertainable reason for the difference), they are justified in concluding that the administration of the Poor Law is faulty in the one and good in the other.

The fact that the Inspectors have the survey of a wide field, while the individual Guardian is shut up in a corner of it with no view over the fence (often one of his own creating), gives to the reports their great value. They have thus been freely quoted from in support of the author's arguments.

The plan of this book is as follows :—It proceeds first of all to show how it was that the Act of 1834 did not meet with all the success which was expected from it, how the principles laid down by the Commissioners of 1832 came to be forgotten, and how the increase of pauperism towards the end of the sixties awoke the Poor Law Board from its long sleep and led it once more to exercise the authority given to it by the Act and Orders as the supervisor of Poor Law Administration.[1] The results of this awakening are next shown.[2] Then follows a restatement of principles too apt to be forgotten.[3] Next the way to secure good administration is indicated,[4] and the vexed question of in-door *versus* out-door relief discussed ;[5] the subject of medical relief being dealt with in a separate chapter.[6] Then follow suggestions for dealing with particular classes of applicants for relief,[7] special attention being given to the question of the "unemployed," which has of late come into so much prominence.[8] Another chapter [9] deals with the causes affecting the increase or decrease of pauperism, and some charts (see p. 196) show very clearly how dependent the amount of it is on particular methods of administration ; depression of trade, bad weather, strikes, etc., affecting only to a small extent the pauperism of those Unions which administer out-door relief very strictly. Various reforms in the law which have been suggested at different times are pointed out,[10]

---

[1] Chap. i.  [2] Chap. ii.  [3] Chap. iii.  [4] Chap. iv.  [5] Chapters v. to x.
[6] Chap. x.  [7] Chapters xi. to xiii.  [8] Chap. xiii.  [9] Chap. xiv.  [10] Chap. xv.

and the concluding chapter[1] has some general remarks on Poor Law Administration. An Appendix contains some of the more important circulars of the central authority, which are of interest at the present time, and various statistics of pauperism. A word of explanation may be necessary as to why the subject of vagrancy has not been dealt with. The consensus of opinion is in favour of the adoption of an uniform system, but the doctors disagree as to which of the present systems it is best to adopt, or, indeed, whether anyone of them works satisfactorily. Nothing less than a departmental inquiry can determine the question. For the same reasons, and also because a Committee is at the present time inquiring into the provisions for the education and maintenance of pauper children, the author has refrained from going fully into this very important and difficult subject.

In conclusion, the author desires to emphasise the fact that the book does not advocate the immediate abolition of out-door relief, but merely its restriction with a view to its virtual abolition. It is asserted that the new Boards of Guardians are likely to adopt an out-door relief policy. It is sincerely to be hoped that before doing so they will consider the beneficial results which are shown in Chapter VII. to have followed on a change from an out-door to an indoor relief policy in certain Unions. If they will pursue the same path, they will assuredly find it leading to reduced pauperism, to reduced expenditure on relief, and better still to a marked improvement in the habits and morals of the poor by the encouragement of thrift, and the discouragement of improvidence and vice.   W. C.

WHARFENDEN, FRIMLEY, *April*, 1895.

---

[1] Chap. xvi.

# CONTENTS.

| Chapter | Page |
|---|---|
| I. The reaction of 1870 in favour of more careful administration | 1-8 |
| II. The statistical results of the reaction of 1870 | 9-10 |
| III. The restatement of principles | 11-15 |
| IV. The conditions of good administration | 16-52 |
|   (1) Adequate accommodation in the Workhouse | 17 |
|   (2) Dealing with applications for relief—the primary duty of Guardians | 20-46 |
|     (a) Personal influence | 21 |
|     (b) Attendance of Medical Officers | 23 |
|     (c) The Relieving Officer and his books | 24 |
|     (d) The need of careful inquiry | 27 |
|     (e) Number of Relieving Officers and size of their districts | 39 |
|     (f) Cross-visiting | 40 |
|     (g) Frequent and systematic visiting | 41 |
|     (h) The distribution of relief | 42 |
|     (i) Relief Committees v. whole Board | 42 |
|     (j) First applications and lists of paupers | 46 |
|   (3) Ample notice of change of policy | 46 |
|   (4) Co-operation between charity and the Poor Law | 49 |
|   (5) Co-operation between public authorities and the Poor Law | 51 |
| V. The evils attaching to Out-door Relief | 53-71 |
|   (1) Affects wages and earnings adversely | 54 |
|   (2) Must be inadequate | 62 |
|   (3) Liable to abuse | 66 |
|   (4) Causes discontent | 68 |
|   (5) Destructive of thrift and providence | 68 |

| Chapter | Page |
|---|---|
| VI. Why Out-door Relief is given | 72-78 |
|     (1) The humane argument | 73-78 |
|         (a) Breaking up of the home | 73 |
|         (b) Danger of starvation | 75 |
|         (c) Harshness generally | 76 |
|         (d) The stigma of pauperism | 78 |
|     (2) The economical argument | 78 |
| VII. The advantages attending the restriction of Out-door Relief | 79-92 |
|     (1) Reduces the number of paupers | 79 |
|     (2) Does not increase in-door pauperism | 79 |
|     (3) Reduces expenditure on relief | 83 |
|     (4) Encourages thrift and providence | 87 |
|     (5) Brings relations to a sense of their duties | 88 |
|     (6) Is not harsh and prompts charity | 90 |
| VIII. How the evils attaching to Out-door Relief may be minimised | 93-103 |
| IX. The Workhouse System | 104-113 |
| X. Medical Relief | 114-130 |
|     (1) It may start a career of pauperism | 115 |
|     (2) Discourages providence | 115 |
|     (3) Subject to abuse | 116 |
|     Possibility of reducing it to a minimum | 119-130 |
|         (a) Compliance with Poor Law Orders | 119 |
|         (b) Attendance of applicant | 121 |
|         (c) Grant of relief on loan | 122 |
|         (d) Establishment of Provident Dispensaries and Medical Societies | 124 |
|         (e) Proper provision for sick in Workhouses | 128 |
|         (f) Public Dispensaries | 128 |
| XI. How to deal with special classes of paupers | 131-159 |
|     (1) The aged and infirm | 132 |
|     (2) Widows with children | 138 |
|     (3) Children | 147 |
|     (4) Deserted wives | 152 |

| | | Page |
|---|---|---|
| Chapter | | |
| (5) Wives of convicts | | 153 |
| (6) Wives of soldiers, etc. | | 154 |
| (7) Single women with illegitimate children | | 154 |
| (8) Aged married couples | | 155 |
| (9) Non-resident paupers | | 157 |
| (10) Members of Friendly Societies | | 157 |
| (11) The able-bodied | | 159 |
| XII. The relief of the able-bodied | | 160-173 |
| (1) The O. D. R. Order, 1852 | | 160 |
| O. D. Labour Test (a) no deterrent | | 161 |
| " (b) idea that the State has to provide work | | 162 |
| " (c) is demoralising | | 162 |
| " (d) discipline cannot be preserved | | 163 |
| " (e) causes discontent | | 164 |
| " (f) advantages of the Indoor Test over the Out-door Test | | 164 |
| (2) The Prohibitory Relief Order, 1844 | | 171 |
| (3) Evasion of the Orders | | 171 |
| XIII. The Unemployed | | 174-194 |
| (1) The permanently unemployed | | 176 |
| (2) The temporarily unemployed | | 178 |
| XIV. Causes affecting increase or decrease of pauperism | | 195-202 |
| (1) Method of administration | | 195 |
| (2) Some causes affecting increase | | 198, 199 |
| (a) Severe weather | | 199 |
| (b) Depression of trade | | 199 |
| (c) Strikes and lock-outs | | 200 |
| (d) Action of Trade Unions | | 201 |
| (e) Improvidence of working-classes | | 201 |
| Some causes affecting decrease | | 202 |
| (a) Growth of Friendly Societies | | 202 |
| (b) Low prices of necessaries | | 202 |
| XV. Suggested reforms | | 203-214 |

| Chapter | Page |
|---|---|
| XVI. General Remarks and Conclusion | 215-223 |
| Appendix A. Statistics showing reduction of general pauperism | 225 |
| ,, B. ,, ,, ,, able-bodied adult pauperism | 226 |
| ,, C. ,, ,, ,, not-able-bodied adult pauperism | 227 |
| ,, D. ,, ,, ,, child pauperism | 228 |
| ,, E. ,, ,, the expenditure on Poor Relief in England and Wales and in the Metropolis | 229-230 |
| Appendix F. Art. 215 of the General Order of 1847 | 231 |
| ,, G. Mr. Goschen's Circular of 1869 | 232 |
| ,, H. Mr. Longley's suggestions for improvements in administration | 235 |
| ,, I. Opinion of Poor Law Board upon relief to members of Friendly Societies | 238 |
| ,, J. Mr. Chamberlain's Circular on Pauperism and Distress | 241 |
| ,, K. Circular of Local Government Board on Workhouse Administration | 243 |
| ,, L. Dr. Downes' Circular of 1892 on Nursing | 249 |
| ,, M. Mr. Fleming's Circular of 1868 on Visiting Committees | 251 |
| ,, N. Opinion of the Local Government Board as to duty of Relieving Officers to inquire as to charitable assistance | 254 |

DIAGRAMS - - *to face p.* 197

I. Showing decrease of Pauperism since 1849 in England & Wales.
II. ,, ,, ,, 1870 in Manchester.
III. ,, ,, ,, ,, Birmingham.
IV. ,, ,, ,, ,, Whitechapel.

INDEX - - - - - - - - - 255

ABBREVIATIONS.

P.L.C. refers to the Reports of the Poor Law Commissioners.
P.L.B. ,, ,, Poor Law Board.
L.G.B. ,, ,, Local Government Board.

# THE BETTER ADMINISTRATION
## OF
# THE POOR LAW.

### CHAPTER I.

THE REACTION IN 1870 IN FAVOUR OF CAREFUL ADMINISTRATION.

THE basis of the English Poor Law is the Act of Elizabeth (43 Eliz., ch. ii.). The Act of 1834 (4 and 5 Will. IV., ch. lxxvi.), which was passed in consequence of the Report of the Poor Law Commissioners of 1832, only provided for its improved administration. It would be outside the scope of this work to point out the causes which rendered a drastic reform in the administration of the Poor Law an absolute necessity. The famous report above referred to, and the many books which have been published on the English Poor Law,[1] are open to all who wish to know what they were. But it is no exaggeration to say that the country was in danger of being consumed by its own children.[2]

---

[1] *E.g.*, Sir George Nicholl's "History of the Poor Law," chap. xv.; Aschrott's "English Poor Law System," part i., section vii.; Fowles' "Poor Law" (the English Citizen Series), 1881, chap. iv.; "Administration and Operation of the Poor Laws," being extracts from the reports received from the Assistant Commissioners by the Royal Commission of 1832 (published by authority); "Dispauperization," by J. R. Pretyman (Longmans), 2nd edition, pp. 27-39.

[2] Rates in some parishes exceeded 25s. in the £. Rents were in fact swallowed up in rates. In 1832 £7,036,969 (or 10s. per head of a population of 14,105,600) were expended for the relief and maintenance of the poor, and that, too, at a time when the general wealth of the country was much less than now (the expenditure in poor relief standing in 1892 at only 6s. per head of population, and this in spite of strikes, lock-outs, and commercial and industrial depression).

The Act of 1834, by establishing the workhouse test for the able-bodied, stepped in to prevent this, and, so far as this class is concerned, has been completely successful in its action. Able-bodied pauperism is to-day practically extinct, and its gradual decrease has been naturally and as a direct consequence accompanied by a decrease in general pauperism. This is a remarkable fact, and bears striking testimony to the wisdom of the framers of the Act. How great the decrease of pauperism has been is shown by the figures given in the Appendix,[1] which (be it noted) do not include lunatics and vagrants.[2]

While, however, the statistics show the progress which has been made since 1834 in reducing the pauperism of the country, this reduction has been most marked since 1870. The reason for this is given by Mr. Longley in his well-known report of 1874.[3]

"During a series of years immediately following the passing of the Poor Law Amendment Act it was the practice of the Poor Law Commissioners to set forth in their annual report, with the utmost precision and distinctness, not merely a narrative of their proceedings during the past year, but

---

[1] Pp. 225-228.

[2] The increase or decrease in the number of lunatics and vagrants has little if anything to do with Poor Law administration. Vagrancy has flourished in this country from the earliest times, and will probably continue to flourish to the end of all time. The life has many attractions, and is suited to our islanders' love of travel and adventure. There is nothing alarming in the number of our vagrants. They do not increase faster than the population increases. Their cost is infinitesimal, and their numbers would be so if *charitable* people, and especially the poor. who do not realise that sufficient legal provision is made for them, would cease to give them alms.

As regards pauper lunatics and imbeciles, the increase in their numbers is serious, but no one would think of attributing it to Poor Law administration. It is, however, a cause for satisfaction that the proportion of them to population is the same now as it was in 1883, showing that there has only been an absolute increase since that date. (See 22 L.G.B., p. 268.) A large portion of the increase (if not the whole) is undoubtedly owing to the better provision which is now made for the treatment of this class; many persons who thirty years ago would have been looked after by their own relations being now relieved in public asylums and institutions.

[3] 4 L.G.B., p. 46.

an enunciation of the fundamental principles which had guided their action; and to elucidate, sometimes in considerable detail, the practical bearing of these principles upon individual cases. This practice was discontinued by the Poor Law Board upon their formation; and though the general policy of the board did not, as far as I am aware, differ from that so persistently recognised and enforced by the commissioners, the need for the practical application of the sound principles on which it was based was gradually lost sight of by boards of guardians, with a few brilliant exceptions, until it was found that the pauperism of the country, which had received a severe check under the administration of the commissioners, was rapidly increasing. The board then thought it expedient to re-enunciate and to recall to the minds of the guardians by means of their circular letter of 2nd December, 1871, those principles of administration which had formerly proved so efficacious in checking pauperism and promoting the independence of the poor."

Among the "few brilliant exceptions" was Atcham (Shropshire), where reform was introduced by the late Sir Baldwyn Leighton, immediately after the passing of the Act of 1834.

In 1836 with a population (1831) of 17,855 the paupers numbered 1,395 [1]
In 1837 ,, ,, ,, 880 [2]
In 1849 ,, (1851) 19,088 ,, 433 [3]
In 1871 ,, (1871) 18,313 ,, 293 [4]
In 1872 ,, (1871) 45,566 ,, 584 [5]
In 1892 ,, (1891) 48,332 ,, 354 [6]

In other words the proportion of paupers to population for those years was: 1836—1 in 13; 1837—1 in 20; 1849—1 in 44; 1871—1 in 62; 1872—1 in 78; 1892—1 in 136. [7]

A comparison of the mean pauperism of the Atcham Union

---

[1] One day in November. (See Report of the Progress of the Atcham Union, p. 21.)
[2] 25th March, 1837, *ib*.
[3] 25th March, 1849, *ib*.
[4] 25th March, 1871, *ib*.
[5] 25th March, 1872, *ib*. Six Shrewsbury parishes with a population of 27,253 were added in July, 1871, to the union. Hence the large increase in its population. In July, 1870, Atcham and Shrewsbury relieved 1062 paupers, and in July, 1871, the combined unions relieved 949 paupers. Thus in nine months only the pauperism of Shrewsbury was reduced owing to improved administration.
[6] 25th March, 1892, *ib*.
[7] The above figures exclude paupers who received *medical relief only*. (See Report of the Progress of the Atcham Union, p. 20.) The practice of taking the number of paupers on the 1st January and 1st of July in each year was not established until 1848. (See 2 P.L.B., p. 8.)

with that of the rest of the country (excluding lunatics and vagrants), for the years ending Lady Day, 1859,[1] and Lady Day, 1871, will be interesting:—

| | Year ending Lady Day. | Population (1861 and 1871). | Indoor paupers. | Outdoor paupers. | Total paupers. | Proportion of paupers to every 1000 of population. | |
|---|---|---|---|---|---|---|---|
| Atcham. | 1859 | 19,314 | 131 | 133 | 264 | 13·67 | Increase of indoor pauperism 5·3% |
| | 1871 | 18,313 | 138 | 119 | 257 | 14·03 | Decrease of outdoor ,, 10·5% |
| | | | | | | | ,, total ,, 2·6% |
| England and Wales. | 1859 | 20,066,224 | 106,762 | 720,745 | 827,507 | 41·23 | Increase of indoor pauperism 31·5% |
| | 1871 | 22,712,266 | 140,467 | 843,799 | 984,266 | 43·33 | ,, outdoor ,, 17% |
| | | | | | | | ,, total ,, 19% |

[1] The particulars of the pauperism of *each* union on the 1st January and 1st July of every year are given for the first time for July 1, 1858. By that date Atcham has been depauperised almost entirely, and therefore the comparison is not so favourable as it would have been had we similar returns for each union, beginning in 1836 or even 1849.

The circular of the 2nd December, 1871, on "Out-door Relief,"[1] referred to by Mr. Longley, attributes the increase of pauperism almost entirely to defective management in the administration of the law, after making "every allowance for the increase of population, stagnation in trades, and temporary disturbances in the labour market, variations in the seasons, etc."[2] Signs of the awakening of the central authority are first noticed in 1869. On the 20th November of that year was issued Mr. Goschen's celebrated circular on a division of labour between Poor Law and charity in the metropolis.[3] On the 13th December of the same year a circular as to the mode in which medical relief was administered in London and other town unions elicited replies from 27 metropolitan unions and 125 provincial unions.[4] In 1870 the board caused inquiries to be made by certain of its inspectors into the manner in which the administration of out-door relief was conducted in their respective districts. The very interesting reports of Mr.

---

[1] 1 L.G.B., p. 63.

[2] See 3 L.G.B., p. 196, for other reasons. The following table shows the variations in the cost of out-door relief and in the number of out-door paupers in England and Wales from the year 1861 to the year 1870:—

| Year ended at Lady Day. | Cost of out-door relief. | Average number of out-door paupers. | Percentage of out-door paupers to population. | Average price of wheat. |
|---|---|---|---|---|
| | £ | | | s.  d. |
| 1861 | 3,012,251 | 758,055 | 3·8 | 55  10 |
| 1862 | 3,155,820 | 784,906 | 3·9 | 56   7 |
| 1863 | 3,574,136 | 942,475 | 4·6 | 52   1 |
| 1864 | 3,466,392 | 881,217 | 4·3 | 43   2 |
| 1865 | 3,258,813 | 820,586 | 3·9 | 39   8 |
| 1866 | 3,196,685 | 783,376 | 3·7 | 43   6 |
| 1867 | 3,358,351 | 794,236 | 3·7 | 53   7½ |
| 1868 | 3,620,284 | 842,600 | 3·9 | 67   6½ |
| 1869 | 3,677,379 | 860,400 | 4·0 | 58   3 |
| 1870 | 3,633,051 | 876,000 | 4·0 | 46   2½ |

[3] 22 P.L.B., p. 9. This circular is set out in Appendix G., p. 232.

[4] 22 P.L.B., p. 38. The circular and replies take up 70 pages of the Blue Book.

Wodehouse, Mr. Henley, Mr. Farnall, Mr. Hawley, and Mr. Longley followed; while the question of out-door medical relief was specially reported upon by Mr. Peel, Mr. Farnall, and Mr. Cane.[1] In 1871 appeared Mr. Wodehouse's invaluable report on the "Administration of Out-door Relief in Seventy Unions in the Country."[2] In 1873 Mr. Longley's report on Poor Law Administration in London was published together with two other interesting and valuable reports on out-door relief in the country districts by Mr. Culley and Mr. Sendall.[3] The beneficial results attending this revival of activity on the part of the central authority in Poor Law administration are shown in a memorandum of the Local Government Board issued in February, 1878.[4] Although it is evident that this interference was by no means welcomed by the local authorities, who thought they knew their own business best. But the necessity for this interference is well put by Mr. Longley. He says:—

"It is, after all, one of the highest and most necessary functions of the board to supply individual boards of guardians with the results of the wide and varied experience which a central authority must inevitably acquire, but which the isolated habits of administration almost universally prevalent among boards of guardians prevent them from gaining for themselves. One main result of the board's wider experience I take to be, that the differences between the circumstances of different localities, great as they are, affect very slightly, if at all, the application of the general principles of Poor Law administration. The special circumstances of the locality and of the case necessarily tend, from their urgency and their proximity, to exercise an overpowering influence on the judgment of local administrators, unless they are enabled, without disregarding these considerations, to take the wider range of view which knowledge of principles, and experience of their practical working in various circumstances can alone afford.

"The board do not, of course, pretend to an exclusive acquaintance with sound principles of administration, or to be the sole possessors of a secret panacea for pauperism, but the necessities of their position have

---

[1] 23 P.L.B., pp. 32-189.
[2] 1 L.G.B., p. 88.
[3] 3 L.G.B., pp. 66-116, 136-209.
[4] 7 L.G.B., p. 217.

placed in their hands a mass of accumulated evidence of the success and of the soundness of those principles which is not to be found elsewhere. In disseminating the experience thus acquired, the board and their representatives do practically incur, and with some show of fairness, the common imputation that they come to the local authorities, saying, in effect, 'We know your own business better than you do yourselves.' This objection, which may, of course, be made to all interference of a central government, is supposed, however, to apply with special force to this interference, when directed to a matter of so purely domestic an interest as Poor Law administration is commonly believed to be. Two answers to this objection appear sufficiently obvious. First, the repression of pauperism and the encouragement of thrift are matters of national, and not merely of local, interest; and next, even if it were otherwise, the wider experience of the board in 'business' identical in character entitles them to be heard when laying down the general principles, at least, upon which the guardians should transact their 'own business.'"[1]

The effect of these reports and circulars was seen immediately. In January, 1873, the Brixworth Board of Guardians appointed a committee to inquire into "the mode of administration of out-door relief in their own and other unions." This committee in their report laid down certain rules for their future guidance.[2] The result is shown in a report made to the Local Government Board by the Rev. W. Bury in 1874. The number of paupers on 1st January had fallen in one year from 990 to 609, the proportion of in-door to out-door paupers from 1 in 12 to 1 in 8, and the proportion of paupers to population from 1 in 14 to 1 in 22.[3]

About the same time, too, Bradfield and St. Neots in the country, and Whitechapel, Stepney and St. George's in the East in London altered their system of administering out-door relief with the extraordinary results set out on page 80. Many unions also passed rules for the better regulation of this form of relief (amongst these were Guildford, Reigate and Manchester);[4] and

---

[1] 3 L.G.B., p. 200.
[2] 2 L.G.B., p. 68.
[3] 3 L.G.B., p. 117. The steady following up of the new policy has resulted in there being on the 1st Jan., 1894, 91 paupers (excluding lunatics and vagrants) or a proportion of paupers to population of 1 in 134.
[4] See 3 L.G.B., pp. 99, 107; 5 L.G.B., p. xvii.

the growth of a sound public opinion has been to a large extent fostered by the firm action of the Local Government Board, and by public discussion at Poor Law conferences which were established at this date.[1]

This improvement in the administration of out-door relief was accompanied by important reforms in the system of in-door relief. We may specially mention the passing of the Metropolitan Poor Act, 1867. The object of this Act was (1) to secure the improved treatment of the sick; (2) to establish stricter and more deterrent discipline in workhouses; and (3) to utilise to the utmost the accommodation provided generally for the in-door poor.[2] This was to have been effected by a classification *by* workhouses. The first object only, however, can be said to be completely attained.

---

[1] See 8 L.G.B., pp. ix.-xii. and 140, and especially Mr. Longley's remarks on the subject in 3 L.G.B., p. 147.

[2] 4 L.G.B., p. 43; 8 L.G.B., pp. xxxii.-xxxviii.; 13 L.G.B., pp. xxxi.-xxxvi. The beneficial changes that the passing of this Act has brought about with regard to the treatment of the sick are ably pointed out in the last two of these reports.

## CHAPTER II.

### THE STATISTICAL RESULTS OF THE REACTION OF 1870.

WE will next draw attention to the great reduction in the pauperism of the country since 1871, the result of the greater attention given to the subject during the last twenty-three years. The following table shows the mean number of paupers of all classes, and also the mean number of paupers excluding lunatics and vagrants [1]:—

| Year ending Lady Day. | Estimated population middle of 1870 and 1892. | Mean number of indoor paupers of all classes. | Ratio per 1000 of population. | Mean number of outdoor paupers of all classes. | Ratio per 1000 of population. | Mean number of indoor and outdoor paupers of all classes. | Ratio per 1000 of population. |
|---|---|---|---|---|---|---|---|
| 1871 | 22,501,316 | 156,430 | 7·0 | 880,930 | 39·1 | 1,037,360 | 46·1 |
| 1893 | 29,403,346 | 192,519 | 6·5 | 566,264 | 19·3 | 758,776 | 25·8 |
| Increase | 6,902,030 | 36,089 | .. | .. | .. | .. | .. |
| Decrease | .. | .. | ·5 | 314,666 | 19·8 | 278,584 | 20·3 |

[1] The second portion of the table is given because the increase in the numbers of lunatics not only keeps pace with the increase of population, but also is accounted for by the large number who take advantage of the comforts afforded by our splendid lunatic asylums. Vagrancy must necessarily fluctuate. The mean number of paupers for any one year is obtained from the number of paupers on 1st July and 1st January in each year *ending at Lady Day.*

| Year ending Lady Day. | Mean number of indoor paupers (excluding lunatics and vagrants). | Ratio per 1000 of population. | Mean number of outdoor paupers (excluding lunatics and vagrants). | Ratio per 1000 of population. | Mean number of indoor and outdoor paupers (excluding lunatics and vagrants). | Ratio per 1000 of population. |
|---|---|---|---|---|---|---|
| 1871 | 139,102 | 6·2 | 838,799 | 37·3 | 977,901 | 43·5 |
| 1893 | 169,155 | 5·7 | 505,448 | 17·2 | 674,603 | 22·9 |
| Increase | 30,053 | | | | | |
| Decrease | .. | ·5 | 333,351 | 20·1 | 303,298 | 20·6 |

*Note.*—In 1871 the mean number of paupers in England and Wales was higher than in all but two of the 22 preceding years, the number being exceeded in 1849 and 1863, the latter being the year when the cotton famine made itself most felt. There have been rises and falls in the mean pauperism of the country since 1871, but the variations have been very small, and not nearly so great as during the period between 1849 and 1871. But since 1871 there have been periods of commercial depression, *e.g.*, in the years 1878-81, 1886-89, and 1892 to the present time; and that pauperism has varied to so small an extent may fairly be attributed to improved administration. The year 1871 has been chosen because it has only been since that time that the effects of improved administration can be seen. For purposes of comparing the pauperism of one union with that of another any year will do, *ceteris paribus*.

The next table shows how great has been the decrease in *adult* able-bodied pauperism during the same period. The figures exclude lunatics and vagrants:—

| Year ending Lady Day. | Mean number of indoor paupers. | Ratio per 1000 of estd. population. | Mean number of outdoor paupers. | Ratio per 1000 of estd. population. | Mean number of outdoor and indoor paupers. | Ratio per 1000 of estd. population. |
|---|---|---|---|---|---|---|
| 1871 | 24,700 | 1·1 | 147,760 | 6·6 | 172,460 | 7·7 |
| 1893 | 30,202 | 1·0 | 69,816 | 2·4 | 100,018 | 3·4 |
| Increase | 5,502 | | | | | |
| Decrease | .. | ·1 | 77,944 | 4·2 | 72,442 | 4·3 |

Some further figures showing the great decrease in the numbers of all classes of paupers since 1870 are given in the Appendices A to D, pp. 225-228.

## CHAPTER III.

### RESTATEMENT OF PRINCIPLES.

THERE can, we think, be little doubt that the principles laid down in the Report of 1834 had been very much neglected, if not forgotten, by boards of guardians,[1] until the reports of the inspectors and the action of the central authority referred to in Chapter II. once more drew attention to them. The Report itself was, indeed, not reprinted until 1885. The reprint of it has made it more accessible to the present generation of guardians, and it is now more frequently referred to than formerly. Yet but few guardians probably have read it. Many know it only by name, though its main arguments are quite as applicable to the pauperism of the present day as they were to the pauperism of sixty years ago. Mr. Baldwyn Fleming remarks:—[2]

"So much unsound doctrine with regard to Poor Law administration has of late been suggested as worthy of acceptance, and so many appeals for a relaxation of the Prohibitory Order have been advanced, that it seems almost impossible that the true position of the question can have been appreciated by those who now advocate a form of relief which had the fullest trial and led to such dire misfortune in the earlier part of this century.

"The condition of affairs in the days when out-relief was administered without the present salutary checks, has been so much lost sight of that guardians are astonished when they are told that before the introduction of the 'New Poor Law' the poor rates in many parishes ranged from 8s. to 21s. in the £ upon the rateable value."

For the administrators of 1874, Mr. Longley restated the principles of the workhouse system as follows:—[3]

---

[1] The Atcham Board, with one or two others, was a brilliant exception.
[2] 17 L.G.B., p. 63.
[3] 3 L.G.B., pp. 138, 140.

"The aim of the English Poor Law is to combine the maximum of efficiency in the relief of destitute applicants with the minimum of incentive to improvidence. Not only is this the abstract principle of the Poor Law, but it is that which has guided the practical and administrative control over the practice of local authorities, which has now for nearly forty years been exercised, under various designations, by the Central Authority.

"That the end thus proposed to Poor Law administrators can be fully reached only by that system of administration which is commonly known as the 'Workhouse System,' has been recognised by the board ever since the passing of the Poor Law Amendment Act, 1834. It is unnecessary that the reasons which have led to this conclusion should be stated at length in this place, and that for two reasons; first, because they are already stated with the utmost precision and clearness in the Report of the Poor Law Commissioners of Inquiry, 1834, a document which is too little known to Poor Law administrators, and the republication of which, or of extracts from which, in a cheap form, would, I believe, materially assist the cause of sound Poor Law administration;[1] and, secondly, because in whatever degree it may fail to govern their practice, the soundness, in theory at least, of the workhouse principle is in fact admitted by all the boards of guardians in London. For the purposes, therefore, of this report, the principle of the workhouse system may be regarded as an axiom of Poor Law administration, and its proof in this place, at least, may be dispensed with.

"For the same reasons it is unnecessary to insist here upon the inherent inferiority of out-door to in-door relief, whether regarded as a test of destitution, as a means of adequately relieving destitution, or as an incentive to thrift.

---

[1] The Report was republished in 1885.

"One observation, however, it may be proper to make here in order to obviate the misapprehension which too commonly prevails as to the practical aspect of the workhouse principle. It cannot be too frequently insisted on, as was pointedly said at one of the recent Poor Law conferences in London, by a veteran Poor Law administrator of unequalled experience, that the imputation so habitually levelled at the advocates of the workhouse system, of adherence to a principle which is, it is alleged, merely abstract, theoretical, doctrinaire, and visionary, is at direct variance with proved and indisputable facts, and betrays the want of acquaintance of those who make it with the reasons publicly given in the report just mentioned, and elsewhere, for the adoption of the principle of which the workhouse system is the expression.

"The workhouse system, as recognised by the founders of the existing system of Poor Law administration, is the direct and logical result of practical experience of its working in various parts of England, *e.g.*, Bingham, Southwell, Cookham, etc. It was found not only that this system had solved the practical problem of Poor Law administration, the solution of which has been suggested above as the aim of English Poor Law, but that no other systems of administration had been equally successful in attaining a similar result; and further, that their success in this direction bore a direct proportion to their degree of approach towards the principle of the workhouse system.

"The practical basis of that system as recommended by the Poor Law Commissioners of Inquiry is abundantly proved by their report, which teems with well-ascertained instances of its success.

"But the case in support of the workhouse system is at the present day far stronger than it was left by that report. The practical experience of nearly forty years has confirmed the judgment of the commissioners who framed that report, and their arguments, hitherto unanswered, have now the support of a much wider area of experience than it was possible to secure for them when first put forth. It is not too much to say, and the assertion may be supported by reference to the earlier reports of the Poor Law Commissioners, that the workhouse system, where fairly and fully tried, has not failed in a single instance to satisfy the conditions of successful administration previously suggested; that all Poor Law administration since the passing of the Poor Law Amendment Act has been successful in proportion to its approach to that system; and that it has not as yet been found that the special conditions of locality, trade, seasons, weather or population, interfere with its universal applicability.

"Such a proposition as this will, no doubt, appear startling to those who entertain the not uncommon belief that the existing Poor Law administration has failed in times of sudden and extreme pressure of distress among the poor. Public expression was given not long ago to this belief at one of the late Poor Law conferences by a speaker whose acquaintance with the working of the several agencies for the relief of destitution in London is probably unequalled, in these words: 'It must be admitted that the administration of the Poor Law has broken down conspicuously in our large towns.' So sweeping an assertion as this appears inconsistent with the passages just cited from the reports of the Poor Law Commissioners and of the Poor Law Board, which testify to the success of Poor Law administration in the large towns of Leicester, Macclesfield, Nottingham, Coventry, and Stoke-upon-Trent, in dealing not merely with their ordinary pauperism, but with destitution aggravated by the disturbance of trade, and the consequent cessation of employment in those large manufacturing towns. One of these passages, which goes to prove the success in these circumstances, not merely of Poor Law administration generally, but of its special and extreme development in the workhouse system, I may be allowed to quote at length. The clerk to the Guardians of the Leicester Union, in a report made to the inspector of the district on the 30th January, 1858, of the course adopted by the guardians in the administration of relief during the depression of trade in the town of Leicester in the year 1857, says:

"'Thus then has the difficulty been met and overcome. The great problem whether in a large and populous manufacturing town the workhouse test can be maintained in times of great commercial depression has been solved in the affirmative, and an example has been given of how easily this may be done (even in a manufacturing town wherein the rate of wages is uniformly low), when the guardians act unitedly and resolutely in carrying out the law.'

"The other passages cited above, while they offer perhaps a less direct testimony in favour of the workhouse system, appear fully to bear out the proposition already advanced, that the administration of the Poor Law has been successful in proportion to the nearness of its approach to the adoption of that system. That since the establishment of the present system of Poor Law administration, destitution has at times failed to be adequately relieved, cannot be denied, but this failure will be found to be due rather to maladministration of the law, or to its administration in the absence of necessary conditions of success, than to any inherent defects in the system of administration prescribed by the existing law, as interpreted and applied by its founders."

## CHAPTER IV.

### THE CONDITIONS OF GOOD ADMINISTRATION.

MR. LONGLEY, from whom we quoted in the last chapter, has also told us what the essentials of good administration are, and the experience and knowledge gained during the last twenty-three years has enforced his conclusions. Everyone has heard of badly administered unions and well administered unions, though few guardians would be inclined to class their own unions in the former category. On most boards, however, there will be found some who, content with nothing less than an absolute decrease in pauperism, will recognise the truth of the following propositions, which apply both to town and country alike:—

"(1) There must be sufficient workhouse accommodation, and the maintenance in workhouses of a deterrent discipline.

"(2) The treatment of applications for relief shall be recognised to be in practice, as it is in theory, the primary duty of boards of guardians.

"(3) Ample and timely notice should be given to the poor of definite changes in the practice of boards of guardians in the administration of relief.

"(4) The co-operation of administrators of private charity with boards of guardians should be placed on a definite and systematic basis.

"(5) Thrift should be encouraged by increasing the facilities at the disposal of the poor for making provision for the future wants of themselves and their families.

"(6) There should be cordial co-operation between Poor Law administrators and other public authorities."[1]

We take these points in turn.

### (1) *Adequate Accommodation in the Workhouse.*

The amount of accommodation should be, *at least*, sufficient to enable the guardians to classify the paupers in accordance with the requirements of the General Order of 1847, Articles 98 and 99. These articles represent what is the irreducible minimum of accommodation.

#### CLASSIFICATION OF THE PAUPERS.

Article 98. The paupers, so far as the workhouse admits thereof, shall be classed as follows:—

Class I. Men infirm through age or any other cause.
Class II. Able-bodied men, and youths above the age of fifteen years.
Class III. Boys above the age of seven years and under that of fifteen.
Class IV. Women infirm through age or any other cause.
Class V. Able-bodied women and girls above the age of fifteen years.
Class VI. Girls above the age of seven years, and under that of fifteen.
Class VII. Children under seven years of age. To each class shall be assigned that ward or separate building and yard which may be best fitted for the reception of such class, and each class of paupers shall remain therein, without communication with those of any other class.

Article 99. Provided

1. That the Guardians shall from time to time, after consulting the Medical Officer, make such arrangements as they may deem necessary with regard to persons labouring under any disease of body or mind.
2. The Guardians shall, so far as circumstances will permit, further subdivide any of the classes enumerated in Article 98, with reference to the moral character or behaviour, or the previous habits of the inmates, or to such other grounds, as may seem expedient.
3. That nothing in this order shall compel the Guardians to separate any married couple, both being paupers of the first and fourth classes respectively, provided the Guardians shall set apart for the exclusive use of every such couple a sleeping apartment separate from that of the other paupers.
4. That any paupers of the fifth and sixth classes may be employed constantly or occasionally in any of the female sick wards, or in the care of infants, or as assistants in the household work; and the Master and Matron shall make such arrangements as may enable the paupers of the fifth and

---

[1] See Mr. Longley's Report, 3 L.G.B., p. 200.

sixth classes to be employed in the household work, without communication with the paupers of the second and third classes.

5. That any pauper of the fourth class, whom the Master may deem fit to perform the duties of a nurse or assistant to the Matron, may be so employed in the sick wards, or those of the fourth, fifth, sixth or seventh classes; and any pauper of the first class, who may by the Master be deemed fit, may be placed in the ward of the third class, to aid in the management, and superintend the behaviour of the paupers of such class, or may be employed in the male sick ward.

6. That the Guardians, for a special reason to be entered on their minutes, may place any boy or girl between the ages of ten or sixteen years in a male or female ward respectively, different from that to which he or she properly belongs, unless the Commissioners shall otherwise direct.

7. That the paupers of the seventh class may be placed in such of the wards appropriated to the female paupers as shall be deemed expedient, and the mothers of such paupers shall be permitted to have access to them at all reasonable times.

8. That the Master (subject to any directions given or regulations made by the Guardians) shall allow the father or mother of any child in the same workhouse, who may be desirous of seeing such child, to have an interview with such child at some one time in each day in a room in the said workhouse to be appointed for that purpose. And the Guardians shall make arrangements for permitting the members of the same family who may be in different workhouses of the Union to have occasional interviews with each other, at such times and in such manner as may best suit the discipline of the several workhouses.

9. *This clause related to casual poor wayfarers admitted by the Master or Matron, and is now replaced by the General Order of the 18th December, 1882, containing the present regulations with respect to casual paupers.*

For married couples special accommodation should be provided. The infirmary accommodation should be adequate, and no infectious cases should be treated within the precincts of the workhouse. For these cases unions should combine to provide isolation hospitals separate from the workhouse.[1]

The actual amount of the accommodation must vary with the needs of the particular union, but the workhouse or labour

---

[1] It is impossible to protect the inmates of workhouses against the spread of an infectious disease, unless there be some means of isolating a suspected infectious case at once. Many workhouses have infectious wards, but in many instances these are not sufficiently isolated. Besides which non-pauper cases come to be dealt with in them, and thus the danger of infection may come from outside. (See 18 L.G.B., p. 129.) As to the importance of isolation hospitals, the difficulties in the way of their establishment, and their use, see 23 L.G.B., pp. 102, 114, 127, and 131.

test cannot be applied unless there is ample margin. In that case it will not be necessary in times of pressure and exceptional distress to employ the out-door labour test. (See Chapter XII.) On the other hand, if the accommodation is inadequate, and the in-door test is applied, the space at the disposal of the guardians has to be turned to the utmost account. One class of inmates has to be lodged in rooms properly appropriated to another class, and all the normal arrangements of the workhouse are turned topsy-turvy.

This course " gradually reduces the workhouse to a condition in which the guardians, I venture to think, instinctively feel that for its purpose as a test for the able-bodied it is nearly useless. Wards bearing the title of able-bodied men's wards are in these cases occupied by aged men; and when the cause is sought, it is generally found that want of room for the sick and more or less helpless infirm is at the root of it. Those not thought to require the trained nurses' care are then found occupying rooms in the main building designed for the aged healthy class, of whom those who are excluded have to be placed in able-bodied inmates' wards, and more or less classed with them, to the great detriment of one of the important classifications in the workhouse. When once the wards intended for the healthy adults of a workhouse become invaded by those requiring the indulgences of the sick wards, and when the wards of those who should be treated strictly as able-bodied become invaded by those requiring to be excused work, then the difficulties of all immediately engaged in the administration of the workhouse become very greatly aggravated."[1]

The evidence is overwhelmingly strong that the absence of a workhouse suitable to the requirements of a union renders proper administration of relief almost impossible, and has much more to do with increased pauperism than the growth of popu-

---

[1] Per Mr. Henley, 18 L.G.B., p. 128.

lation.¹ "It is a matter of every-day experience that the numbers of the in-door poor are but slightly, if at all, increased by a more frequent application of the workhouse test."² "We are satisfied," the Conference of Metropolitan Guardians of 1872 reported,³ "that it is of the first importance that boards of guardians in the east of London should be enabled to offer the workhouse to *able-bodied* paupers far more freely than, for want of room, they have been enabled to of late years. In an able report published by the 'Leicester' guardians of the experience gained by them during the monetary crisis of 1857-58, after showing the great advantages which had resulted both to the ratepayers and the poor from the erection of a new workhouse, and the almost uniform maintenance of the workhouse test in dealing with the able-bodied applicants for relief, they go on to say, 'Valuable as an auxiliary, as the test of destitution an out-door labour test usually fails, and is equally unsatisfactory to the guardian and the recipient of relief. . . .' In-door relief, whilst it amply provides for the wants of the applicant, effectually removes him from the labour market, and prevents him competing therein with the independent workman who is called upon to pay the rates."

The timely and useful circular letter of the Local Government Board of the 29th January, 1895, which we have inserted in Appendix K, contains an admirable *précis* of the Poor Law orders relating to adequacy of accommodation, classification, nursing, etc., in workhouses.⁴

(2) *Dealing with Applications for Relief—The Primary Duty of Guardians.*

In considering this—the primary duty of guardians—we

---

¹ *E.g.*, 1 L.G.B., p. xviii.: 17 L.G.B., pp. 73, 79; 18 L.G.B., pp. 109, 126, 127.
² See 3 L.G.B., p. 140, per Mr. Longley.   ³ 2 L.G.B., pp. 8, 9.
⁴ As to the improvement in workhouse administration, see 23 L.G.B., p. 99.

have to touch on many details, such as the improper use of personal influence in cases of which a guardian professes to have a personal knowledge, the attendance of the medical officers at the meetings of the board, the filling up of the application and report and other books by the relieving officers, the need of minute and careful inquiry, the number of relieving officers, the size of relieving officers' districts, frequent visiting and cross-visiting, the delivery of out-door relief, and the settlement of cases by the whole board rather than by relief committees.

Boards of guardians are very apt to neglect the case work on account of the greater interest attaching to general business. The case list is hurried through in the shortest possible time, the old cases often receiving not the least attention. Such slackness on the part of a board reacts upon the relieving officers, and they become careless, and neglect to look up the old cases. The natural result is that pauperism increases. It is quite possible that the effect of the new Local Government Act will be to cause still less interest to be taken in case work, especially in country unions, where so much additional work has been thrown upon the rural district councils, who will in most cases be constituted of the same members as boards of guardians. This makes it all the more important to impress again upon guardians what their primary duty is.

### (*a*) *Personal Influence.*

It often happens that cases are *well known* to individual guardians. This happens most frequently in rural or small urban unions, and the case may be decided upon the report of one guardian alone. This is not enough. "Such personal knowledge on the part of the guardians is no doubt of great benefit in many respects, but it is not unaccompanied by some counterbalancing drawbacks. There cannot in the first place fail to be instances in which a guardian well acquainted with the circumstances of some case from his own parish is tempted to divest himself of his judicial character as a member of the board, and assuming that of an advocate of the applicant, to urge some relaxation of the mode in which the guardians would under ordinary circumstances deal with the case. His brother guardians are, in the absence of the pauper, unable to support their own views by questioning him, and ascertaining his condition for themselves, and being compelled to rely solely upon the report of the relieving officer, and the opinion which has been expressed by the guardian of the parish, give way against their better judgment, and assent to the relief which he has proposed. The guardian, whose views have thus been adopted, is naturally willing to assent to the wishes of each of his brother guardians in turn under similar circumstances, and thus without being consciously actuated by any improper motives, boards of guardians are constantly led to depart in practice from what they would in theory acknowledge to be sound principles of Poor Law administration. At a meeting of a board of guardians, which I attended in an agricultural union in the west of England, I took occasion to call their attention to the exceptionally high rate of pauperism which prevailed in their union, and to several points which appeared to me objectionable in their mode of administering relief. A large number of guardians were present, and in the course of the discussion which ensued one member of the board stated it as his belief that the large majority of the guardians agreed individually with what I had said and were prepared to assent to the principles which I had endeavoured to enforce, 'but somehow,' he added, 'when we come to act as a board, we don't carry them out.' None of the other guardians expressed any dissent from this statement, and I have no reason to doubt that it was correct.

"As another drawback from the advantages resulting from the personal acquaintance which the guardians in agricultural unions possess with the circumstances of those who apply to them for relief, I may mention that I have met with instances in which relieving officers have advanced this fact as a reason for not themselves visiting the homes of persons in receipt of relief so frequently as they ought, and have excused themselves for neglecting this duty, which is one of the most important which has been imposed upon them, upon the ground that the guardian of the parish is sure to be aware of any alteration in the circumstances of their cases."[1]

The personal knowledge then of the guardian should be only considered as part of the evidence.

### (b) *Attendance of Medical Officers.*

Next, the services of the district medical officers should be utilised much more than is done at present. In country unions it would, perhaps, be impossible to exact their attendance at every meeting of the board, but where they are obliged to give the whole of their time to Poor Law work, as in London and other large towns, there is no reason why they should not be ordered to be present at each meeting. Few boards, however, require the personal and regular attendance of these officers during the hearing of applications for relief, and yet the practice has always been attended with the best results.

"A large proportion of the real or alleged destitution of applicants for relief is connected with the sickness of the applicant or of some member of his family, and the guardians can obtain much more precise and satisfactory information upon this point from the medical officer, personally, than from his certificate.

---

[1] 1 L.G.B., pp. 92, 93, per Mr. Wodehouse. See also 3 L.G.B., p. 70, on advantage of whole board dealing with a case.

"A medical examination, too, of the applicant upon the spot, often furnishes the guardians with most material information. I have also seen cases in which imposture has been detected, where the applicant has told one story to the relieving officer, and another to the medical officer when visited by him. In these cases, unless the medical officer had been present and had heard the statement of the relieving officer, the fraud would probably have remained undetected. An active and intelligent medical officer may, in this way, be of much service to the guardians. Much, no doubt, depends upon the tact and discretion of the medical officer, and any interference with the peculiar duty of the relieving officer should be carefully guarded against. No such mischief, however, has arisen where the practice in question has been adopted, and it seems highly desirable that it should become general. The guardians may probably be trusted to confine the medical officer to his proper sphere on these occasions."[1]

(c) *The Relieving Officer and his Books.*

The main reliance of the board, however, "must ultimately be placed in the regular and unremitting routine of inquiry pursued by paid and responsible officers."[2]

The official employed to investigate the cases of applicants for relief is the relieving officer. His duties in this regard are clear. "He has to examine into the circumstances of every case by visiting the house of the applicant (if situated within his district) and by making all necessary inquiries into the state of health, the ability to work, the conditions and family, and the means of such applicant, and to report the result of such inquiries in the prescribed form to the guardians at their next ordinary meeting, and also to visit from time to time as

---

[1] 3 L.G.B., p. 153.   [2] 3 L.G.B., p. 167.

requisite all paupers receiving relief, and to report concerning the same as the guardians may direct." [1]

He is supplied with a book called the "Application and Report Book," in which he should enter all the information that he has obtained. If this book is properly kept, the particulars it contains should be sufficient to enable a board of guardians to decide upon the right form of relief.[2] But, unfortunately, as is well known, it often contains only the most meagre and insufficient information. Where this is so, the fault lies entirely with the guardians.

---

[1] General Order of 1847, Art. 215, No. 2. This article deals with the duties of the relieving officer as regards relief generally, and is printed in full in Appendix F., p. 231.

[2] The heads of information are as follows :—

1. Date of the application.
2. Names of applicants, their wives, and children under 16, dependent on them.
3. Age.
4. Residence, where or with whom.
5. How long resident in the union without relief or interruption.
6. Calling or occupation.
7. If adult, whether single, married, widow, or widower. If child, whether orphan, deserted, or illegitimate.
8. If ordinarily able-bodied.
9. If partially or wholly disabled, and the description of disability.
10. If receiving medical relief only.
11. If receiving regular or temporary relief, and any other, and what relief from clubs, charitable institutions, government pensions or otherwise ; such relief, pension, allowance or contribution to be described, and the amount stated.
12. Present cause of seeking relief, or nature of application.
13. *Observations*, and names of relations liable by law to relieve the applicant, distinguishing those apparently capable of assisting the applicant.
14. Present weekly earnings or other income of applicant, and family dependent on him or her.
15. Date of last visit at the residence of the pauper.
16. Quantity and description of relief in kind.
   (*a*) Reported as given by overseers.
   (*b*) Given by relieving officer.
      (Note, in both cases the date when given and the value has to be stated.)
17. Relief ordered by guardian.
   (*a*) Money.

"One cause of a lax administration of out-door relief is the imperfect manner in which applications for relief are often presented by the relieving officers to the guardians. This remark is intended to point, amongst other things, to the frequent omission to enter in the proper column of the application and report book the names of the relatives of applicants for relief who are legally liable for their support; and in order to show the importance of insisting upon this information, the Board may mention that cases have occurred in which the mere inquiry as to the relatives of the applicant has at once led to the withdrawal of the application for relief. Another illustration of laxity is the practice of issuing tickets on shopkeepers in urgent cases between the meetings of the guardians, and the omission to state on the tickets and enter in the application and report book the articles so ordered and given. Sometimes these tickets have been known to be given, where the guardians meet fortnightly, to the amount of as much as 14s. In all cases of emergency it is the duty of the relieving officers, after careful investigation, to specify the precise articles required for the relief of the applicant, and when this precaution is neglected, experience shows that serious abuse too often follows.

"The guardians need scarcely be reminded of the broad and general principle of the English Poor Law, *viz.*, that no person has a claim to relief from the rates, except in case of actual destitution. To ensure relief being strictly limited to the class for whom it is intended, it is only requisite that those who are entrusted with the administration of the law should, by diligent and minute inquiry, ascertain the exact condition and circumstances of each applicant, and to enable the guardians to do this effectually it is essential that they should have the aid of competent and painstaking relieving officers, whose districts should not be so extensive as to preclude them from visiting each recipient of relief at his own home, and at frequent intervals, in conformity with the regulations of the board. An adherence to these simple requirements has been the main cause which has led to such gratifying results in those unions where pauperism has been so largely reduced."[1]

Mr. Longley's remarks, too, on the subject are by no means out of date. He says:—[2]

"In order that the board of guardians should have an effectual control over the administration of relief, it is not sufficient that they should examine, however carefully, the cases which are brought before them, or in which relief may have been actually given. Care should be taken that

---

    (b) In kind.
        (Note, quantity, description and value to be stated.)
    (c) For what time allowed, or nature of the order made.
18. Other orders of the board of guardians.
19. Date when order made.
20. Initials of chairman or clerk.
21. Observations.

[1] See 7 L.G.B., pp. 225, 226.
[2] 3 L.G.B., pp. 166, 167.

every application for relief, however dealt with, should pass under their review, and this can best be accomplished by the strict adherence of the relieving officers to the directions of the board already adverted to, for keeping the application and report books. These books will never, as a rule, be strictly and punctually kept by the relieving officers, unless they are encouraged to do so by a regular examination of the entries in them, and an inquiry as to omissions from them by the guardians. Too much stress cannot be laid upon the fact that, as the relieving officer is neither more nor less than the agent of the guardians in the administration of relief, so the application and report book is the only authorised record of the acts of the relieving officer on their behalf, and it is for this reason that I am disposed to suggest that this book should contain, not only a full, but an exclusive, account of the whole of the relieving officers' dealings with applications for relief. Such an examination of the application and report books as is here recommended is carried out most efficiently, and with the best effect upon the practice of the relieving officers, by some of the most active of the union clerks, and much information is afforded to the guardians, when the mode in which the book is kept is criticised by the clerk during the hearing of applications for relief. There are, however, unfortunately, but very few instances in which the guardians, or even the chairman, enter upon this examination of the application and report book, with which, indeed, the majority of the guardians have but an imperfect acquaintance."[1]

This book should in all cases be laid before the chairman of the board. Some relieving officers keep diaries. "These are very useful for reference, especially during a revision of the relief list. They are, however, seldom kept, and it is too common to find that column of the application book which should record the date of the last visit of the relieving officer to the house of the pauper left blank."[2]

(d) *The Need of Careful Inquiry.*

The relieving officer should be closely examined on his report.[3] Many boards are content when he has stated the cause of distress (sometimes expressed by the single word "destitution"), the number in the family, the wages earned, and the rent paid. But these are often the mere statements of the

---

[1] See also 23 P.L.B., pp. 37, 38; 1 L.G.B., p. 93; and 3 L.G.B., p. 78.
[2] 3 L.G.B., p. 77; *contra.* see 2 L.G.B., p. 62, and 3 L.G.B., p. 148, because it might be unadvisable to multiply books.
[3] As to the necessity of this see 3 L.G.B., p. 82.

applicant, and have not been verified, and it is forgotten that it may be to his interest to conceal the truth, or to give a special colour to facts. He will not, of course, like to have every statement examined, and it may go against the grain with many guardians not to accept his word. But they must remember that they are trustees of public funds contributed by compulsory taxation, which should not be given away needlessly, nor wasted on unworthy objects. Good administration depends on close investigation and thorough inquiry, and if pauperism is to be checked, too much stress cannot be laid upon this. How few boards verify the applicant's statements by reference to his former employer! How few ascertain what the actual cause of distress is, or inquire whether charitable bodies or individuals are giving assistance![1] How the number of our paupers would decrease if an applicant had to give upon oath definite answers to the following questions which are taken from a form used by the Parochial Board of St. Cuthert's, Edinburgh!

Q. 1. What is your name, and where do you reside?
A.
Q. 2. In what country were you born, at what place, and in what parish?
A.
Q. 3. If married, state the place or parish of your wife's or husband's birth.
A.
Q. 4. What is your age, and, if married, the name and age of your husband or wife? Give the precise date.
A.
Q. 5. Who are your parents (and grand-parents if alive), what their occupation, and where do they reside?
A.
Q. 6. If married, what are the names of your husband's or wife's parents, their occupation, and present place of residence?
A.
Q. 7. Are you single; or, if married, have you been so oftener than once?

---

[1] See Mr. Longley's remarks on the point, 3 L.G.B., pp. 167, 168, and *infra.* pp. 49-51.

# THE POOR LAW.

State when, where, and by whom, you were married; or, if a widow, or widower, how long have you been so? And where did your husband or wife die?
*A.*

*Q.* 8. If you have children to support, or living in a family with you, state their names, the places and dates of their births, and whether they are all by one marriage, or otherwise?
*A.*

*Q.* 9. Have you any children not living with you? Are they single or married? What are their number, names, ages, earnings, and residence, and date and place of their birth?
*A.*

*Q.* 10. What is your trade or employment, or how do you, or, if married, your spouse earn a living?
*A.*

*Q.* 11. What are your weekly earnings, and how much do the other members of the family earn?
*A.*

*Q.* 12. Have you any other relations who do or might be expected to support or assist you?
*A.*

*Q.* 13. Have you any household furniture, or other property, or claim to property of any description, and to what extent? Have you any claim to any pension, or right to any relief from any charitable institution? Have you any money in bank, or otherwise? Are you heir to, or have you any expectation of succeeding to, any description of property?
*A.*

*Q.* 14. Where have you resided for the last ten years, minutely specifying in the order in which you occupied houses, or lived as servant or lodger, also the names and addresses of your landlords, masters, mistresses, or lodging-house keepers, as the case may be (landlords' receipts to be produced, or other satisfactory certificates).

If the application be made by a married woman in answer to this question she will state the residence of her husband, and if for a child or children, then the residence of the parent of such child or children.
*A.*

*Q.* 15. Have you ever had parish aid? If so, when, from what parish, and the reason why?
*A.*

*Q.* 16. Have you any parish aid at present, or supply from any society or individual, or from any other source, and to what amount or extent?
*A.*

*Q.* 17. What are the particular circumstances of distress at this time which make the present application necessary? If from disease, state the nature of it, and how long you have been affected with it?
*A.*

*Q.* 18. What is the kind of relief expected,—is it temporary or permanent? and why?
*A.*

Q. 19. What place of worship do you attend? how long have you done so? and are you a communicant?
A.

Q. 20. Are you willing to become an inmate of the poorhouse?
A.

Q. 21. Can you name any parties in Edinburgh, or elsewhere, to whom you are personally known, or who can give information respecting your case?
A.

Q. 22. Are you willing to make oath to the truth of the foregoing statement?
A.

REPORT BY THE INSPECTOR, OR ASSISTANT INSPECTOR.

Having investigated this case, I find—1st, That the applicant is entitled to Interim Relief, on the ground of destitution, and being at present resident in the parish of.................. ; 2nd, That the Parochial Settlement of the applicant is in the parish of..............., on the following grounds, viz. :—
...................................Inspector.

It may be objected that a close investigation would occupy too much time,[1] and that it would be impossible for a board to get through its work. Undoubtedly more work would be entailed to begin with, but the decrease in the number of applications would be so great that, in no very long time, the board would find that it got through its work much more quickly than it did at the outset. This has been proved by experience.

We have already referred to the Atcham Union as one where the principles laid down in the great Report of the Commissioners of 1832 have been practically applied from the very first, with the result that the pauperism of the union has been reduced to a minimum.[2] The system followed in this union for thorough investigation of cases before any decision is come to on them has largely contributed to bring about this result.

---

[1] One of the scandals of our present system of administration is the small amount of time given to the consideration of applications for relief. (*Cf.* 3 L.G.B., p. 152.)

[2] *Supra.* pp. 3, 4.

Three special books are kept in addition to the official relief order and application and report books.[1] The first is the "Relieving Officer's Pocket Book." In this the relieving officer enters the result of his inquiry under five heads, as follows:—

    1st column. Names, including children under 16.
    2nd   ,,   Age.
    3rd   ,,   Names of children not dependant.
    4th   ,,   Residence and settlement.
    5th   ,,   Wages.
    6th   ,,   Particulars.

This book is practically a memorandum book, and from it is filled in the particulars required for the second special book.

This second book is called the "Relief Order Book," and is laid before the guardians at their meetings. The columns to be filled in are headed as follows:—

    1st column. Number of case.
    2nd   ,,   Names of applicants and children under 16 dependant upon them.
    3rd   ,,   Age.
    4th   ,,   Names of children not dependant on them and other relations.
    5th   ,,   Parish in which residing and length of continuous residence within the union.
    6th   ,,   Supposed place of settlement and date of last relief (if any) received by the applicant.
    7th   ,,   Weekly earnings.
    8th   ,,   Other receipts.
    9th   ,,   Particulars of application.
    10th  ,,   Amount of relief ordered.

The orders of the board are put in by the chairman at the end of each case, and initialed by him. The book contains an index at the beginning of it. The following short case will illustrate how this book is used:—

---

[1] These official books are only kept in compliance with the Poor Law orders, but are of no practical use, as they are virtually supplanted by the three special books here described.

| 1st Column. | 2nd Column. | 3rd Column. | 4th Column. | 5th Column. | 6th Column. | 7th Column. s. D. | 8th Column. s. D. | 9th Column. | 10th Column. s. D. |
|---|---|---|---|---|---|---|---|---|---|
| 999 | D— H— E— (his wife) | 62 66 | | Meole New Road, Pulley Many years | | | 1 0 2 6 | Applicant has not worked for 5 years—nearly blind—is in no club. Rent, £4 10s.—one bedroom—keeps a pig—wife earns about 1s. weekly by washing—rent paid by a daughter—other children help. Has 2s. 6d. per week for keeping the illegitimate children of his daughter. Applies for out-door relief | |
| | | 41 | M— S | London | | not known | | Married—husband, cabinetmaker—5 children—ages not known | |
| | | 35 | A— G | Ellesmere | | 14 0 | | Married—husband, labourer—wages 14s.—5 children at home | |
| | | 34 | E— | Liverpool | | | | Single—in service— wages, £13 | |
| | | 29 | E— | Asscott | | | | ,, ,, 12 | |
| | | 26 | M— | Manchester | | | | ,, ,, 16 | |
| | | 24 | E— | Shrewsbury | | | | ,, ,, 10 | |
| | | 22 | H— | London | | | | ,, Grenadier Guards—time up in August | |
| | | | | | | | Order | Offer Workhouse | |
| | | | | | | | | [Signature of Chairman] | |

The third book is kept for the entry of the names of those paupers who are on what is commonly called the "Permanent List." This book has entries for each parish, and the pauper is entered in the parish of residence. But the cases entered are all revised and considered every three months.[1]

Another equally good system is employed with the best possible effects in the Paddington Union, and is known as the "case paper" system.[2] Its object is to get a complete record of every case assisted by the guardians, and it is therefore applied both to in-door and out-door paupers. It is worked as follows :—

The name of every person who has applied for relief is entered in index books in alphabetical order, and on the vowel system. One index book is kept by the general relieving officer for in-door cases, and others by each of the relieving officers for the out-door cases in their respective districts.

*As regards in-door cases*, every case admitted to the workhouse, infirmary, lunatic asylum, or other Poor Law institution, has to be reported to the clerk on the day of admission, and it is at once numbered and indexed. If it be a *new* case, it is the duty of the relieving officers to fill in the particulars of the case on the specially printed forms (see Forms A, B, and C, *infra.*), and to send them to the clerk when filled in. These forms, together with any letters or communications about the case, are before the relief committee when it comes up for their decision, and, together with another printed orm on

---

[1] The R.O. districts used to be divided into three parts for the purposes of revision, so that one division of the union could be revised each board day, but as there are now only ten permanent cases throughout the union, it is all done at one meeting. [From information kindly supplied by Mr. J. Everest, the clerk to the Atcham Board of Guardians.]

[2] An elaborate account of the system will be found in a paper read by Mr. C. W. Empson, at the South Eastern Poor Law Conference, 1894. (See Poor Law Conferences Report for 1894.)

which their decision is noted, make up the "case paper." The paper is then numbered with the number of the case and filed.

If the case be an *old* one, the index shows it, and the original "case paper" can be produced.

*As regards out-door cases*, the same course is followed, and the same forms are used, but through the medium of the relieving officers *only*, who have charge of the case papers and of the indexes relating to cases in their own districts.

If an out-door case should become an in-door case, the papers relating to it are at once transferred to the clerk's office.

Where any relative of the applicant lives outside the boundaries of the union, the inquiry as to his or her means is made by the general relieving officer.

Every in-door case is put on for a certain number of weeks, and at the expiration of the time has to come again before the committee for a further order. Thus no case can be lost sight of.

The forms used are as follows :—

FORM A. FOR BOTH IN-DOOR AND OUT-DOOR CASES.

## PARISH OF PADDINGTON, LONDON.

*Relief Office, 289 Harrow Road, W.,* _____189 \_\_\_\_

No.

Report respecting                                       born

Admitted to                        on the        day of                      18

Calling (if any)                          Married or single

Religious Persuasion                 Name of Husband or Wife

When Married                        Where married

Wife's Maiden Name             If a Widow, Name and ⎫
                                        Occupation of Husband ⎭

Names of Children

   and, if a child,

When born

Where born

When and where Baptised

Previous Residence and how long there

When and where last chargeable

   In the case of a Lunatic—

Name of Justice              Date of Order       Exam. Exs.   £   :   :
                                                                                   Removal Exs. £   :   :

Name of nearest Relative

Address of     do.

Other particulars of the case, in- ⎫
   cluding names and addresses ⎪
   and financial circumstances of ⎬
   Relatives able to assist. ⎭

FORM B. FOR SETTLEMENT OR ADJUDICATION INQUIRIES ONLY.
PARISH OF PADDINGTON, LONDON.

No.———

*Guardians' Offices, 289 Harrow Road, W.,* ————— *189*——

Report respecting                                                         Aged
   When born?                          Where born?
Name of Husband or Wife
   When born?                          Where born?
Names and Ages of Children
   When born?
   Where born?
Date of Admission to Workhouse                    By whose Order?
If a Lunatic { Name of Magistrate                 Date of Order
             { Name of Asylum                   When sent?
Residence before Admission to Workhouse, and how long there?
Previous residences, given in order }
   backwards, as far as may be neces-
   sary for showing settlement.
Calling or Occupation                             Married or Single
Able-bodied, temporarily disabled, or permanently disabled
If married, When?
      Where?
Wife's Maiden Name?

      *Christian and Surname.*      *Address.*      *Occupation.*

Names and Addresses of { Father
                           Mother
                           Husband
                           Wife
                           Children
                           Friends, or any Relatives not }
                              above inserted

If Apprenticed, or if Father was Apprenticed
   Name of Master
   Address
   Date of Apprenticeship?
   Residence during last 40 days?
If rented a House, or if Parents rented a House }
    before Pauper was 16 years old?
   When?
   Where?
   Landlord's Name?
         Address?
   Rent?
   Rates and Taxes?
If possessed of an Estate?
   Value?
   Where?
Parish Relief at any time?
   When?
   Where?
If removed before?
   When?
   From what Parish?
   To what Parish?
Where was Father born?
       When?
      (if not known)
Where was Mother born?
       When?
Where was Father living at time when }
   Pauper became 16 years of age?

## Form C.

A REPORT on the Circumstances of _____
a Relative liable to maintain _____ his _____
who is at present chargeable to the PARISH OF PADDINGTON, in the _____
_____ at a cost of _____ per week.

| | |
|---|---|
| Name and Age of the liable Relative | |
| His place of Residence | |
| What is his Occupation? | |
| Is he at present in Employment? | |
| What are his Earnings? | |
| What other Sources of Income? | |
| Has he a Wife? | |
| Is she able to Work; and if so, has she Employment, and what does she earn? | |
| How many Children has he? | |
| What are their Ages? | |
| What does each Child earn? | |
| What Rent does he pay? | |
| Is he a Member of a Club, or Friendly Society? | |
| Is he in Debt? | |
| Is there a Bill of Sale on his Furniture? | |
| Does he Maintain, or contribute to the Maintenance of, any other Relative? | |
| Other particulars (if any) | |

Dated _____ 189   _____
*General Relieving Officer of the*
_____ *Union.*

FORM D.[1]

Name:—

PARISH OF PADDINGTON.

No. ————

NORTH No.
SOUTH No.
WEST No.

*Relief Office, 289 Harrow Road, W.,* ———— *189*—

| Date. | Nature of Application and Order of Committee. | Date. | Initials of Chairman or Clerk. |
|---|---|---|---|
|  |  |  |  |

[1] *Note.*—When it is decided to order *in-door* relief this form is stamped as follows:—

> Approved
> for......weeks
> [Date
> of decision]
> ............
> *Chairman.*

Under this system, which works smoothly and without the least friction, the guardians have always a full history of the case before them. It has been found to be a great check on fraud and imposture, and has been most successful in reducing the pauperism of the union.[1]

Some boards of guardians, of which that of Whitchurch (Hants) is an example, keep a "Record Book," in which is entered the names of all paupers who have applied for, been refused, or granted relief, and full particulars of the cases. This is a most useful practice, and the history of every case is before the guardians from the time of the applicant's first appearance up to date. When the book has once been started, there is very little trouble connected with keeping it posted up.

---

[1] We have to thank Mr. H. F. Aveling, the clerk to the Paddington Guardians, for the information with regard to the "case paper" system.

*(e) Number of Relieving Officers and Size of their Districts.*

It is evident that a relieving officer will never be able to perform his duties of inquiry and investigation properly if his district be too large either as regards area or population. Not only has he to examine new applications for relief, but he has also to visit the houses of those already in receipt of relief. *Therefore a union must have a sufficient number of relieving officers.*

It is impossible to lay down any general rule as to what the number should be, because a relieving officer can of course look after more cases in a town than in the country; but the relief districts should be so arranged "that no relieving officer

---

It was at first established in 1890, and applied only to in-door cases; but two years later it was extended to out-door cases. Mr. Empson, one of the Paddington Guardians, has kindly supplied us with the following description: "The present system has now been in working order for about two years, and has proved a great success. At first one of the R.O.'s raised an objection to it on the ground that it was not part of his duty to adopt such a system. The L.G.B. was applied to by the guardians in the matter, and ruled that it was within the power of the guardians to order the R.O.'s to use the system. No difficulty has risen since this ruling, and the R.O.'s admit the usefulness of the system. The L.G.B. declined, however, to allow the Application and Report Book to be superseded in any way, and the guardians recently passed a resolution directing the R.O.'s to keep that book in such a way as will satisfy the requirements of the L.G.B. No more than is absolutely necessary is inserted in that book, the additional information required by the guardians being given on the case paper, to which is attached all correspondence relative to the case. The guardians have, therefore, the whole history of a case before them without trouble of reference, and they are often able thereby to avoid mistakes. Every indoor case is put on for a certain number of weeks; at the expiration of the time, if the case is still chargeable, it comes up automatically before the Indoor Relief Committee, who see that all orders on the case have been complied with, and consider whether any difference of treatment is desirable. It is then "approved" for a certain number of weeks again, at the end of which time the process is repeated. In this way no in-door case can be lost sight of, as so frequently happens otherwise. Out-door cases necessarily are brought up before the Relief Committee, when the relief order has expired, should further help be asked. Every case, whether in or out, has its distinctive number, and can be easily found by reference to the index."

shall have under his charge a greater number of cases than it will be possible for him to visit and thoroughly to investigate, at least once in every quarter, in addition to visiting and reporting upon every fresh application, after careful inquiry into all the circumstances of each case."[1] "It is of essential importance to any sound system of out-door relief that the relief districts should not be too large, or the number of relieving officers too small. If a relieving officer's district be too large it will be impossible for him, however zealous and vigilant he may be, to investigate with sufficient care the circumstances of each applicant for relief, or pauper in receipt of relief; and nothing can be more objectionable than that an officer should be compelled to perform his duty in a hurried and incomplete manner."[2] It has been said that no relieving officer ought to have more than 150 or at most 300 paupers on his list, in order to enable him to do his work of inquiry and visiting properly.[3]

As regards area, it is most important that a relieving officer's district should be of a manageable size; but again, when one has "to deal with such discordant elements as area, population, character of population, and personal ability, it is very difficult to say what is and what is not a workable district."[4] Each board then must decide what number of relieving officers is sufficient for its own union.[5]

### (f) Cross-visiting.

Several unions have adopted the system of cross-visiting.

---

[1] Per Mr. Doyle, 2 L.G.B., p. 66. See also 1 L.G.B., p. 102, and 3 L.G.B., p. 77. The appointment of assistant relieving officers is not recommended. For reasons see 3 L.G.B., p. 150.

[2] 1 L.G.B., p. 68, and 23 L.G.B., p. 99 (Peterborough).

[3] See Aschrott's "Poor Law System," 1st edition, p. 92, note; and Report of Conference of Metropolitan Guardians, 2 L.G.B., p. 7.

[4] 3 L.G.B., p. 77.

[5] To assist them in coming to a decision, we refer them to 23 P.L.B., p. 104; 2 L.G.B., pp. 62-66; 3 L.G.B., p. 77; and 17 L.G.B., p. 84.

This has been found of great assistance in detecting imposture, and it keeps the relieving officers up to their work. The cross visitor is an officer whose duty it is to check by independent visits the inquiries made by the relieving officers, to pay surprise visits at irregular intervals to all recipients of out-door relief, and also to make special investigations. Such an officer would render the guardians great assistance in large urban unions, but he would also be found very useful in scattered country unions, where the districts of relieving officers are very extensive.[1] Where a cross-visitor has been appointed, the best results have ensued, and pauperism, especially out-door pauperism, has been much reduced.

### (g) *Frequent and Systematic Visiting.*

A proper supervision of out-door relief implies the frequent visiting of homes. Art. 215 of the General Order of 1847 says that it is the duty of the relieving officer to visit from time to time all paupers receiving relief, and to report concerning the same. This duty has not been properly performed in the following cases:[2]—(1) When he has seen the pauper but has not visited the home, (2) when he has visited the home and has not seen the pauper, (3) when he has neither seen the home nor the pauper *because he knows all the circumstances of the case*, and (4) when he is satisfied with the report of any guardian upon the case, and being thus satisfied, neither visits nor makes further inquiry. . . . . " In a country district a relieving officer soon becomes acquainted with the whole of the habitual pauper class. He does not, therefore, realise the necessity of domiciliary visits, probably considering an interview at his weekly round to the village or an occasional con-

---

[1] See 18 L.G.B., p. 143; and 21 L.G.B., p. 162.
[2] See 23 P.L.B., p. 96.

versation with the guardian to be sufficient." Nothing is more important for purposes of good administration than that the visiting of the homes of out-door paupers should be *systematic*, and yet in very few unions have the guardians any system at all in regard to it.[1] One painstaking relieving officer attributed to it the success he had met with in reducing his out-door relief list. He saved nearly £1,500 to the rates by visiting the poor at their homes, not only once a quarter, but continually, whenever and wherever there was a doubt that the relief given was not used for the purpose intended.[2]

### (h) *The Distribution of Relief.*

The guardians should also exercise great care as to the mode of distributing out-door relief. The ideal system is that the relief should be delivered at the home. But the impossibility of doing this renders it necessary to have pay stations in the country, and to utilise the union offices for this purpose in towns. In no case, however, should a public-house be used as a pay station.[3]

### (i) *Relief Committees v. Whole Board.*

In populous urban districts, owing to the number of applications for relief, boards of guardians usually work by relief committees. But the settlement of cases by the whole board is preferable, and, if the applications are dealt with on some regular system or well-understood lines, and after full and searching investigation, the division of the board into

---

[1] *Cf.* 1 L.G.B. p., 101; 3 L.G.B., pp., 83, 84; and 19 L.G.B., p. 134.
[2] 19 L.G.B., p. 134.
[3] As to the evils attaching to the pay station system, see 3 L.G.B., pp. 80, 81.

relief committees may be indefinitely postponed, for the cases will not so increase in number as to make this necessary. Relief committees are likely to administer relief in different ways and on different principles, and the knowledge of this encourages speculative applications from the poor. If, therefore, the system is adopted, a board should agree to clear and definite bye-laws with regard to the grant of out-door relief, and no departure from them should be allowed except on the decision of the whole board.[1]

Thus, Mr. Culley, writing in 1873 of the Hartlepool system, says, that that town had an advantage over some other urban unions,

"in that the applications are heard by the whole board of guardians instead of by small relief committees. Putting aside the evident chance of more uniform treatment, I am convinced that the examination of applicants by the chairman before the full board is the only means by which a board of guardians can ascertain that they are administering the law equally and fairly throughout their union. I have frequently heard the report of relieving officers usefully supplemented by such an examination, and still more frequently the opinions of individual guardians utterly upset. Where the population of unions is so large as to make the appointment of relief committees necessary, I would recommend that each committee (when acting) should not consist of less than three guardians, and that the committees should occasionally change their districts, or that one or two responsible members of the board (such as the chairman or vice-chairman) should attend the different committees in turn."[2]

Mr. Longley expresses the same opinion:—

"A hesitating and variable course of administration of relief tends to promote speculative applications from the poor, and so to encourage them in improvident habits, while, at the same time, it frequently inflicts much injustice on them by a sudden return to principles which have been for a

---

[1] *Cf.* 3 L.G.B., pp. 159, 160. And see 18 L.G.B., p. 114.
[2] 3 L.G.B., pp. 70, 71. Mr. Culley has the following note: "In York Union, which has for many years been especially well administered, there were formerly separate relief committees for the city and rural districts, but this practice was abandoned 'because it was found that the rural guardians were more inclined to give out-relief than the city guardians, and the administration was not equal throughout the union.'" See also Appendix, p. 236.

time abandoned. The larger the number of distinct bodies by which relief is administered, the greater, of course, is the risk of variance of practice among them : but the extent of the mischief in this respect which results from the multiplication of relief committees can scarcely be conceived by anyone who has not seen two committees of the same board of guardians, sitting, sometimes, at the same time in adjoining rooms, the difference of whose practice in administering relief is such that a bystander might be led to doubt whether the same law governed the proceedings of both."[1]

### Mr. Baldwyn Fleming writes of his district :—

" The out-relief in Hants and Wilts is very excessive—though to a more moderate extent. It could readily be reduced in the three counties, but only by the expenditure of a great deal more time, trouble and impartiality, than is at present given. I observe with extreme regret the growing practice of 'dividing the board' of guardians into committees for hearing the relief cases, and also how frequently a large number of guardians who attend what is known as 'the public business,' take little or no share in the actual administration of the relief. Of all the duties the guardians have to perform, none is, in any degree, so important as the careful hearing of the applications for relief, and the impartial decision of a full board upon them. Instead of this the cases are very often heard by a few guardians, and are practically decided by the guardian of the parish from which each application comes. Most country guardians 'stick up' for the cases in their own parish, and the result of the above practice is to make each guardian the advocate and judge of the case. I was recently at a large urban board of guardians when the question of relief by committees was considered. The argument in favour of committees was that it would save time. I urged the great objections to the administration of relief by a small section of guardians instead of a full board, but without avail. I then begged them to lay down a rule that no guardian should sit on a committee for his own parish, in order that the administration might be impartial, and that relief should be granted solely upon the merits and necessities of each applicant without the influence of any personal knowledge or prejudice. The guardians, headed by the chairman, appeared to think my suggestion ridiculous. It was said immediately, 'Oh! of course, we must each look after the cases from our own parish.' But it is just the 'looking after' and the 'own parish' which cause such unfortunate results. The looking after cannot be effectually done unless very much time is given to it, and it is especially the province of the relieving officer, and the 'own parish' introduces the personal influence which it is so important to eliminate. This lack of time and impartiality is specially noticeable when the cases are 'revised.' "[2]

---

[1] 3 L.G.B., p. 160.
[2] 18 L.G.B., pp. 113, 114.

Mr. Knollys writes :—

"The mode of administration as regards relief by committees in populous unions is, at such times as the present, of special importance. It seems desirable that where relief is dispensed by committees, those committees should have, in addition to the general regulations laid down by the Local Government Board, certain clear instructions for their procedure framed by each board of guardians, and not a general understanding only, to ensure similarity of administration, and that any departure from these should be dealt with by the full board of guardians only."[1]

And again :—

"In the Middlesborough Union there is an understanding that the guardians from time to time shall change the committee on which they sit, and in the Auckland Union, where the guardians divide themselves at the time of the board meeting into four sections for relief purposes, there is a regulation that each relieving officer shall bring his cases before each of the four sections in turn : but otherwise the practice in the district is for the guardians to sit on the relief committee for the district including the parish they represent and on no other. The practice of dividing the board into sections for relief purposes is, as a rule, adopted, I am happy to say, in four unions only in my district, at Hexham, Tynemouth, Auckland and Durham, and the practice is one that appears open to many objections. If duly constituted relief committees, sitting on some other day than the board day, are not formed, all cases should, I think, come before the full board, but if a board is divided into sections, such a practice as that followed by the Auckland Guardians seems a very desirable one."[2]

Finally, Mr. Dansey says :—

"I also took the opportunity of comparing the pauperism of some of the more strictly managed unions in Shropshire with that of the Cheshire unions, and urged the adoption of bye-laws for the administration of out-relief, more especially as the relief in money of the Cheshire unions was administered by committees ; and my experience of the work of relief committees is not encouraging except where they are guided by bye-laws adopted by their respective boards."[3]

---

[1] 18 L.G.B., p. 133.
[2] *Ib.*, p. 134.
[3] 20 L.G.B., p. 232.

*(j) First Applications and Lists of Paupers.*

When the applicant has made a first application for relief he should always be present so that he may answer personally any questions which the guardians may desire to put to him. This should be the rule not only when general relief but also when medical relief is asked for. The enforcement of this rule is a great check upon unnecessary applications. It often happens that when the case is brought forward the applicant is not in attendance, and this usually means that he is not destitute.

In some unions it is the practice to post up lists of all paupers relieved during the half year on the doors of churches and chapels. As to the utility of this plan there is some divergence of opinion, but it is certainly a good practice to furnish once a quarter to every friendly society in the union a list of persons receiving relief.[1] These methods are likely to reduce the number of applications and to facilitate the detection of imposture and fraud.

### (3) *Ample Notice of Change of Policy.*

When a board of guardians which has been very free in granting out-door relief has become convinced of the evils attaching to this course, and wishes to change its practice, it must be careful not to bring about the change too rapidly, otherwise more harm than good will be done.

As Mr. Longley says:—

"It has always appeared to me that the poor have good cause to complain when, having been induced, and as it were educated, by the practice of a board of guardians to rely unduly upon Poor Law relief, a sudden and abrupt change of practice alters the position in which they have been placed, not by themselves, but by the past practice of the guardians, for whose lax administration they are now to suffer. I am not now arguing that a pauper has a vested interest in the maintenance of an unsound system,

---

[1] As to guardians printing weekly lists of out-door paupers, see Appendix, p. 234.

but merely that the system, whatever it is, should be conducted on principles which shall be, or which may be, as well known to him as to the guardians, and that due warning should be given of any change in the rules on which relief is administered."[1]

Mr. Bland Garland, the late chairman of the Bradfield Board of Guardians, has described how the change was made in his own union. There was in his union in 1871, as in all other unions, a permanent list on which the names of all out-door paupers were placed. There they remained for life. The board of guardians could not pretend to revise this list properly, nor could the relieving officers deal with it on account of the numbers, which were very great.

It was determined to close this list and to add no new names to it, but relief was not withdrawn from those paupers who were already on it. In course of time they died off, and the permanent list came to an end.[2]

The report of the Whitechapel Board of Guardians for the year ending Lady Day, 1893, shows how the change was made in that union. The guardians "began by gradually restricting out-door relief in 'out of work' cases, until they were able (in 1870) to entirely close the out-door labour yard, and it has not since then been re-opened. In this process of restriction it was found that only one in ten of those who were offered in-door, in place of out-door relief, entered the workhouse, and these, in turn, gradually withdrew themselves, so that eventually the in-door pauperism resumed its normal condition. Following this was a further review of the out-door relief lists, the gradual application of other forms of limitation side by side with efforts to bring the more deserving within reach of helpful charity.

[1] 3 L.G.B., pp. 146, 147.
[2] "From Pauperism to Manliness," an address delivered at the annual meeting of the London Charity Organisation Society on April 23rd, 1891.

"The guardians were especially mindful to guard the entrance to the out-door relief list, and, where the circumstances seemed to necessitate present relief in the home of the applicant, it was sought to make it in the first place adequate to the necessities of the case, and next, temporary in duration; and it was usually given upon some condition of personal effort to avoid future recourse to the rates for support. Sick men with families dependent upon them, if not offered in-door relief, were relieved temporarily in money and kind, upon the distinct promise to join a benefit club. Widows with dependent children were, in some cases, afforded relief out of the workhouse for a strictly limited period pending inquiries as to their circumstances and possibilities of communication with relatives and late employers, and efforts to place them in positions to achieve independence.

"In some cases employment was offered in the infirmary as a scrubber or washer at weekly wages; or, failing other means of meeting the necessities of the case, the guardians undertook to receive a portion of the family into the district school, leaving the mother free to enter service, or otherwise to provide for herself and one, or sometimes two children.

"The aged and infirm were only relieved out-of-doors when there was evidence of thrift, and when guardians were satisfied that there were no children or relatives legally or morally bound to support them, and able to do so; but even these exceptions and limitations became non-existent and unnecessary with the organisation of voluntary charity, which gradually undertook the benevolent work of saving the really deserving poor from the Poor Law. Thus the door of out-relief became gradually closed, and as a fact no cases—other than those of sudden or urgent necessity relieved by the relieving officers in kind—have now for some twenty-three years been added to the out-door relief lists; and now (in 1893) there remains but one aged woman, the sole remnant of a former system, in receipt of permanent out-door relief."[1]

### (4) *Co-operation between Charity and the Poor Law.*

Another essential to good administration is that there should be close co-operation between a board of guardians and the administrators of public or private charities in the union.[2]

No proper co-operation can be said to exist unless there is a division of the field of work between the Poor Law and charity. A case should either be taken off the rates altogether or else left to the guardians to deal with. So long as out-door relief continues to be given no perfect co-operation can exist. The great advantage of the restriction of out-door relief to certain definite limits, as for instance to urgent cases, cases of relief during the first month of widowhood, etc., is that it spurs on charity to deal with those cases which should not be allowed to come on the rates, and, as often happens, eventually to drift into the workhouse.[3] Out-door relief is a charity that is no charity, a charity that makes use not of freely given alms, but of funds compulsorily levied from taxpayers. So far then as out-door relief is administered like charity it is opposed to the principle of our Poor Laws, the fundamental doctrine of which is "that relief is given, *not as matter of charity but of legal obligation*, and to extend this obligation beyond the class to

---

[1] Whitechapel Report, 1893, p. vii.
[2] See as to this an interesting report by Miss Octavia Hill to the Local Government Board, on "Official and Volunteer Agencies in Administering Relief," which is printed in 3 L.G.B., pp. 126-30, and especially affects large towns.
[3] For reasons see the very able paper entitled, "Why is it Wrong to Supplement Out-door Relief?" (occasional paper No. 31, Charity Organisation Society's Series). Also Mr. Goschen's circular on the subject, printed in Appendix G., p. 232 (22 P.L.B., p. 9). *Cf.* 3 L.G.B., pp. 118, 145; 18 L.G.B., p. 115; 20 L.G.B., p. 225.

which it now applies, namely the actually destitute, to a further and much larger class, namely those in receipt of insufficient wages, would be not only to increase to an unlimited extent the present enormous expenditure, but to allow the belief in a legal claim to public money in every emergency to supplant in a further portion of the population the full recognition of the necessity for self-reliance and thrift."[1]

Few boards, however, have had the courage to place close and definite limits upon out-door relief, and thus reduce it to a minimum. Where they have done this charity has accepted new and more complete duties, and both Poor Law and charity have been benefited. But if this, the best policy, is not adopted, the only way in which charity may interfere legitimately is by giving any necessary assistance which the guardians have no power to give themselves;[2] but in so doing it must act in concert with the guardians.

But how are the guardians to find out what charity is doing? It is the duty of the relieving officer to obtain this information for them, and submit it to them in detail.[3] And individual guardians, too, should not conceal from the board the fact that charitable relief is being given, from a mistaken idea that the Poor Law has to take no note of what charity is doing. In short, *a constant interchange of information should be established between the guardians and the administrators of charity.* This interchange may be greatly assisted by a

---

[1] See 22 P.L.B., p. 10.

[2] (1) In establishing any person in trade or business.
    (2) In redeeming tools, clothes, or other articles from pawn.
    (3) In purchasing tools, etc.
    (4) In purchasing clothes (guardians can only do this in cases of urgent necessity).
    (5) In paying the cost of conveyance to any part of the United Kingdom.
    (6) In paying rent or lodging.

[3] See Appendix N., p. 254, for the opinion of Local Government Board on the point.

periodical publication by the guardians of the names of persons in receipt of relief.[1]

Unfortunately, the old, bad, and justly censured system of out-door relief still exists in the majority of unions, and as long as this is so the Poor Law cannot be said to be well administered in them. In such unions charity relies upon the rates, and the rates are used as a charity. Charity relieves inadequately because it hopes the guardians will allow something, and the guardians give their miserable dole on the chance of charity supplementing it with another one.[2] Little or no communication passes between the board and the givers of charity. And pauperism thrives.

(5) *Co-operation between Public Authorities and the Poor Law.*

In close connection with the subject we are considering is the need of cordial co-operation with public authorities. The aid of the magistrates is often called in to maintain the discipline of the workhouse, to enforce the repayment of loans, the payment of contributions by relations, and so on. There is no doubt that the guardians are the best judges as to what amount a relation can afford to pay, as to whether the means of the recipient of the loan will enable him to repay it, and yet the magistrates often ignore the opinion of the guardians and order what they may consider right and just. Far be it from us to dispute the discretion of the bench in such matters, but unless there is some very good reason for it, such as a knowledge of prejudice and unfairness on the part of the guardians, the magistrates should as a rule uphold their decision. Nothing is

---

[1] See 3 L.G.B., p. 145; and *supra.* p. 46. The objection that such periodical publication affixes the stigma of pauperism too publicly on paupers is nowadays too ridiculous a one to argue upon. (See *ib.*, p. 146.)

[2] See 18 L.G.B., p. 115; and *cf.* 3 L.G.B., p. 169.

so detrimental to good administration of the Poor Law as uncertainty, and appeals from the orders of guardians are sure to multiply as soon as it is found out that the bench are in the habit of overruling their decisions. Besides which the guardians are discouraged from doing their duty by such action on the part of the magistrates.

It is unnecessary to enlarge here upon the necessity of close co-operation between boards of guardians and public bodies such as vestries, local boards, etc., in times of exceptional distress. The subject is touched upon in Chapter XIII.

## CHAPTER V.

### THE EVILS ATTACHING TO OUT-DOOR RELIEF.

HAVING then pointed out how inquiry and investigation into application for relief should be made, we will now consider how a board of guardians should be guided in deciding the two apparently simple questions which arise on every application for relief:—*Firstly,* Is the applicant destitute? and if so, then, *secondly,* How shall he be relieved?

*As to the first question,* no definition of what constitutes destitution is given (so far as we know) in any Poor Law Act or Order. But a person (and the same may be said of a family of persons) may be considered destitute who has not the means of procuring the necessities of bare existence, and whose life may be endangered in consequence. The law makes the guardians the judges of destitution, and every board has naturally a different opinion on the question. In most unions no distinction is made between destitution and poverty, and thus the poor as well as the destitute become the recipients of relief from the parish. There is, however, one way in which destitution can be detected, and that is by the offer of the house. This is known as the workhouse test. An applicant for relief will refuse the offer if he has any means of supporting himself. As a relieving officer has full power to give relief in kind, or an order for the doctor in cases of sudden or urgent necessity, the law has provided against any harm happening to a person, or family of persons, between the meetings of a board; and when he has reported his action in the case to the guardians, and they have ordered how he is to act, his responsibility in the matter other than to carry out the order ceases.

*As to the second question,* good, fair, or bad administration of the Poor Law depends upon the way in which boards of guardians habitually decide it. There are only two modes of giving poor relief, the first by relief inside the workhouse, and the second by relief outside the workhouse. There is no third course. Out-door and in-door relief are correlative terms, and must be dealt with together. Out-door relief may, however, be subdivided into ordinary out-door relief and medical out-door relief, and as different considerations govern the grant of the latter we shall consider it by itself. In this and the two following chapters we refer only to ordinary out-door relief.[1]

This form of out-door relief is given either in money or in kind, or in both money and kind. The evils attaching to it are manifest, and generally admitted, but most boards of guardians prefer giving it to the possibility of breaking up the "little home" by "hard and cruel" offers of the house. We propose to show why the epithets "hard and cruel" should rather be attached to out-door than to in-door relief; how, if the "little home" *is* broken up, it is generally for the benefit of its occupants; and how beneficially the enforcement of the "workhouse test" works.

(1) *Out-door Relief must affect Wages and Earnings adversely.*

This was more apparent as regards wages under the old

---

[1] Out-door relief is at present regulated by two orders—(1) the Out-door Relief Prohibitory Order of 1844, and (2) the Out-door Relief Regulation Order, 1852. The former, which is stringent, applies to country unions and small towns, and the latter, which is more lax, to London and large towns. For a clear and concise summary of the orders see Aschrott's "English Poor Law System," 1st edit., p. 132, *et seq.*

system prevailing before 1834 than it is now.[1]  Owing to the enforcement of the workhouse test for the able-bodied, wages cannot be so much affected now as they were then; but in the case of women, especially widows, and those who are infirm or crippled, out-door relief does undoubtedly affect wages. That it affects earnings is well known. The following extracts bear upon the subject.

Mr. Wodehouse says:[2]

"I endeavoured to ascertain, as far as I was able, within what limits, and to what class of cases, relief is given in aid of earnings. Some distinction may, I think, be drawn between relief given in aid of earnings and relief given in aid of wages. Relief in aid of earnings is clearly inseparable from any system of out-relief.

"Thus in all unions relief is afforded to able-bodied widows with children, and it is clear that all such relief is in aid of an income obtained by the widow by washing, charing, or other similar employments. So again, in almost every union that I visited relief is given to old and infirm men, who, though past regular work, are from time to time employed in occasional odd jobs of various sorts. Relief to these two classes of paupers may, I think, be distinguished from that system of relief in aid of wages which was so generally prevalent prior to the introduction of the present Poor Law. Relief in aid of the earnings of widows and aged persons is relief given to supplement an income derived from employment obtained at irregular intervals, and remunerated at a variable rate, whereas the relief formerly given in aid of wages was given to persons who were in regular employment and were paid at a comparatively fixed rate. Of the former class of relief it may at least be said, that it does not tend so directly to keep down the rate of wages as the latter, although it cannot be doubted that it has an indirect tendency in that direction, by encouraging the employment at reduced wages of old and infirm men, and in some cases of women and children upon work which would otherwise be performed by able-bodied labourers. A class of cases lying half-way between the two that I have mentioned is that of cripples to whom some employer of labour may have given constant employment at a rate of wages reduced in consequence of infirmity to so low a point that they are obliged to apply for parochial assistance. The simple question to be decided in each case of this nature is what portion of the cripple's maintenance ought to be provided out of the pockets of his employer, and what portion should fall upon the rates? If the guardians are not careful to see that the cripple receives an amount of remuneration fairly proportionate to the value of the work which he is able to perform, any relief they may allow will be relief in aid of the wages of the employer, who, in many

---

[1] See 1st Report of Poor Law Commissioners, 1834, pp. 143, 144.
[2] 1 L.G.B., p. 98.

cases, it is to be feared, gets the best of the bargain. In most of the unions which I visited, the answer which I received to my inquiries upon these points was, that although relief was granted in aid of the earnings of widows and aged persons, yet it was not given, with the exception of some few cases of cripples, to any persons who were in regular and constant employment. In some unions, however, the line which I have attempted to draw between relief in aid of earnings and relief in aid of wages, was clearly over-stepped. Thus in some cases where a widower has a large family, some of the children are taken into the workhouse although the father is in constant work and receiving regular wages.

"At Stratton I was told relief was given 'to some who were in regular employment, such as men at work on the roads or at reduced wages.' At Axminister, on the day of my visit, a labourer with six children, whose wife had been sent by the guardians to a hospital, and who was himself in regular employment, and receiving the ordinary wages of the district, applied for relief upon the ground that he could not afford to pay anyone to look after his children. The board granted him 1s. 6d. per week. The case was certainly one of great hardship, but the relief given was without doubt relief in aid of wages."

Mr. Longley writes :—[1]

"In London, as in all large towns, there is a distinct demand for female labour, which is no doubt frequently ill remunerated, but which, it can scarcely be denied, would be better remunerated if the operation of the general principles which regulate the price of this, as of all other labour, were not disturbed by the existence of a special class, who are known to be able to sell their labour at a lower rate than that at which the independent labourer can afford to work. The inference is so obvious as scarcely to need any instances in its support. I may, however, mention a case which occurred in my presence, where a widow who applied for a renewal of out-relief stated that her occupation was to clean an office in which she lived rent free, though she received no wages for her work. The relieving officer told the guardians, as indeed was evident, that 'her relief paid her wages,' and that if it were discontinued her employer must pay her. The relief, however, was renewed."

Mr. Murray Browne says :—[2]

"I will venture to make one more remark, *i.e.*, upon the effect of out-relief in keeping down the general rate of wages. This is a point which has been often adverted to, but has not, I think, always attracted as much attention as it deserves. Before the introduction of the 'new Poor Law' in 1834, it is not denied that wages were largely and intentionally kept down by the use of out-relief. Since the reform introduced by that measure, this

---

[1] 3 L.G.B., pp. 180, 181.
[2] 20 L.G.B., pp. 255, 256.

effect has been produced to a comparatively small extent only. Yet it is on record that the virtual abolition of out-door relief in the union of Bradfield raised the wages of charwomen throughout the union by 6d. a day. And I think that anyone who considers the matter will be able very well to understand that a similar policy in any highly pauperised union would be very likely to produce a similar result.

"Charwomen who are widows with children (a numerous class) would in such cases appeal to their employers for increased pay, on the ground that now, when they could get nothing from the 'parish,' they could not afford to work for so little. And after more or less demur, the claim would be allowed. The wages of charwomen who are not widows would then rise in like manner; and it would become apparent that the wage of the very poorest class in the community is now kept down by the grant of out-relief.

"The remuneration of other kinds of female labour is probably to some degree reduced by the same cause. And the like observation applies to all those 'odd jobs' and other labour of an inferior kind which are at present performed by old men in receipt of out-relief.

"Were out-relief abolished these old men would probably get better paid, the conclusion being that the wages of such poor people are at present paid partly out of the rates, while their competition keeps down the price of the labour of the independent poor. Indeed I think that I have at times detected, in the minds of farmer guardians and others, a conviction that this was the case, and a deliberate preference for out-relief on that account. I have been told that out-relief 'keeps people in the country, etc.,' a saying which I can only interpret as implying that out-relief prevents the poor from going out of the union to other places where their labour is more in demand, and so keeps them ready for any employment which may offer, at any wages which can be obtained. On the injustice thus done to the poor I need not dilate. It is in the interest of the poor rather than of the rich, that I plead for the practical abolition of out-door relief."

An extract from the interesting "Report of the Progress of the Atcham Union" (see *infra.* p. 143) supports this view.

Mr. Stevens, in drawing attention to the great amount of pauperism in Lincolnshire, says:—[1]

"I am convinced that the administration of relief in Lincolnshire is mainly what causes the pauperism to be high there, and that much of the out-relief given has a tendency to keep down wages, thus relieving ratepayers who largely employ low wage earners at the expense of other ratepayers."

The small pittance which out-door relief represents when

---

[1] 21 L.G.B., pp. 166, 167. See further, 23 P.L.B., p. 37.

the sum is divided among the recipients shows, too, that the "old abuse of relief in aid of wages" still prevails, the smallness of the amount being conclusive evidence of the fact.[1]

We do not of course suggest that, where the wages paid for labour are low, the grant of out-door relief is the exclusive cause. It would be absurd to do so. But that they are affected by it there can, we think, be no doubt whatever.[2] It may be urged that the rate of wages regulates the amount of pauperism.[3] In unions where out-door relief is the rule and not the exception no doubt it does; but in comparing differently administered unions in this regard we find that although wages *are the same*, pauperism is rampant in one and almost non-existent in the other.[4] The argument of the following table is, we think, conclusive that wages do not in any way regulate pauperism :—

| Union. | | Population 1881. | Population 1891. | Paupers 1st Jan., 1893, excluding lunatics, vagrants, and children. | | | Proportion of paupers to population. |
|---|---|---|---|---|---|---|---|
| | | | | Indoor. | Outdoor | Total. | |
| Bradfield | Berks. | 17,972 | 18,017 | 58 | 22 | 80 | 1 in 225 |
| Hungerford | | 17,802 | 17,017 | 65 | 328 | 393 | 1 in 43 |
| Brixworth | Northamptonshire | 13,336 | 12,186 | 44 | 19 | 63 | 1 in 193 |
| Daventry | | 18,514 | 17,648 | 78 | 327 | 405 | 1 in 43 |

[1] See 10 L.G.B., p. xvii. ; 11 L.G.B., p. xxi. ; and 21 L.G.B., p. lxxi.
[2] See 3 L.G.B., p. 182.
[3] See 23 P.L.B., pp. 149, 150.
[4] See 17 L.G.B., p. 82 (interesting comparison of the pauperism of Skirlaugh and Patrington Unions); also 20 L.G.B., pp. 239, 240; 3 L.G.B. pp. 68-70.

The unions bracketed are agricultural and contiguous unions, where the rate of wages is much the same.

Mr. Murray Browne's remarks on this subject (reporting on the pauperism of the North Wales district in 1887) are to the point :—

"I regret to say that the profuse out-door relief which characterises the greater number of the North Wales Unions still continues. It is impossible not to believe that it arises mainly from laxity of administration on the part of the guardians. The condition of life, wages, etc., appear much the same in North Wales as in the country unions of Cumberland and Westmoreland, Cheshire, etc., where out-relief is low. Moreover, in some unions within North Wales itself, as Wrexham, Forden, and Hawarden, out-relief has been reduced within something like reasonable limits, while in other unions large reductions (at any rate) have been made. It is not pretended, to my knowledge, that the condition of the poor is worse in these unions than is the case where the flood of pauperism runs highest. It follows that out-relief might be reduced without hardship to at least as low a point in the one class of unions as has been done in the other. The Welsh are naturally a thrifty, industrious, persevering people. If freed from the demoralisation produced by the lavish granting of out-relief, they would attain to as high a standard of independence and self-reliance as their neighbours."[1]

So also Mr. Davy :—

"The explanation of the somewhat striking variations in the percentage of pauperism on the population in rural unions, where the conditions of life are practically the same, is to be found in the different methods of administering the Poor Law which are adopted by the guardians. In the Petworth Union, for instance, the percentage of pauperism on the population is 4·5 per cent., whereas in Thakeham it is 2·4, simply because the Petworth Guardians give nearly 87 per cent. of their relief outside the workhouse, whereas the Thakeham Guardians give but 71 per cent. In the same way West Hampnett and Ticehurst have both over four per cent. of paupers, whereas Hollingbourne and Tenterden have under 2·5, because in the former unions over 80 per cent. of the pauperism is out-door, whereas in the latter the out-door pauperism is not much more than 50 per cent. of the whole. In fact, the rate of pauperism, on the population in rural unions, is now very much what the guardians choose to make it."[2]

---

[1] 17 L.G.B., p. 87. See also L.G.B., pp. 71, 72, for reasons for not giving out-door relief to certain classes of the non-able-bodied.
[2] 22 L.G.B., p. 70.

Again Mr. Stevens makes a quotation from a local newspaper, which bears out what he had said in a former report :—

"Where are we to look for the cause of the great discrepancy in unions in the same county? For instance, Holbeach and Spilsby are both similarly situated, both are agricultural unions, neither has within it a town possessing a population exceeding 5000, and Spilsby covers a much wider area than Holbeach, and yet whilst the South Lincolnshire Union has 42·7 paupers per 1000, Spilsby has only 23·0. Again Spalding and Glanford Brigg are very similarly constituted, although the latter is double the size of the former ; but Spalding comes out with 40·4 per 1000 against 24·6 in the Brigg Union. It is difficult to account for the striking differences in these figures unless they arise from the fact that the guardians in the Holbeach, Spalding, Boston, and Louth Unions are more considerate and generous than are those of some of the other unions referred to." [1]

The same differences existed in 1870, and the cause given is the same. Thus Mr. Henley reports :—

"You will observe that on the first day of January, 1870, the pauperism in the Faringdon Union was 1 in 32 of the population, in the Eton Union 1 in 20, in Bicester Union 1 in 18; whereas in the Henley Union it was 1 in 12, in the Buckingham Union 1 in 11, and in the Wokingham Union 1 in 12. It might be alleged that one year was not a fair comparison; I have, therefore, added a column for the previous year, which proves that the proportion is nearly the same.

"I have been unable to ascertain that any local cause exists for this great discrepancy, farm labourers' wages appearing from Mr. Culley's report (23,822) to be lower in Faringdon, where the pauperism is 1 in 32, than in Henley and Wokingham where it is 1 in 12, thus :—

| | | |
|---|---|---|
| In West Berkshire | 13s. to 14s. per week | (Faringdon). |
| In South Oxfordshire | 14s. to 15s. ,, | (Henley). |
| In East Berkshire | ,, ,, | (Wokingham). |

Neither can I gather any reason from the table marked (C)

---

[1] 22 L.G.B., p. 87. See further *ib.*, pp. 94, 100 ; and 23 L.G.B., p. 106 (Warwickshire, Oxon, Bucks, and Berks).

THE POOR LAW. 61

annexed.[1] The acreage to the population is much the same; the rateable value to the population closely approximates. In the neighbouring unions of Bicester and Buckingham the

[1] COMPARISON OF UNIONS IN BERKS, BUCKS, AND OXON.

| Unions. | Condition of pauperism, highest or lowest in three Counties. | Population. | Area. | Rateable value. | Number of paupers on 1st January, 1870. | Paupers to population. | Population to acres. | Rateable value per head. | Out-door paupers to population. | Out-door relief per head on population.* | Total relief to the poor expended per head.† |
|---|---|---|---|---|---|---|---|---|---|---|---|
| **BERKS:** | | | | £ | | 1 in | 1 person to | £ s. | 1 in | s. d. | s. d. |
| Faringdon | Highest | 15,688 | 64,207 | 119,803 | 487 | 32 | 4 | 7 13 | 47 | 0 10¾ | 7 4 |
| Wokingham | Lowest | 14,455 | 42,226 | 82,698 | 1,324 | 12 | 3 | 5 14 | 12 | 3 10 | 14 7 |
| **BUCKS:** | | | | | | | | | | | |
| Eton | Highest | 22,353 | 41,589 | 141,891 | 1,107 | 20 | 2 | 6 7 | 26 | 1 6 | 8 0 |
| Buckingham | Lowest | 13,735 | 51,909 | 94,990 | 1,267 | 11 | 4 | 6 18 | 12 | 4 3 | 13 1 |
| **OXON:** | | | | | | | | | | | |
| Bicester | Highest | 15,555 | 64,127 | 90,268 | 856 | 18 | 4 | 5 16 | 21 | 2 2 | 8 2 |
| Henley | Lowest | 18,200 | 61,662 | 98,765 | 1,494 | 12 | 3 | 5 9 | 14 | 3 7 | 13 2 |

\* Calculated from Return C., In-Maintenance and Out-Relief, Lady Day, 1870.
† For year ended Lady Day, 1869, P.L.B. Report.

pauperism is relatively 18 and 11 to the population, the acreage to the population is the same, and the rateable value higher per head in Buckingham, which is the more pauperised of the two. I may, therefore, assume that a more vigilant discrimination is exercised in the first-named unions than in the latter."[1]

Mr. Lockwood holds the same views:—

"There has been, I regret to report, a continued high average percentage of pauperism, and its cost per head on population in the eastern district during the year 1889. While, however, the mean is high, the variations are considerable, ranging from 1·7 and 1s. 9½d. in Ipswich, and to 5·5 and 5s. 3d. in Docking. It is difficult to believe that variations so wide are to be accounted for by the mere fact that a particular union has an urban and another a rural population, or by any difference in local trade and labour conditions; my own conviction is that the rate of pauperism obtaining in a given union is for the most part a question of administration, and in support of this view it is worth noting that in the Depwade Union, which, like that of Docking, has an almost exclusively agricultural population, the rate of pauperism has since the beginning of 1887 been steadily declining, while in Docking Union and others it has been steadily going up. In the Sudbury Union again (in which of late years agricultural and trade depression has been, at least, as severely felt as elsewhere in the district), the guardians have succeeded in the course of the last three years in reducing the cost of out-relief by nearly £1,000 a year (and this without any increase in the indoor poor), and had the administration of relief in the district at large been equally vigilant and discriminating, the average percentage of pauperism on population would probably have been nearer 2½ than 4. There is, however, a belief too prevalent among guardians, in rural unions especially, that to 'satisfy' the individual applicant (usually with a dole of eighteenpence, and a varying allowance of loaves or flour) is at once the most beneficent and the most economical method of dispensing the poor rate, and I have little doubt that this belief, and the sort of administration it induces, is mainly responsible for the fact that in the Parliamentary return for the quarter ended Michaelmas, 1889, the eastern district alone shows an increased pauperism, and that Norfolk with its 45 paupers per 1,000 is, with the exception of Dorset, the most highly pauperised county in England."[2]

### (2) *Out-door Relief must be Inadequate.*

The cost per head for the year ending Lady Day, 1892, was

---

[1] 23 P.L.B, p. 100.
[2] 19 L.G.B., p. 112.

£4 14s. 3½d. on the mean number of out-door paupers, excluding lunatics in asylums.[1] Thus the dole to the out-door pauper was 3·1d. per day. Not only must out-door relief be inadequate to meet the necessities of every case, but guardians know it. They depend, however, upon it being supplemented from other sources, but they seldom inquire as to what those sources may be.

Mr. Longley, speaking of London, says:—

"Efficient relief may be taken to be that which is neither inadequate nor excessive, and the latter condition can be effectively secured only where the amount of aid derived from other sources is accurately known to the guardians, or where the recipient is known to the guardians to be exclusively dependent upon the relief given. It is one of the inherent vices of out-relief that the knowledge necessary in the former case cannot, in practice, be secured, and exclusive relief seems, therefore, to be the only mode of satisfying the required condition.

"That exclusive relief is, practically, in-door relief, will not be denied, and it is interesting and important to observe that some boards of guardians have been led to recognise in practice the abstract conclusion at which it has been thus attempted to arrive. For it is an implied rule with almost every board of guardians, and is openly stated by some, that if an applicant needs to be wholly maintained by relief, or if the relief which appears to be adequate for the case is unusually large (two cases which generally coincide), he shall receive in-door relief only. In other words, where the guardians are compelled by the circumstances of the case to give adequate relief, they find it necessary, in order to guard against excess, that it shall be also exclusive.

"Two instances of language used in my presence will illustrate the view thus taken by the guardians of adequate and exclusive relief. A chairman of a board of guardians, addressing a widow with two children applying for renewal of relief, said, 'If you can't earn enough to keep you with what we give you, you must come into the workhouse; we don't profess to give enough to keep you out of the workhouse.'

"In another case the view of the guardians was thus frankly explained to me by one of their number:—'Relief in aid is our principle for out-relief; we can only give adequate relief in the workhouse.'

"This system of giving relief which is notoriously and admittedly inadequate, which has been termed the 'dole system,' specially illustrates, in their most aggravated form, the mischiefs some or all of which are in a greater or less degree inherent in all out-relief. It encourages a fraudulent concealment of the circumstances of the applicant; it is generally given in aid of wages or earnings, with the inevitable injury to the labour market

---

[1] 22 L.G.B., p. lxxv.

which is inseparable from relief so given; it promotes, if it does not suggest, mendicancy; and, lastly, it tends to foster among the guardians an erroneous estimate of the measure of their responsibilities in dealing with applications for relief."[1]

Mr. Courtenay Boyle in his report upon the eastern district in 1878, says:—

"Out-relief in very small amounts is given in a large number of cases in the district, doles even to the minimum of sixpence and half a stone of flour per week being frequent. I have thought it my duty to combat very strongly the principle of giving small doles, and have contended that if out-relief is required at all it should be given liberally. The following cases which were dealt with in my presence are instances of the system which obtains in more:—

- A. B., a widow, aged 59, living alone, pays 1s. 6d. per week rent, reported partially able by the doctor, states she earns nothing, has no friends, gets nothing from the clergyman of her parish, cannot go charing, might do a little if she could get it. Granted 1s. per week and half a stone of flour. 'Thank you, sir.'
- C. D., a widow, aged 76; six daughters who do nothing but pay rent, allowed 1s. and half a stone of flour.
- E. F., aged 25, scrofulous, all face covered up; granted 6d. and half a stone of flour.
- G. H., aged 51, nearly blind, lives alone, cannot do anything, pays 1s. 6d. per week rent, which her daughter helps to pay; granted 1s. and half a stone of flour per week.

It is difficult to believe that the out-relief in these cases was not either unnecessary or insufficient."[2]

Mr. Murray Browne, referring to the almost entire abolition of out-door relief in the four unions of Reading, Bradfield, Wallingford, and Oxford, remarks:—

"That in practice out-relief is hardly ever given in sufficient amount to be, alone, enough to live upon. A moment's thought will show this to be the case. It is obviously impossible that people can live on the miserable pittance of 2s. 6d. or 3s. 6d. per week, which is the usual out-door dole. And as a rule those unions which give most out-relief give least to each recipient. They pauperise a multitude, but give no one enough to live upon. The assumption which underlies all this is that the paupers have

---

[1] 3 L.G.B., pp. 168, 169.
[2] 8 L.G.B., p. 109.

some other means of support besides their relief, either from their own earnings, from friends, children, or otherwise. If then this is the case, if, that is to say, out-door relief is only one of several sources of income, it is more easy to understand how, if one source of income be taken away, a small increase in the others may fill up the void. A little more wage, a little more help from children or friends, and the thing is done. Meanwhile, it should be borne in mind that, whether out-door relief on the whole be good or bad, it is open at any rate to two objections. These are, first, that it tends to keep down the rate of wages among the poorest classes, and, secondly, that it damps the exertions of the recipient to rise permanently into a better position.

"On the first point, I may be allowed to refer to my own report for 1890, published in the Twentieth Annual Report of the Board.[1] The second point, I think, is clear. If a man knows that the result of an improvement in his circumstances will be that he would lose his 'little pension,' he is very apt not to exert himself to improve his circumstances as keenly as he might otherwise have done. That such a tendency has a demoralising effect will hardly be denied."[2]

If out-door relief were always made adequate to the necessities of every case, the rates would rise so high that the ratepayers would make short shrift of the guardians. The latter are quite alive to this, and consequently in most unions there are tables or scales by which the amount of relief, according to the number of children, and to the age or condition of the applicant is regulated. These scales vary in every union, some boards being more liberal than others.

Mr. Culley's remarks on the point, made in 1873, are quite applicable to the state of things at the present day. He says:—

"The scale of allowances (by which I mean the allowance usually granted in different classes of cases when the relief given by the guardians is, or is supposed to be, the only source of income) differs to a degree which I think there is nothing in the surrounding circumstances to justify. To take, for example, the important class of able-bodied widows with children, as dealt with by the guardians of contiguous and similar unions, I know no reason why the boards of guardians for Berwick Union should give relief in such cases at the rate of 1s. 6d. for each child if the Glendale guardians are right in giving only 1s., nor why the guardians for South

---

[1] See *supra.* p. 56.
[2] 22 L.G.B., p. 74.

Shields should give only 1s. if 1s. 6d. is necessary in Tynemouth. The scales of relief to the various classes of paupers are given in my special reports, and, after examining them, I think you will agree with me that the allowances are highest in the best administered unions.

"Where boards of guardians, from want of adequate workhouse accommodation, or from any other causes, are unwilling to apply the workhouse test, there remains only one apparent check on expenditure, and that is to offer the smallest amount of relief which, in the opinion of the relieving officer, will prevent the applicant from coming to the workhouse. 'Try 1s. 6d.,' or 'try 2s.,' are sounds only too familiar to our ears. In unions where such action as this takes place, out-relief is often given where it should have been refused, and often, though I hope not so often, given in a niggardly way to deserving applicants."[1]

(3) *Out-door Relief is very liable to Abuse.*

It is almost impossible for the relieving officer or the guardian to prevent out-door relief being used for any other purpose than that for which it was intended. Grocery and food tickets have a market value; and the nourishment intended for the sick may be disposed of by the sound. There is no end to the abuses attaching to out-door relief.

Mr. Sendall, reporting on the Wantage Union in 1873, says that there

"Meat is contracted for, and distributed by order on the contractor.

"Nobody knows, says the relieving officer of No. 1 district, if the 'patient gets the meat ordered in cases of sickness.' Believes that in most instances the meat is cooked for the family, and states the following case:—A woman, whose husband was dying, received 2 lbs. of beef for beef-tea, ordered by the doctor for the husband. The relieving officer happened to visit the house two hours after, and found all the beef in the frying-pan."[2]

The permanent relief list (abolished now in a few unions) is much open to abuse.

The same inspector relates two amusing stories in regard to it. He says:—

"That many cases on the permanent relief list remain imperfectly in-

---

[1] 3 L.G.B., pp. 73, 74. For a glaring instance of inadequate out-door relief, see 23 L.G.B., p. 138.
[2] 3 L.G.B., p. 95.

vestigated may also be inferred from the fact that the appointment of a new relieving officer is not seldom attended by discoveries of which the following may be taken as examples. One of the officers of the Guildford Union, engaged, shortly after his appointment, in looking up his cases, came upon a pauper of long standing at work in the well-stocked garden of his cottage. The following dialogue ensued:

"'You have got a nice bit of garden here?'

"'Yes, it is pretty good.'

"'And are those your pigs in the sty there?'

"'Yes, they be mine.'

"'And there is a horse and cart, is that yours too?'

"'Oh, yes, that is what I goes to market with. And who be you, sir?'

"'Well, I am the new relieving officer, and I think you had better come up and see the guardians next board day.'

"It is needless to add that the invitation to meet the guardians was not accepted, and that the pauper, who had been for some ten years in receipt of parish relief, has contrived from that date to maintain himself without assistance from the rates. On another occasion the same officer found a man who had been twenty years in receipt of relief (given in the first instance on account of some bodily infirmity), and who eked out his parish allowance by keeping a mangle, to work which he employed two grown women. A hint to present himself at the board had the immediate effect of severing the long connection between the parish and this enterprising pauper. It is difficult to write with becoming gravity of cases such as these which, however, in respect of all essential features, may easily be paralleled in other districts."[1]

Mr. Stevens points out how many opportunities there are for cheating the rates, and gives, as an example, what he states to be *not an imaginary case* :—

"A relieving officer does not always find the recipient at home; he is 'somewhere about'; time is precious; there are others to be called on; the money is left with the daughter or wife; but something arises for which the recipient is wanted urgently by a friend, and he is found to be miles away, harvesting at 30s. a week."[2]

The recipient of relief is often unable to attend at the Relief Office, owing to illness, old age, or infirmity. This may open another door to abuse, as witness what Mr. Wodehouse relates in his admirable report of 1870 :—

In such cases,

"The relief is taken to the paupers by some neighbour, and in several

---

[1] 3 L.G.B., p. 83.
[2] 20 L.G.B., p. 240.

of these unions the pauper pays 1d. or 2d., and in some cases a higher amount, to the person who brings his relief. Thus at Bethnal Green a case lately occurred in which it was found that 'an old woman had been receiving 2d. a week from each of four paupers to whom she took relief, and in one of these cases, in which relief had been raised, she had kept back 6d. per week for five weeks.'

"In Shoreditch 'a case occurred the week before my visit in which the guardians received a letter, from which it appeared that a pauper receiving 2s. 6d. a week paid 6d. to a person for bringing it to him.'

"The relieving officer also told me that he knew cases in which paupers 'paid 3d. a week for having their relief brought to them.' It will be seen from the detailed reports that a similar practice prevails to a greater or less extent in several other unions."[1]

### (4) *Out-door Relief causes Discontent.*

The report of 1834 shows how out-door relief at that time was the cause of many of the riots which took place in villages.[2] Wages are indeed not *directly* paid out of the poor's rate at the present time, but any one who has had anything to do with Poor Law administration cannot but have noticed the discontent which out-door relief excites. Especially is this so where out-door relief is granted on no system or principle, but according to the opinion of individual guardians interested in the case. The poor cannot understand why one family should receive the weekly parish dole and the other not. Out-door relief "places the individual who is not ashamed to come upon the rates in a distinctly better position than the more thrifty and independent breadwinner who makes the necessary effort to keep himself and family above the degradation of pauperism."[3]

### (5) *Out-door Relief is entirely destructive of Thrift and Providence.*

In the circular from the Local Government Board to the

---

[1] 23 P.L.B., p. 42.
[2] See Report, pp. 31, 32.
[3] 19 L.G.B., p. 117.

Poor Law Inspectors, dated the 2nd December, 1871, the following passage occurs :—

> "A certainty of obtaining out-door relief in his own home whenever he may ask for it extinguishes in the mind of the labourer all motive for husbanding his resources, and induces him to rely exclusively upon the rates instead of upon his own savings for such relief as he may require. It removes every incentive to self-reliance and prudent forethought on his part, and induces him, moreover, to apply for relief on occasions when the circumstances are not such as to render him absolutely in need of it."[1]

It is perhaps hardly necessary to labour the point here, especially as we shall have more to say on the question of thrift and providence and how it may be encouraged later on,[2] but the evidence shows that friendly, benefit, and medical societies and clubs have great difficulty in obtaining a foothold in an union where out-door relief is easily obtained. Directly it is restricted, up they spring mushroom-like. A remarkable instance is given by Mr. Fawcett[3] of how out-door relief prevents the establishment of such societies :—

> "An event which lately happened in a western county will serve as a striking illustration of the extent to which prudential habits are discouraged by the distribution of large parochial funds among those whose improvidence is their sole title for public support. Not many months since, a report appeared of a large meeting which had been held of Somersetshire colliers. The meeting appears to have been suggested, and everything connected with it arranged, by the workmen themselves. The object of the gathering was to promote the formation of a friendly society. There was at first an unanimous feeling in favour of the proposal; presently it was mentioned by one of the speakers that those who became members of the friendly society would lose all chance of obtaining parochial relief. The whole tone of the meeting changed; the hint having once been given, it was quickly seen that the amount which they might subscribe to the friendly society would simply reduce the rates. A resolution was ultimately passed that the society should not be established so long as a claim to a share of the rates was forfeited by belonging to it. It is difficult to over-estimate the mischief which such an occurrence must produce.

---

[1] 1 L.G.B., p. 66.
[2] See *infra*, pp. 87, 88.
[3] See "Pauperism," p. 40.

Colliers are proverbially an improvident class, and a movement which must have promoted the development of prudential habits amongst them was prematurely nipped in the bud by an extraneous circumstance which legislation has created, and has power to control."

It is in out-door relief unions that clubs, to which the epithet "rotten" is commonly applied, flourish, *i.e.*, clubs where the members' payments are too small for the benefits to be adequate, and the parish is looked to to amplify the weekly payments. Indeed, the fact of the applicant being a member of one of these clubs is generally used as an argument for giving him out-door relief, the income which he is receiving from the club being generally taken at only half its value. Where no out-door relief is given, these clubs cannot stand; they soon break up, and are replaced by the lodges and courts of the great friendly societies.

Again, can anyone doubt that the grants of out-door relief to widows, and to the infirm and aged, has made it difficult for the friendly societies to provide for the wants of these classes of the poor.

Every guardian must have come across cases similar to the following one related by Mr. Stevens:—

"The wife of a working-man in regular employment and on good wages, when a friend surmised that she and her husband must have a nice bit of money saved, as they had no children, scouted the idea, saying they meant to spend all they earned, and then go 'on the parish.'"[1]

This discouragement to thrift and providence is perhaps the greatest evil attaching to out-door relief. The children of parents, who are receiving relief from the parish, are often employed to fetch it, and thus not only learn to regard relief as no disgrace, but are led to depend upon it themselves

---

[1] 20 L.G.B., p. 240.

in times of trouble or old age. The applicant who comes to the board with a demand for his " parish pay " is less frequently seen now than in the past, but he appears sometimes, and what is more he usually gets what he asks for.

## CHAPTER VI.

### WHY OUT-DOOR RELIEF IS GIVEN.

HAVING shown, then, how many disadvantages attach to the grant of out-door relief, why is it that it still continues to be given? The reasons given vary in each union, and Mr. Courtenay Boyle has drawn attention to the contradictory nature of the excuses made as follows :—

> "'We are purely agricultural here, sir,' said the chairman of one board of guardians to me. 'We have no towns or factories where work can be had; our population has to trust exclusively to field work, and finds it very difficult to lay anything by.'
> "'We are peculiarly situated,' said another chairman about a week after. 'We have several large factories in our union which give employment to a considerable number of hands who come upon us directly they are out of work, owing to sickness or other temporary causes.'"

Again,

> "Our high rate is due to the fact that we have a considerable seafaring population, the women and children of which are apt to become chargeable to the rates if anything interferes with their husband's earnings, and even when they are at sea."
> "Your arguments may apply to districts where there is extra employment such as fishing, but here we have none such, therefore out-relief is naturally high."

Once more,—

> "We have no large proprietors here to give extra employment."
> "We have several large proprietors in our union, and we find that their charity does much to increase dependence on relief."[1]

---

[1] 8 L.G.B., p. 107.

But the arguments in favour of out-door relief may be ranged under two different heads; (1) that it is *humane*, and (2) that it is economical.[1]

### (1) *The Humane Argument.*

It is alleged that out-door relief operates less *harshly* on the poor than in-door relief, and saves the little home from being broken up.

#### (a) *The breaking up of "the Home."*

"This phrase, which represents a process for the most part imaginary, is the familiar bugbear of boards of guardians, and has exercised a most prejudicial influence on their practice. In the first place it assumes, and in many cases erroneously, that the applicant has a home at all, or such a home that its loss will be otherwise than to the ultimate benefit of himself and his family. Next, though the objection which this argument embodies might have some weight if the offer of in-door relief by way of test were, as it unfortunately is in some cases, something strange and almost unheard of, it loses much of its force when a system of administration has been established which leads the applicant to rely mainly, if not wholly, upon relief in this form, and to govern himself accordingly. That this is so is evident from the fact that the 'breaking up of homes' is most commonly mentioned by boards of guardians who fail to administer in-door relief upon principle. Again, it seems to be invariably assumed by those who make use of this objection that all to whom the workhouse is offered will accept it, and that the breaking up of homes will be co-extensive with the orders given for admission. In other words, they fail to appreciate the value of in-door relief, as a test of, as well as a mode of, relieving destitution. But even if the hardship inflicted in breaking up a home be recognised as an element for consideration in determining the form of relief, the special conditions of the life of the pauper class in London seem to be such as to reduce it to a minimum. A change of home, which is a serious matter to the rural poor, is a matter of constant occurrence with the poor in London, whose migratory habits, combined with their forced residence in lodgings, and the comparative facility of resource with which they establish themselves in a new locality, all combine to render the loss of a home at once less distressing and less irretrievable in London than elsewhere. My own experience coincides entirely with Mr. Wodehouse's statement as to the extreme rarity of *bona fide* cases of breaking up of homes under the direct and exclusive pleasure of an offer of in-door relief, and I cannot but

---

[1] See L.G.B., pp. 96, 97; 3 L.G.B., p. 170; and 8 L.G.B., p. 107.

think that the terrors with which the argument in question often inspires boards of guardians are founded rather in imagination and anticipation than on experience. Assuming, however, that in a given case the question of breaking up a home by the offer of in-door relief is fairly raised, within the limits indicated by the previous remarks, recourse should, I think, be had to the general considerations which have appeared, on a balance of advantage and disadvantage, to render in-door preferable to out-relief. On the one side is to be set the inconvenience and hardship to the individual, great and undeserved as they may be in the particular case; on the other are to be ranged the general good which accrues from the discouragement to improvident habits offered by a deterrent form of relief; the protection afforded by it to the, too often, semi-pauperised ratepayers, and in the case of relief to able-bodied to the interests of the labour market; and lastly, the inducement to a struggle for independence which the discipline, if not the disgrace, incident to residence in the workhouse will offer to the pauper himself, in a far greater degree than does a merely weekly pittance the receipt of which cannot but sap the independence and self-reliance of all but the most active and energetic, the very class who are conspicuous by their absence from the ranks of pauperism."[1]

Mr. Stevens says:—

"Out-door relief is often thought to be more humane than the workhouse order, the humanity of it being in its saving the applicant's home when all other means have failed to do so. Where there is little doubt that it is the home of destitution, I have at times tried, seldom with any success, to obtain an assurance that the convenience of the household generally, especially of those who will not handle the money, and who are too young or feeble to speak, is best consulted by its preservation, and I am sure that such matters as its sanitary condition, the state of its inmates (especially children and sick), the history of its decline, the prospects of its future, and the consequences of its precedent, should be more closely considered than they sometimes are before the claim of the home receives the tribute that it does from the rates. Cases in which an application for relief has been met by an offer to take some of applicant's children for a time into the workhouse are very rare in this district."[2]

In scattered districts out-door relief is defended on this ground alone. Thus Mr. Bircham, speaking of the South Wales district, says:—

"The small workhouse is often situated at a great distance from pauper

---

[1] 3 L.G.B., p. 171. See also 1 L.G.B., p. 97; 17 L.G.B, p. 64; 199 L.G.B., p. 116; 20 L.G.B., pp. 222, 239.
[2] 20 L.G.B., p. 240.

homes, which are scattered widely over thinly populated and very extensive areas, while the paupers themselves are all personally known to those to whom they apply for relief, and as they are content to exist on a small dole of out-relief in the cottages where they and their forbears have lived probably for generations, our Welsh country guardians find it extremely difficult to see where the economy lies in refusing out-door relief in such cases. Still, that such a system is open to a certain amount of abuse is undoubtedly true."[1]

To this, however, may be opposed the opinion of Mr. Murray Browne, who was at the time inspector for the North Wales district, a district by no means dissimilar from that of South Wales. He attributes the amount of out-door pauperism to nothing but bad administration of out-door relief, and his comparison of the pauperism of Cumberland and Westmoreland with that of his own district is very happy:—

"In the former the peasantry are, for the most part, self-reliant. They resort to the aid of the Poor Law only under the pressure of the most extreme necessity. And as a matter of fact there is in the north of England, as a rule, very little out-relief. In Wales, on the contrary, there sometimes seems to be a scramble among the poorer classes to get as much as possible out of the union. Each guardian too frequently fights to get as much out-relief as he can for his own parish. Self-respect is lost, and the result is too often general deterioration."[2]

### (b) *The Danger of Starvation.*

Another "humane" argument used by guardians is as follows:—

"The poor, rather than come into the house, will starve outside."

Mr. Baldwyn Fleming answers this argument as follows:—

"As to the statement that applicants would rather die than go into the workhouse, and that their independent spirit should be commended for such a determination, it may be questioned whether such independence of

---

[1] 18 L.G.B., p. 143. He thus admits the abuse; and makes it clear that the infrequent use of the workhouse test in South Wales is owing to insufficient workhouse accommodation. (See *supra.* pp. 17-20.)

[2] See 20 L.G.B., p. 254; and *cf.* 2 L.G.B., p. 60.

spirit is in truth deserving of the smallest encouragement. The objection on their part is not to become a burden upon their fellow-creatures, but to the receipt of relief in a form which is unacceptable to themselves. The individuals who are too independent to go into the workhouse are perfectly willing to burden the ratepayers with as much out-relief as they can succeed in obtaining from the guardians. No admiration can be too great for the real independence of spirit which prefers to suffer any extremity rather than admit defeat in the battle of life, or consent to become a burden upon others; but this real independence has no place in the class of case now under consideration. I have watched these and similar statements with great care, and I have found almost invariably that the argument is only advanced in unions where the guardians are weak enough to allow the paupers to choose between in-door and out-door relief, or where a persistent refusal of in-door relief had led eventually to the grant of out-door relief."[1]

We deal with this question more fully in Chapter IX.[2]

### (c) *Harshness generally.*

On the charge of the harshness attaching to the restriction of out-door relief Mr. Davy has some weighty remarks.[3] He says:—

"The charge of harshness to the poor, which is often brought against the advocates of a strict administration of out-door relief, is due for the most part either to a confusion of thought or to a want of practical acquaintance with the procedure of an ordinary board of guardians. Strict administration as a settled policy implies a high standard of public duty on the part of the guardians, for it involves an amount of patient labour which can hardly be expected from an average board of unpaid administrators. In the first place, the principles which all experience shows are the only safe guide in the administration of public relief, must be mastered, and what is more difficult, must be constantly borne in mind. It is very easy to make things pleasant all round by the grant of public money; pleasant to the applicant, pleasant to the guardians who advocate the case, and pleasant to the guardians themselves, who, in granting the relief, feel the joy of a benevolence, which though it is vicarious, is none the less genuine after its kind. The hard task is that of the boards who administer relief as conscientious trustees of the public money; who insist that their officers shall give the fullest information with regard to each case; who form a painstaking judgment as to the amount and the kind of relief which is necessary; and finally, who,

---

[1] 17 L.G.B., pp. 64, 65; see also 20 L.G.B., p. 221.
[2] *Infra*, pp. 108-110.
[3] 22 L.G.B., p. 71.

in coming to their decision, hold the immediate interest of the individual applicant subordinate to the general well-being of the class from which the applicant comes. It is easy to get rid of an application by a small weekly dole; it is a work involving much vigilant care to make certain that in every case where relief is given the relief shall be sufficient for the necessities of the applicant, and shall be given in accordance with sound public policy. To insure this in the first place, the arrangements of the workhouse, especially for those for the sick and infirm, must be beyond reproach; and this implies a constant and kindly supervision by the visiting committee. Next there must be no slackness on the part of the medical officers or relieving officers. It is a difficult and often an invidious task for a board of guardians to insist that medical officers shall give personal attention to the cases on their list, or that relieving officers shall devote their whole time to the duties of their office, shall personally distribute the weekly relief, and shall not only occasionally visit, but shall constantly watch, the necessities of each out-door pauper. Members of a board of guardians might by experience and reflection become convinced that out-door relief tends to lower wages, to damage the position of the independent labourer, and to impede every impulse towards temperance and thrift; but for any board of guardians to adopt a policy of indiscriminately refusing out-door relief would be impossible. The current administration must be improved to the highest point before any general policy of restriction could have any chance of even a temporary success; and as such a policy would be unpopular among certain classes—not probably the labouring classes—the guardians must in self-defence take care that there is nothing to be said against their machinery of relief. Then, apart from all question of general policy, as the administration approaches the highest standard, the proportion of out-door relief will diminish, for the simple reason, that not only will the cases that are not destitute be discovered and struck off the lists, but the guardians, as their knowledge of the circumstances of each case increases, will come to realise how impossible it is to adequately relieve a large proportion of them by any grant of out-relief. The typical boards of guardians, who think that systematic in-door relief is a hardship to the poor, do not scruple to give small weekly grants out of the common purse to every applicant whose circumstances are said to be known to any member of the board, and against whose character the relieving officer has nothing very specific to allege. The applicant is in fact got rid of by a weekly dole, the amount of which is in most cases ludicrously out of proportion to the plea of absolute destitution which is the alleged cause of the application for relief. Often the value of the relief given would not do much more than pay the rent. In many cases, perhaps the majority, it is painfully evident that either the pauper must starve on the amount of relief given, or that the relieving officer has not sufficiently mastered the facts of the case to enable him to advise the guardians of the exact circumstances and sources of income of the applicant. If any relief is given at all to an applicant, it is the plain duty of the guardians to take precautions to ensure that the relief is adequate, and that the pauper is sufficiently fed, clothed and lodged. This responsibility is discharged in the case of inmates of workhouses, whereas in the case of out-door paupers too much is left to the chance that the relief given will be supplemented by other sources of income. The worst form of this supplementation is when the pauper earns money by his own work, for then it is obvious he is kept on the labour market, and enabled to do work which would otherwise be done by independent labourers, by means of a subsidy paid out of the poor rates. The best form of it is when the pauper is helped by his relations. But even then the guardians should take the utmost care to ascertain whether he is properly looked after."

### (d) *The Stigma of Pauperism.*

It is said to be inhumane to clothe the workhouse inmates in a special dress. The objection is one more founded on sentiment than on reality. It must not be forgotten that the application of the workhouse test is intended to act as a deterrent. Some boards of guardians allow a non-distinctive dress to well-conducted inmates when they go outside the workhouse, and perhaps there is not much objection to this.[1] The danger lies, of course, in the possibility of the exception becoming the rule. It is quite certain, however, that even supposing there to be any strong feeling among the poor upon the subject, it would not lead those boards of guardians, which grant out-door relief because they consider that in-door relief "pauperises," to abolish the distinctive dress with a view of making a more frequent use of the workhouse test. The Commissioners of 1832 were quite alive to the danger of converting workhouses into almshoufes. (See *infra*, p. 136.)

### (2) *The Economical Argument.*

The argument of economy is not so often used at the present day; it has been so often and so completely confuted. We deal with it at length later on.[2]

---

[1] See *infra*, p. 247. The instructional letter of 5th February, 1842, merely says that paupers "are to be clothed in a dress furnished by the guardians." (See S. P. L. C., p. 107.)

[2] See *infra*, pp. 83-86.

## CHAPTER VII.

THE ADVANTAGES ATTENDING THE RESTRICTION OF OUT-DOOR RELIEF.

HAVING pointed out the evils which must attach to out-door relief and the reasons which induce most boards to grant it, we will now point out the great advantages attaching to its restriction.

(1) *The Restriction of Out-door Relief reduces the Number of Paupers.*

It is hardly necessary to prove this statement. No one denies the fact. The evidence is too strong for it to be disputed.[1] If the mean number of paupers of all classes had borne the same ratio to estimated population in 1893 as it did in 1871, the number in the former year would have been 1,351,114 instead of 758,766. The figures are more remarkable when the rise in the number of lunatics from 48,506 in 1871 to 79,301 in 1893 is considered.[2]

Again, if the mean number of adult *able-bodied* paupers (excluding vagrants) had borne the same ratio to estimated population in 1893 as it did in 1871, the number in the former year would have been 225,360 instead of 100,018.[3] (Compare Charts A. B. C. and D., p. 197.)

(2) *The Restriction of Out-door Relief does not materially increase, and often decreases the Number of In-door Paupers.*[4]

In many cases, and in rural districts almost always, a decrease

---

[1] *E.g.*, 18 L.G.B., p. 138 (Sheffield); 20 L.G.B., p. 234 (Lancashire); and 21 L.G.B., p. 155 (Birmingham).
[2] See 22 L.G.B., p. 268.     [3] See 22 L.G.B., p. 265.
[4] See 8 L.G.B., p. 106 (Eastern District); 19 L.G.B., p. 111 (Birmingham and Reading); 18 L.G.B., p. 138 (Sheffield); 21 L.G.B., p. 150 (Kent and Sussex Districts), and the valuable report of Mr. Murray Browne

in the number of in-door paupers accompanies the decrease of out-door paupers. In large towns, owing to the influx of able-bodied labour, the effect is not so noticeable, but still even in them the restriction of out-door relief causes a comparatively small addition to the number of in-door paupers. As this curious fact is not generally admitted we must prove it by giving instances of some unions (and they by no means exhaust the number) which have followed an *anti*-out-door relief policy, and by comparing the figures of pauperism at the time they initiated the reform with similar figures at the present time. As the number of vagrants and lunatics does not depend in any way on the administration of out-door relief, no note of them is taken in the following table :—

### MEAN PAUPERISM.[1]

(1) *Five Unions which practically give no Out-door Relief.*

| Union. | Year ending Lady Day. | Population (census years). | In-door paupers. | Out-door paupers. | Total paupers. | Decrease in total of average daily pauperism. |
|---|---|---|---|---|---|---|
| Stepney | 1871<br>1893 | 57,578<br>57,376 | 887<br>1004 | 2830<br>146 | 3717<br>1150 | 2567 |
| Whitechapel | 1871<br>1893 | 76,332<br>74,462 | 1081<br>1071 | 3281<br>120 | 4362<br>1191 | 3171 |
| Brixworth | 1872<br>1893 | 13,856<br>12,186 | 55<br>57 | 1056<br>19 | 1111<br>76 | 1035 |
| Bradfield (Berks) | 1872<br>1893 | 15,852<br>18,017 | 221<br>89 | 839<br>27 | 1060<br>116 | 944 |
| St. George's-in-the-East | 1874<br>1893 | 48,235<br>45,795 | 1059<br>1135 | 1635<br>181 | 2694<br>1316 | 1378 |

[1] The mean pauperism is obtained by taking the number of paupers on the 1st July and the 1st January in any one year ending Lady Day, adding the number together and dividing by two.

---

on this special subject; 7 L.G.B., p. 228; also 3 L.G.B., pp. 117, 118 (Brixworth); 21 L.G.B., p. 156 (Bradfield); 2 L.G.B., p. 57 (Wellington); 19 L.G.B., p. 125 (Lancaster); 20 L.G.B., pp. 239, 240 (Leicester and Spilsby).

(2) *Eight Unions which administer Out-door Relief strictly.*

| Union. | Year ending Lady Day. | Population (census years). | In-door paupers. | Out-door paupers. | Total paupers. | Decrease in total of average daily pauperism. |
|---|---|---|---|---|---|---|
| Atcham [1] | 1871<br>1893 | 45,561<br>48,346 | 318<br>317 | 713<br>50 | 1031<br>367 | 664 |
| Paddington | 1872<br>1893 | 96,784<br>117,846 | 565<br>793 | 1782<br>251 | 2347<br>1044 | 1303 |
| Wallingford | 1872<br>1893 | 14,641<br>14,706 | 141<br>117 | 757<br>91 | 898<br>208 | 690 |
| St. Neots | 1872<br>1893 | 18,511<br>15,239 | 112<br>71 | 727<br>151 | 839<br>222 | 617 |
| Manchester [2] | 1873<br>1893 | 173,965<br>145,100 | 2606<br>3076 | 3238<br>688 | 5844<br>3764 | 2080 |
| St. George's, Hanover Square | 1875<br>1893 | 155,936<br>134,138 | 1674<br>2346 | 2882<br>487 | 4556<br>2833 | 1723 |
| Birmingham | 1883<br>1893 | 246,352<br>245,503 | 2380<br>2602 | 4555<br>740 | 6935<br>3342 | 3593 |
| Reading | 1885<br>1893 | 43,494<br>60,054 | 387<br>459 | 601<br>114 | 988<br>573 | 415 |

[1] The figures for the year ending Lady Day, 1871, give the pauperism of Atcham and Shrewsbury Unions combined. The Atcham Union itself has followed the policy of restricting out-door relief since 1836 with the results mentioned on p. 3. But in 1871 six Shrewsbury parishes were added to the union with a large population and pauperism. Therefore, as regards these parishes, we may consider the reform to have begun since 1871.

[2] The great decrease of population is accounted for by the demolition of dwelling-houses to make room for warehouses, railway stations, etc., and by the pulling down of insanitary dwellings. The population now consists mainly of the labouring classes, and there is a large common lodging-house population. (See Report on the Out-Relief Department of the Manchester Union for the year ending March 25th, 1891.)

The next table gives the percentages of increase or decrease of population, and of the decrease of pauperism, and the number of paupers per 1000 of population for the same unions during the periods named.

F

| Union. | Percentage of increase of population. | Percentage of decrease of population. | Percentage of increase of in-door pauperism. | Percentage of decrease of in-door pauperism. | Percentage of decrease of out-door pauperism. | Percentage of decrease of total pauperism. | Number of paupers per 1000 of population. |
|---|---|---|---|---|---|---|---|
| Stepney | — | 35 | 13 | — | 95 | 69 | 1871—64<br>1893—20 |
| Whitechapel | — | 2·4 | — | 9 | 96 | 73 | 1871—57<br>1893—16 |
| Brixworth | — | 12 | 3·6 | — | 98 | 93 | 1872—80<br>1893— 6 |
| Bradfield | 13·6 | — | — | 60 | 97 | 90 | 1872—66<br>1893— 6 |
| St. George's-in-the-East | — | 5 | 7 | — | 89 | 51 | 1874—56<br>1893—28 |
| Atcham | 6·1 | — | stationary | | 93 | 64 | 1871—22<br>1893— 7 |
| Paddington | 21·7 | — | 40 | — | 86 | 55 | 1872—24<br>1893— 8 |
| Wallingford | 45 | — | — | 17 | 88 | 77 | 1872—61<br>1893—14 |
| St. Neots | — | 17·7 | — | 36·6 | 79 | 73 | 1872—45<br>1893—14 |
| Manchester | — | 16·5 | 18 | — | 78 | 36 | 1873—33<br>1893—26 |
| St. George's, Hanover Square | — | 14 | 40 | — | 83 | 38 | 1875—29<br>1893—21 |
| Birmingham | — | 34 | 9 | — | 84 | 52 | 1883—28<br>1893—13 |
| Reading | 38 | — | 18·6 | — | 81 | 42 | 1885—22<br>1893— 9 |

This last table shows, among other things, that decrease of pauperism is entirely independent of fluctuation in population.

### (3) *The Restriction of Out-door Relief reduces Expenditure, and so relieves the Rates.*

This fact is often denied. Guardians say it is cheaper to relieve outside than inside the house. This fallacy has been frequently exposed, and it is surprising that it still holds the field in so large a number of unions.

Mr. Wodehouse has put the argument in its simplest form, as follows :—

"A family applies for relief; if they are given out-relief to the amount of 4s. a week, they will be satisfied; if they come into the workhouse their maintenance will cost 10s. a week. The economists, therefore, argue, that by giving out-relief they will save 6s. a week."

Here is his answer to it :—

"Now the very same guardians who have used this argument have frequently acknowledged to me that when the workhouse test is offered it is not accepted in more than one case out of ten. By offering the workhouse then in ten such cases the guardians would indeed lose 6s. a week in the one case in which it was accepted, but in each of the remaining nine cases they would save 4s., so that their total gain would amount to 30s. a week. I believe, however, that transparent as the fallacy is, this mistaken notion of economy lies at the root of a large proportion of the out-relief at present given throughout the country, and that if the guardians were generally convinced of the fallacy of the argument employed, they would be more willing than they are at present to make a proper application of the workhouse test."[1]

The reports are full of instances showing how economical the restriction of out-door relief is,[2] but we will take the same unions as before and prove it.

---

[1] 1 L.G.B., p. 97.
[2] *E.g.*, 10 L.G.B., pp. xxiv., xxv.; 20 L.G.B., p. 240; 18 L.G.B., pp. 138, 139. See also 23 P.L.B., p. 36; 3 L.G.B., p. 170; 7 L.G.B., p. 228; and 17 L.G.B., p. 62. Mr. Murray Browne's report, entitled, "Report on the Proportionate Amount of In-door Relief in Different Districts as Compared with the Population," and which is printed in 7 L.G.B., p. 228, is particularly interesting.

| Union. | Year ending Lady Day. | Population. | Cost of in-maintenance. | Cost of out-maintenance. | Total cost in and out-maintenance. | Rate per head of population. | Decrease of expenditure. |
|---|---|---|---|---|---|---|---|
| | | | £ | £ | £ | s. d. | £ |
| Stepney | 1870 | 57,578 | 12,537 | 11,931 | 24,468 | 8  6 | 12,518 |
| | 1892 | 57,376 | 11,180 | 770 | 11,950 | 4  2 | |
| Whitechapel | 1870 | 76,332 | 13,076 | 6,864 | 19,940 | 5  2½ | 2,299 |
| | 1892 | 74,462 | 16,842 | 799 | 17,641 | 4  9 | |
| Brixworth | 1870 | 13,856 | 474 | 5,425 | 5,899 | 8  6 | 4,800 |
| | 1892 | 12,186 | 868 | 231 | 1,099 | 1  9½ | |
| Bradfield | 1870 | 15,852 | 1,929 | 4,373 | 6,302 | 7  11 | 4,964 |
| | 1892 | 18,017 | 1,123 | 215 | 1,338 | 1  5¾ | |
| St. George's-in-the-East | 1872 | 48,235 | 13,684 | 7,334 | 21,018 | 8  8½ | 7,038 |
| | 1892 | 45,795 | 13,598 | 382 | 13,980 | 6  1 | |
| Paddington | 1871 | 96,784 | 6,161 | 9,900 | 16,061 | 3  3¾ | 474 |
| | 1892 | 117,846 | 13,362 | 2,225 | 15,587 | 2  7½ | |
| Wallingford | 1871 | 14,641 | 1,290 | 5,515 | 6,805 | 9  3½ | 5,204 |
| | 1892 | 14,706 | 1,231 | 370 | 1,601 | 2  2 | |
| St. Neots | 1871 | 18,511 | 1,349 | 4,277 | 5,626 | 6  1 | 4,004 |
| | 1892 | 15,239 | 963 | 659 | 1,622 | 2  1½ | |
| Atcham [1] | 1872 | 45,561 | 2,961 | 1,857 | 4,818 | 2  1 | 58 |
| | 1892 | 48,346 | 3,580 | 180 | 4,760 | 1  11½ | |
| Manchester | 1872 | 173,965 | 24,953 | 18,799 | 43,752 | 5  0 | 12,158 |
| | 1892 | 145,100 | 29,592 | 2,002 | 31,594 | 4  4¼ | |
| St. George's, Hanover Square | 1874 | 155,936 | 25,596 | 12,249 | 37,845 | 4  10 | 4,624 |
| | 1892 | 134,138 | 30,106 | 3,115 | 33,221 | 4  11 | |
| Birmingham | 1883 | 246,352 | 25,055 | 16,176 | 41,231 | 3  4 | 11,497 |
| | 1892 | 245,503 | 26,214 | 3,520 | 29,734 | 2  5 | |
| Reading | 1884 | 43,494 | 4,160 | 2,383 | 6,543 | 3  0 | 1,109 |
| | 1892 | 60,054 | 4,618 | 816 | 5,434 | 1  9½ | |

[1] See note (2) *supra*, p. 81.

It will be noticed that none of these unions show any increase in expenditure for in and out maintenance, while most of them show large decreases. Although in some cases they may be spending more now than formerly, other similar unions where an opposite policy is followed are doing the same. Indeed, it is quite possible that no great decrease of expenditure may occur when a large urban union goes in for a policy of restricting out-door relief, because the guardians may spend the money thus saved in improving the administration of their in-door relief. Taking the Whitechapel Union as an example, it is more than probable that its expenditure on relief would be much greater than it is at the present time had its guardians continued in their old policy. Thus comparing its expenditure with that of the adjacent union of Bethnal Green (where an out-door relief policy prevails) for the years ending Lady Day, 1872 and 1892, and not taking into account the sums received from the Metropolitan Common Poor Fund, we find that while the expenditure of Whitechapel has increased from £46,773 to £48,910 or 4·5 per cent., that of Bethnal Green has increased from £53,200 to £72,640, or 36·5 per cent.[1] During the same period the increase in expenditure on relief in England and Wales has been from £8,007,403 to £8,847,678, or 10 per cent.

---

[1] The following tables give the items of expenditure which make up the above totals, and to show how little the population arguments affect the figures, we have added the expenditure in both unions during the year ending Lady Day, 1882.

| Year ending Lady Day. | Union. | Population. | In-maintenance. | Out-relief. | Lunatics. | Loans. | Salaries. | Other expenses. | Total. |
|---|---|---|---|---|---|---|---|---|---|
| 1872 | Whitechapel | 75,552 | 12,040 | 4,692 | 4,436 | 10,784 | 5,501 | 9,320 | 46,773 |
| 1882 | ,, | 71,350 | 14,724 | 1,293 | 5,621 | 3,376 | 6,951 | 15,844 | 47,809 |
| 1892 | ,, | 74,462 | 16,842 | 799 | 5,954 | 4,478 | 12,641 | 8,376 | 48,910 |
| 1872 | Bethnal Green | 120,104 | 15,979 | 7,328 | 10,281 | 3,519 | 6,440 | 9,673 | 53,200 |
| 1882 | ,, | 127,006 | 21,433 | 3,551 | 10,444 | 1,543 | 9,753 | 12,442 | 59,166 |
| 1892 | ,, | 129,134 | 30,051 | 5,288 | 12,853 | 6,391 | 12,414 | 5,643 | 72,640 |

In some of the recent criticism on our Poor Law system a great deal has been made of the point that the expenditure per head of population has risen in some unions which have adopted an in-door relief policy.

Mr. Wodehouse has shown what a false test this is of good or bad administration. He says:—

"Every case in which out-relief is granted has a direct tendency to encourage other persons to apply for similar assistance, while the offer of relief in the workhouse is not attended with the same consequences to any appreciable extent. While, therefore, the cost per head in unions where out-relief is freely given will undoubtedly be less than in unions where the workhouse is frequently used as a test of destitution, yet the actual number of paupers, and the aggregate cost of their maintenance will not only be greater in the former unions than in the latter, but will also have a tendency to increase more continuously and more rapidly." (23 P.L.B., p. 36.)

But the figures we have given above show that we can beat our opponents even on this ground.

| | | | | | |
|---|---|---|---|---|---|
| Increase in total expenditure of Whitechapel, | . | 1872 to 1882 | £1,036 or | 2·2 | per cent. |
| ,, | ,, ,, | . 1882 to 1892 | 1,101 or | 2·3 | ,, |
| ,, | ,, ,, | . 1872 to 1892 | 2,137 or | 4·6 | ,, |
| ,, | ,, Bethnal Green. | 1872 to 1882 | 5,966 or | 11·2 | ,, |
| ,, | ,, ,, | . 1882 to 1892 | 13,474 or | 22·7 | ,, |
| ,, | ,, ,, | . 1872 to 1892 | 19,440 or | 36·5 | ,, |
| Decrease in expenditure on 'in and out maintenance in Whitechapel, | | 1872 to 1882 | 717 or | 4·3 | ,, |
| Increase ,, ,, ,, | . | 1882 to 1892 | 1,624 or | 10·4 | ,, |
| ,, ,, ,, ,, | . | 1872 to 1892 | 909 or | 5·5 | ,, |
| Increase in expenditure on in and out maintenance in Bethnal Green, | | 1872 to 1882 | 1,677 or | 7 | ,, |
| ,, ,, ,, ,, | . | 1882 to 1892 | 10,355 or | 41·4 | ,, |
| ,, ,, ,, ,, | . | 1872 to 1892 | 12,032 or | 51·5 | ,, |

Thus we see that with an increase of population, since 1881, of 4·3 per cent. in Whitechapel, its expenditure has only increased 2·3 per cent, while in Bethnal Green, with an increase of population since 1881 of only 1·7 per cent., its expenditure has increased as much as 22·7 per cent.

(4) *The Restriction of Out-door Relief encourages Thrift and Providence.*

The poor soon get to know what they may expect from the Poor Law, and take care to provide for themselves; whereas "when once relief has been found to be obtainable to tide over a difficulty, reliance is placed upon that resource for the future to the great detriment of individual thrift and exertion."[1] The weak benefit societies, which depend upon the Poor Law to supplement their inadequate payments, have to wind up their affairs, and the strong benefit societies step into their shoes.[2] It is very difficult to get exact data on this subject, although the improvement in the habits and morals of the poor in a county union following upon the abolition or restriction of out-door relief is soon noticed. The late Mr. Bland Garland, however, did go into this question.

"As to proofs of increased thrift, you will, of course, see that it is difficult to give you much data on that subject. However, in 1888 I got returns from all the friendly societies in the union area, including all the old clubs, which were diminishing in numbers, and from all our medical officers, as to the membership of their medical clubs. I am happy to say that the medical clubs showed an increase of membership during the time of our reform of 148 per cent. The friendly societies showed an increase of membership of 150 per cent. Of course, I could not get at the data of the large collecting societies, and the savings banks, and building societies, and, therefore, cannot say what effect our policy has had upon that class of thrift. But I see no reason to suppose that the deposits of savings banks, and the contributions of these collecting societies and building societies, have not increased in like manner. I have no doubt in my own mind that they have."[3]

And Mr. Baldwyn Fleming says:—

---

[1] See 19 L.G.B., p. 117.
[2] See 20 L.G.B., p. 213.
[3] "From Pauperism to Manliness" (a pamphlet published by the Charity Organisation Society), p. 5. See also 21 L.G.B., p. 156.

"Upon one of the questions of the hour, namely, thrift by means of friendly societies, the unnecessary grant of out-relief has a distinctly hostile influence. A working man might truly say that he saw little good in joining a friendly society, because the amount he received from it would be deducted in estimating any claim for relief from the rates. If he did not belong to a benefit society he would at once get a proportionately larger amount of relief, and, therefore, it is a pure waste of money to him to pay into a club. This may be answered by saying that the guardians need not take club payments into account, but if they did not, they would compel the ratepayers to give the man more than his necessity required, which would be indefensible. Hence the grant of out-relief militates against friendly societies in two ways:

"1. It is a positive inducement not to enter, because the provision it affords is better than is given by friendly societies, inasmuch as medical attendance, and what are known as medical extras (stimulants, meat, expensive medicines, etc.) are supplied free of cost.

"2. The members are actually placed in a worse position than those who are not members, if the necessity for relief should arise. They have spent money upon club payments, and have to keep on so spending money, while they get less relief than men who are not in a club. Thus, out-relief must compete, and compete very mischievously, with provident societies. On the other hand, in-door relief does not, and cannot, compete with them."[1]

The decrease in drunkenness goes hand in hand with the increase of thrift and providence. The two cannot exist together for long, and this is not the least of the advantages attaching to the restriction of out-door relief.

For further information see *supra*, pp. 68-71.

### (5) *The Restriction of Out-door Relief brings Relations to a Sense of their Duties.*

It is a most remarkable fact that, when out-door relief is refused, someone related to, or connected with, the family generally comes forward to assist.

"It is," says Mr. Longley, "within the experience of many boards of guardians that, while there are persons who, even when in prosperous circumstances, readily permit their aged relatives to receive out-relief, an offer of in-door relief is frequently found to put pressure upon them to rescue

---

[1] 21 L.G.B., p. 160.

themselves, if not their relatives, from the discredit incident to the residence of the latter in the workhouse."[1]

There can, indeed, be no doubt that the persistent neglect of sick and aged parents by their children is one of the great evils of the age, requiring the strict attention of the administrators of Poor Law relief;[2] and that out-door relief helps to encourage this neglect. The application of the workhouse test is the only remedy.

"The workhouse test is not made use of so frequently as it might be, as a means of inducing persons to contribute towards the support of their relations, in order to prevent the necessity of their having to come into the workhouse. On the day on which I attended a meeting of the guardians of the West Fairle Union, an application was made for relief under the following circumstances. The family desiring relief consisted of the following members:—An old man aged 67, confessedly past work, and unable to earn anything. His wife, ten years younger, earned, and admitted she earned, 4s. a week. An unmarried son, aged 23, living with his parents, and earning 13s. 6d. a week. Another son aged 17, also living in the house, and earning 10s. a week. Two younger children under 8 years of age. The family, therefore, consisted of six persons, for whose support there was coming in a weekly income of 27s. 6d. It appeared to me to be clearly a case in which the workhouse ought to have been offered, and that, in the event of it being accepted, legal proceedings ought immediately to have been taken against the eldest son. The guardians, however, did not take this view of the case, and granted a weekly allowance of 2s. and two gallons of flour. I noted down the facts of the case at the time, and took an opportunity of stating them to other boards of guardians, whose meetings I subsequently attended, and inquiring what they would have done under similar circumstances. I was surprised to find that in several of these unions the guardians informed me that, if a similar case were brought before them, they would not be unwilling to grant out-relief."[3]

Every guardian is acquainted with similar cases to the illustrative one given by Mr. Knollys. He says:—

"I have found an inclination in some unions to grant out-door relief in cases where the application is in truth only an appeal to guardians to interfere in family quarrels. There may be several sons all more or less able to

---

[1] 3 L.G.B., p. 188.
[2] See 19 L.G.B., p. 132.
[3] 1 L.G.B., p. 100, per Mr. Wodehouse.

maintain a parent, and A is willing to do his share, but B, C, and D, refuse to do theirs. The guardians grant say 6s. a week in out-relief, and obtain a magistrate's order for repayment of 1s. 6d. a week each against all the sons. They consider, I sometimes fear, that by such an arrangement all cost is saved to the union, but they overlook these facts that, if A was in a position himself to maintain his parent, the applicant was probably never really destitute at all, that the collector of the guardians has probably to be paid his percentage on the sums refunded, so that if all be punctually repaid the relief is only refunded less 10 per cent. for its collection, that much of the officer's valuable time is taken up by payment of the relief, and its subsequent collection, that a pauper is needlessly made, and that, if the relief is easily collected, a great temptation is put in the way of the relieving officer to retain a pauper on his books after the necessity has ceased."[1]

(6) *The Restriction of Out-door Relief acts kindly and not harshly on the Poor, and advances the Cause of True Charity.*[2]

"Figures do not represent the whole of the case. They may show a satisfactory balance-sheet to the ratepayers, but they tell nothing of that side of the question which as guardians we ought never to lose sight of, and that is the effect, moral as well as otherwise, upon the poor themselves. It is possible that in attempting a reform we have forgotten the humanity which is due from us, and the reduction in rates and pauperism may represent an increased amount of suffering to the poor, which we have no right to inflict. This most important side of the question cannot be omitted if we would rightly estimate the work of our reform, while the difficulty of it would be apparent to all. I have been able, however, with the assistance of the relieving officers, in some measure to meet it. Each case that has been permanently struck off the out-door relief list has been watched as far as it was possible to do so, and the subsequent condition and manner of living carefully recorded. It appears that during the year ending December 31st, 1873, out-door relief has been permanently discontinued from 241 paupers; of these 2 have died, 3 have accepted the offer of the house, 12 have left the district (this includes a family of 6 persons), 9 are maintaining themselves with occasional help from relatives, 55 are supported by relatives who seem well able to do it, the remainder, to the number of 160, are entirely supporting themselves in the district, and of these only 7 appear to have any difficulty in doing so, while 4 out of the 7 are acknowledged to be cases requiring relief, but for whom the house is manifestly the proper place, the offer of which has been made, but persistently refused.

"The above statement serves, I think, to exonerate the board from any suspicion of harshness, and is a sufficient justification of the course that has been adopted.

"It appears from this that of 241 persons who were supported by the

---

[1] 19 L.G.B., p. 134.
[2] See also *supra*, pp. 73-78.

rates on January 1st, 1873, only 3 were being so supported on January 1st, 1874, or in other words, that 236 persons who on January 1st, 1873, were paupers, on January 1st, 1874, were independent.

"I am aware that it may be urged that many of the cases, where there is little or no evidence of distress, would have undergone a great amount of suffering had it not been for the aid afforded by charitably-disposed persons. No doubt this is so, and to a certain extent I think it ought to be so. There are cases which the board cannot relieve without doing violence to principles, and opening the door to various abuses; these *true* charity will trouble itself to find out and help. Charity outside the board-room can be safely and wisely exercised in many instances where relief through the rates would be manifestly injurious. The best form of charity is that which, giving not money only but time and trouble, helps others to help themselves, and the worst as it is the easiest, is that which is given at the expense of the ratepayers in individual cases regardless of the injury done to a whole community by a sacrifice of principle.

"It must, however, be acknowledged that a reform so radical as that which has been described, cannot have been effected without a certain amount of suffering, often endured in silence, escaping, therefore, the notice of the most careful investigation, and difficult to estimate as it was impossible to prevent. Yet, at the same time, it should be remembered that such consequences, however much to be deplored, are really due, not to the reform itself, but to the neglect in former years which rendered such reform necessary."[1]

### Mr. Baldwyn Fleming says:—

"To those who desire improved administration, out-relief stands condemned for two chief reasons. Firstly, because it perpetuates the misery it professes to relieve, and secondly, because of its cruelty. The opponents of in-door relief may talk of the cruelty of driving people into the workhouse. I have endeavoured to show that no one wishes to drive people into the workhouse, but granting the assumption for a moment, can the cruelty of driving people into the workhouse, where they will be provided with every necessary of life, be for one moment compared with the cruelty of forcing people to try to live upon 2d. or 3d. a day?

"One of the strongest arguments against out-relief is the cruel inadequacy of the amount given. This argument might, no doubt, be met by increasing the amount, but if adequate out-relief were given to all the present recipients the burden upon the rates would become intolerable. It is amusing to watch the assumption on the part of the advocates of out-relief that they are the poor man's friend, and that those who wish to restrict out-relief are trying to injure and to oppress him.

"The opponents of out-relief object to it because they know how terribly injurious it is to the well-being and improvement of the poorer

---

[1] Report of Brixworth Board on the effects of their change of system, 3 L.G.B., pp. 118, 119. See also 19 L.G.B., p. 138 (Sheffield and Bradford).

classes, and because they hold it to be demoralising and most oppressive to pretend to relieve a man by the grant of an amount upon which it is absolutely impossible that he can live.

"The question is above all others a poor man's question. Out-relief as now administered must remove the natural inducement to thrift and self-reliance. It must divert charity from other and better ends in order that the recipients of out-relief may not starve. It must depreciate the value of labour, as it is relief in aid of wages. It must compel the thrifty man to contribute from his hardly-earned means to the support of his unthrifty fellows. It must encourage begging, and recourse to every sort of questionable means by which its inadequacy may be eked out. It must become the fruitful source of fraud and misrepresentation. For these and kindred reasons which affect the lower classes much more closely than any others, those who see the evil desire the general application of the remedy, which lies in a sounder administration of the law, a remedy which has been tried under almost every conceivable variety of conditions, and which has never failed to raise many to independence who would otherwise have remained paupers."[1]

---

[1] 19 L.G.B., pp. 121, 122.

## CHAPTER VIII.

### HOW THE EVILS ATTACHING TO OUT-DOOR RELIEF MAY BE MINIMISED.

WE have in the three last chapters drawn attention to the evils attaching to out-door relief, and to the benefits which attend the application of the workhouse test. We must, however, admit that in the present state of public opinion, misled by the sentimental school of Poor Law reformers, it would be, perhaps, impossible to do away with out-door relief entirely; and, therefore, we shall, in the present chapter, show how the evils attaching to it may be minimised.

Thus if out-door relief is granted at all, it should only be given under the very strictest regulations, and should be made the exception and not the rule. Many unions, unwilling to adopt the workhouse test system in its entirety, but impressed with the necessity of administering out-door relief most carefully and on some settled principles, have adopted rules for its regulation, which, when strictly conformed to, have produced wonderful results.[1]

"I am persuaded," says Mr. Dansey, "that one of the chief points in the strict and sound administration of relief is the adoption by boards of guardians of by-laws or sets of precedents, and that in this way alone will such anomalies as those just mentioned be done away with. By-laws for the administration of relief are now adopted in nearly all the well-managed unions, with the best results, for it is found that relief is then given on a principle, and that no guardian is able to complain that a pauper in his parish has been treated differently to one in another parish, while the ap-

---

[1] See *supra*, pp. 80-86.

plicants for relief are taught to feel that their chances of obtaining relief are not dependent upon the presence of any particular guardian at a meeting." [1]

In 1871 the Local Government Board, in a circular to their Poor Law inspectors,[2] adverted to some considerations which ought to be borne in mind by guardians in the administration of out-door relief.

"The most important, in the opinion of the board, is the application of an efficient workhouse test to all able-bodied applicants for relief, whether male or female, and the most strict and careful inquiries into the destitution and circumstances of all paupers to whom out-door relief is granted at their own homes. The board request you, therefore, to bring these points and the following recommendations under the notice of the guardians :—

1. That out-door relief should not be granted to single able-bodied men or to single able-bodied women, either with or without illegitimate children.
2. That out-door relief should not, except in special cases, be granted to any woman deserted by her husband during the first twelve months after the desertion, or to any able-bodied widow with one child only.
3. That in the case of any able-bodied widow with more than one child, it may be desirable to take one or more of the children into the workhouse in preference to giving out-door relief.
4. That in unions where the Prohibitory Order is in force the workhouse test should be strictly applied ; and the guardians should be informed that the board will not be prepared to sanction any cases which are not reported within the time limited by the order, and in which the reports do not contain a detailed statement of the paupers to which they refer, showing the number of their respective families, with the ages and number of children employed, amount of wages of the several members of the family at work, cause of destitution, period during which they have been without employment, amount of relief, if any, given previously to the transmission of the report, and what extent of accommodation for all classes exists in the workhouse at the time.
5. That out-door relief should be granted for a fixed period only, which should not in any case exceed three months.
6. That all orders to able-bodied men for relief in the labour-yard should be only given from week to week.
7. That out-door relief should not be granted in any case unless the

---

[1] 19 L.G.B., p. 124.
[2] See 1 L.G.B., p. 67.

relieving officer has, since the application, visited the home of the applicant, and has recorded the date of such visit in the relief application and report book. Cases in which the relieving officer has not had time to visit should be relieved by him in kind only, or by an order for the workhouse.

8. That the relieving officer should be required to make at least fortnightly visits to the homes of all persons receiving relief on account of temporary sickness, and of able men receiving relief in the labour-yard, and to visit the old and infirm cases at least once a quarter; and the relieving officer should be required to keep a diary with the dates and results of such visits.
9. That the provisions with respect to the compulsory maintenance of paupers by relations legally liable to contribute to their support should be more generally acted upon.
10. That as the recommendations of medical officers for meat and stimulants are regarded as equivalent to orders for additional relief, they should, in all cases, be accompanied by a report from the medical officer in a prescribed form, setting forth the particulars of each case ascertained by personal inquiry.
11. That in the most populous unions it may be expedient to appoint one or more officers to be termed 'inspectors of out-relief,' whose duty would be to act as a check upon the relieving officers, and ascertain also the circumstances connected with the recipients of relief. Such appointments have already been tried in Liverpool, and found to answer very successfully."[1]

The rules which have governed the administration of outdoor relief in the Atcham Union will be of interest. They are as follows :—[2]

"We give no permanent relief out of the workhouse
1. To any who rent more than half an acre of land.
2. To orphan children, *i.e.*, without both parents.
3. To deserted wives or deserted children.
4. To applicants residing out of the union.

"In cases of funeral we do everything or nothing, *i.e.*, we will not give the coffin and allow the relatives to do the rest.

"If a cottage is very dirty, we endeavour to get it made clean under the threat of refusing out-relief. If rent is £4 10s., or even £4, we only grant relief for a short time, until the pauper can obtain a cheaper place.

"We never grant out-relief on the plea of no work.

"We do not give clothing except to children going to service."

---

[1] These rules, with certain variations in minor details, were recommended for adoption by all metropolitan boards at a conference of metropolitan guardians held in London in 1872. (See 2 L.G.B., p. 5.)

[2] 2 L.G.B., pp. 67, 68.

On the 15th April, 1875, the Manchester Board of Guardians adopted the following standing orders with regard to the administration of out-door relief:—

"1. Out-door relief shall not be granted or allowed by the relief committees (except in case of sickness) to applicants of any of the following classes:—

*(a)* Single able-bodied men.
*(b)* Single able-bodied women.
*(c)* Able-bodied widows without children, or having only one child to support.
*(d)* Married women (with or without families) whose husbands, having been convicted of crime, are undergoing a term of imprisonment.
*(e)* Married women (with or without families) deserted by their husbands.
*(f)* Married women (with or without families) left destitute through their husbands having joined the militia, and being called up for training.
*(g)* Persons residing with relatives, where the united income of the family is sufficient for the support of all its members, whether such relatives are liable by law to support the applicant or not.

"2. Out-door relief shall not be granted in any case for a longer period than thirteen weeks at a time.

"3. Out-door relief shall not be granted to any able-bodied person for a longer period than six weeks at a time.

"4. Out-door relief shall not be granted on account of the sickness of the applicant or any of his family for a longer period than two weeks at a time, unless such sickness shall be certified in writing by the district medical officer as being likely to be of long duration or to be of a permanent character.

"5. Where relief is allowed to a parent through the admission of a child or children into the Swinton Schools or the workhouse, such relief shall not be granted for a longer period than six months at a time; and if at the expiration of such period a continuance of the relief is required, the relieving officer shall visit and inquire into the circumstances of the parent, and bring the case up for re-consideration by the relief committee in the same manner as if it were a case of out-door relief."[1]

Many boards of guardians object to be bound down by rules. They prefer, as they say, to deal with every case which comes before them "on its own merits." But the merits of

---

[1] See 5 L.G.B., p. xvii. Rules passed by other boards. See 3 L.G.B., p. 99 (Guildford); *ib.*, p. 108 (Reigate); 8 L.G.B., pp. 123-30 (Dorking and Dunmow); 18 L.G.B., p. 133 (Middlesborough); *ib.*, p. 134 (Sunderland); 21 L.G.B., p. 164 (Northwich).

any case depend entirely upon the constitution of the board at the time it is under discussion, and frequently solely on the opinion of individual guardians. The advantage of having rules is that similar cases will be dealt with in a similar way. We will quote Mr. Longley on the subject:—

"There is no point which I have discussed more frequently with the boards of guardians than that now under consideration, and my efforts to procure adherence to rule in the administration of relief have been commonly met by general objections to 'hard and fast rules,' and by the counter proposition that each case should be dealt with on 'its own merits.' The question of the applicability of general rules to Poor Law administration has already been discussed, but the latter objection seems to need some further notice, because its terms seem to imply that administration according to rule is, in some way or other, opposed to, and inconsistent with the consideration of the circumstances of an individual case. The chief value of a rule, on the contrary, appears to be this, that it affords a ready means of applying to the circumstances of a given case, when duly ascertained, the experience gained by previous dealing with other similar cases, and it will be observed that inasmuch as a knowledge of the circumstances of one case must precede their identification with those of another, they are little likely to be overlooked by any competent and candid administrator who seeks to apply a rule to them. The absolute disregard of rule which seems to be contemplated by some of these objectors, and for which they are sometimes disposed even to claim credit, involves, as it seems to me, a course of dealing with each case which shall be debarred from all the advantages of accumulated experience."[1]

It is the rule of most boards to have a permanent list. This is a bad practice even when the list is revised every thirteen weeks. The relieving officer feels himself under no obligation to visit cases of this nature until the time for revision comes round. But in the meantime the circumstances of the paupers may entirely change. Thus Mr. Kennedy, speaking of his district, says:—

"It is to be regretted that in nearly all the unions in the north of England the guardians still continue to grant relief in those cases they consider of a permanent character for periods of twenty-six weeks; this system, which is at all times opposed to an economical administration of

---

[1] 3 L.G.B., p. 146.

relief, is especially so in such times as the present, when the circumstances of the relations of many recipients of relief are rapidly changing; for example, it is clear that if, when relief is first granted, a son is able to contribute 1s. 6d. or 2s. per week towards a parent's maintenance, if he subsequently obtains a rise of 10 or 15 per cent. in his wages, his ability to contribute will have been correspondingly increased, and I have shown that such rises have been frequent during the past year. There are only two of the more populous unions in the district in which it is the rule never to give relief for longer periods than thirteen weeks—Sunderland and Newcastle, and it is noteworthy that in these two unions the percentage of pauperism to the population is considerably lower than in the other large urban unions, being 1·3 and 1·8 against 2·4 in the Tynemouth Union, which is the next lowest."[1]

Mr. Baldwyn Fleming says:—

"In most unions there is a revision about once a quarter. Very often the revision consists in a reading over of the names by the chairman with a statement that the cases have all been gone through by the guardian of the parish and the relieving officer and that none can be altered. Such revision is altogether insufficient.

"Quarterly 'revisions' are very unnecessary, very troublesome and very inefficient; a standing rule that relief shall in no case be given for more than a fortnight, or at the outside a month, without reconsideration, is worth all the revisions that could be devised. It is absurd to say that circumstances cannot change even in the most unlikely cases. We know perfectly well that the endless vicissitudes of life affect the lowest as well as the highest.

"If no order be given for more than a fortnight and the investigation each time be careful and complete, two advantages will be secured:

"(1) The case will be regularly visited and attended to by the relieving officer.

"(2) Attempts at imposition will be defeated. Of course this cannot be done without time and trouble, but I maintain that time and trouble should be given."[2]

"I have not failed," says Mr. Knollys, "to call the attention of the guardians of those unions in my district where relief was still in some cases granted for periods of twenty-six weeks to the desirability of making it an established rule that in no case should fourteen weeks be exceeded as the limit of time for which an order should be made; and in addition to those unions in which this was previously the rule, the guardians of the following unions have changed their practice in this respect:—Alnwick, Auckland, Chester-le-Street, Hexham, Middlesborough, Pickering, South Shields and Whitby. I am glad to say that now the guardians of all the most important unions in the district, except Tynemouth, have adopted the thirteen or four-

---

[1] 19 L.G.B., p. 133. See further as to necessity for frequent revision, 1 L.G.B., p. 90; and 3 L.G.B., p. 75.
[2] 18 L.G.B., p. 114.

teen weeks' limit. I have also urged upon boards of guardians the advantages which appear to me to attend the system by which the cases of a certain number of those paupers who are practically permanently in receipt of out-door relief are brought up for consideration at each board meeting, as opposed to the practice of having a long list which is brought for revision once a quarter. In the latter case not only is there the danger of the guardians dealing with the cases in a somewhat perfunctory manner upon the reiterated *ipse dixit* of the relieving officer, in case after case there is 'no alteration,' but they do not and cannot receive that careful investigation from the relieving officer immediately before they are brought before the guardians for consideration which they should. The visits at the residences of these paupers when the cases are numerous, must either have been made in some instances some time previously, or many visits must have been made in the same place on the same day, when they will not only have been unduly rapid and perfunctory in their character, but, being expected by the paupers, preparations may have been made to prevent the officer from obtaining an accurate knowledge of facts. The alterations of the circumstances of relatives are also apt to be overlooked, and in some cases I have found the names and earnings of such relatives not repeated in the application and report book after the first application."[1]

The unrevised permanent list is so universally condemned that we need say nothing about it.

Whenever the circumstances of the case show a probability of the applicant being at some future time in a position to repay the relief granted, it should always be given on loan, and when there is ability to pay, the repayment should be enforced.

In all new applications for relief it is very important that the applicant, and if possible the head of the family, should attend the meeting of the board.

"I am convinced that the examination of applicants by the chairman before the full board is the only means by which a board of guardians can ascertain that they are administering the law equally and fairly throughout their union. I have frequently heard the report of relieving officers usefully supplemented by such an examination, and still more frequently the opinion of individual guardians utterly upset."[2]

Relief in kind instead of money is far too seldom given. It

---

[1] 20 L.G.B., pp. 244, 245.
[2] 3 L.G.B., pp. 70, 71; see also 1 L.G.B., p. 92.

gives more trouble. The advantages resulting from it were pointed out in the report of 1834, and "no change of circumstances has made the remarks of the commissioners of less administrative force now than in their day. Advances in money, it should be always recollected, are advances only of the means of obtaining relief, which means the pauper is under constant temptation to misapply, and in a large proportion of cases is incompetent to apply properly. Relief in kind, if well adapted, may be considered as the relief itself, the object of the *bona fide* applicant being not money, but bread, or the immediate means of sustenance. It has been a frequent source of complaint, that of relief in money only a small portion reached the wives and other members of the family for whose sustenance it was given; and that, in the rural districts, the greater portion was spent in the beer shops, and in the towns was expended in the gin shops. Relief in kind we found less liable to misapplication. If instead of giving to a pauper a weekly allowance in money, an allowance be given in food or other necessaries of the same value, he can only obtain a reduced amount of his wonted description of indulgence by the misappropriation of the relief in kind. This misappropriation is necessarily attended with increased trouble, loss and risks of detection. Under this form of relief we find that the temptation to fraud is diminished to the extent of the additional trouble incurred in the misappropriation, and the reduction of the amount of beer, spirits, or other objects of desire obtained by it. Another advantage seldom noticed as connected with relief in kind, and which has presented itself to our consideration as a reason for bringing this form of relief as early as possible into general operation, is that in the present condition of the country it diminishes the fluctuations of allowances in the way of unintended and unwarranted increases."[1]

---

[1] 11 L.G.B., p. xiii.

Mr. Longley's suggestions for improvements in administration generally where out-relief is granted, and which are particularly applicable to urban unions, are set out in Appendix H., p. 235.

It has been frequently suggested that the regulations with regard to out-door relief should be made more stringent.[1] Mr. Baldwyn Fleming thinks the present regulations quite sufficient, if they are steadily and intelligently applied. His words will have weight :—

"Guardians who wish to work upon right principles find their good intentions defeated by the elasticity of the exceptions to the orders prohibiting out-relief. In their difficulty they turn to the board with the perhaps natural appeal, 'You are always telling us that out-relief is bad, but your own regulations give such loop-holes for out-relief that we are unable to resist the pressure put upon us to grant it. Cannot you do something to help us by making out-relief positively illegal except in cases of emergency, which cannot otherwise be dealt with?'

"Such an appeal excites sympathy, and the inclination to help if possible, but a very little consideration will show that it is the cry of weak administration struggling with opposition it has not yet learned to conquer.

"Any new regulations the board might issue must be either of general or local application. A general order prohibiting out-relief would create so much opposition, and at first so much hardship, that probably a revulsion of public feeling would very rightly set in, and much more harm than good would grow out of such an effort to help guardians who will not help themselves. If new regulations were only of partial application the effect would be that one Poor Law would prevail in one union and another in another. It may be said that there are already different regulations in force in different unions, and this is true to the extent that in some unions orders are in force which have not been issued to others. This has come about from a variety of causes, but it is scarcely open to question that in the general interests of good administration it is much to be desired that uniform regulations should be in force throughout the extra metropolitan unions. Clearly any extension of the existing differences would be regrettable, and would increase the inconvenience arising from the divergencies which already exist. The following question then presents itself:—Do unsatisfactory results really come from defects in the Poor Law, and the regulations for enforcing that law, or are they to be attributed to the bad administration of the law, and of the board's regulations? There can be but one answer.

---

[1] *E.g.*, see resolution of Central Poor Law Conference of 1876 (6 L.G.B., pp. xxv., xxvi.); and the reply of the Local Government Board thereto (7 L.G.B., p. 51).

"The present law and regulations have produced excellent results whenever they have been properly used, and they can be well administered in any union.

"The principles which should govern their operations have often been misunderstood, and the powers they confer have been misapplied, but the fault lies with the administration and not with the law.

"It is a strange anomaly, but an intelligible one, that though public opinion at this moment is opposed to centralisation, guardians who are not strong enough to apply principles which they cannot deny to be sound, should wish the board to take action which would be centralisation and nothing else. This is intelligible enough, and for the following reason, guardians on principle are unwilling to part with any portion of the discretion and responsibility they possess, but in practice their ready good sense tells them that the long experience and wide field of observation open to the board, does place the board in a position which no local authority can occupy. In some unions it might be useful that the guardians should have faster rules to aid their desire for better work, but all the arguments hitherto advanced upon this subject do not affect these two conclusions.

"It has been abundantly proved that no alteration in the law is needed to ensure good results, inasmuch as good results have been brought about under a variety of circumstances by the present law. The absolute prohibition of out-relief would certainly be evaded by the ingenuity of hostile administrators, would entail some real hardship, and would arouse such opposition that in the long run it would probably be mischievous instead of advantageous.

"All that is needed is the steady and intelligent application of the powers which guardians already possess. Many guardians are satisfied with the present condition of affairs, and this is the most difficult feature to deal with in Dorsetshire and Wiltshire. Probably many others are not satisfied, but they find themselves outnumbered, and have grown tired of futile attempts. Many again say that in all the discussions they hear upon Poor Law, they learn nothing of a practical character, that theories sound very well at a public meeting, but break down when they come to the board room. This is not a very just statement of the case, for no heroic action is required to bring about a largely improved administration, and the matters of everyday practice upon which success depends have been stated very frequently.

"Guardians can require that every case shall be thoroughly investigated in the first instance, and that it be constantly watched whilst receiving relief. They can refuse to act upon the uncorroborated statements of the applicant. They can make orders for short periods only. They can seek out all relatives legally liable and make them contribute. They can gradually break up 'permanent lists.' They can ensure thorough revision when application is made for renewal of relief. They can abolish pay stations, and have the relief given at the homes of the poor. They can cause the frequent and unexpected visitation of the paupers at their own houses by the relieving officers. They can insist upon 'extras' and articles in kind being actually supplied to the cases for which they are ordered.

They can give relief upon loan, and enforce repayment where the case should be so treated. Such details as these are what really tell in the long run. They are troublesome, if you will, and need time, patience, energy, but when these are given the reward comes. If the true facts of the case are fully learnt and kept under observation, the relief will generally be appropriate and adequate. The weakness of ordinary rural administration is the want of thorough knowledge in each particular case, and the tendency to leave too much to the guardians of the parish. The very object for which the board of guardians is constituted, is defeated when a guardian is allowed undue weight in dealing with the cases from his own parish. The board and not the guardian is to give the decision, in order that it may be impartial and independent of local knowledge and prejudices."[1]

It is a question, however, whether the time has not arrived when the Prohibitory Order of 1844 should be applied universally.

---

[1] 20 L.G.B , pp. 226, 227.

## CHAPTER IX.

#### THE WORKHOUSE SYSTEM.

WE have shown in the last chapter how the evils attaching to out-door relief may be minimised by very strict administration. Searching inquiry and investigation before any out-door relief is granted, coupled with a free application of the workhouse test, is, perhaps, the most that can be expected from boards of guardians at the present time. By the adoption of such a policy pauperism will be greatly diminished, if not entirely got rid of. We shall devote this chapter to a consideration of how the workhouse test should be applied.

It was undoubtedly the expectation of the commissioners who drew up the celebrated report of 1834, that the result of improved administration of the Poor Law, in accordance with the principles then laid down, would be the almost entire abolition of out-door relief. Hard-headed men themselves, they may have forgotten that the large majority of civilised beings are governed in matters relating to the relief of distress by the heart and not by the head. The principles they were so careful to formulate were soon forgotten, their workhouses became unpopular, and in spite of prohibitory and out-door relief regulation orders, out-door relief still continued to be freely given. The following are the principal considerations which led, and still lead, guardians to adopt this course :—[1]

(1) Insufficiency of workhouse accommodation.
(2) The feeling that it is a hardship to compel those who may be

---

[1] See 23 P.L.B., p. 36.

persons of deserving character to come into the workhouse, especially in cases where it would have the effect of breaking up a home.

(3) That it is cheaper to give some assistance in the shape of out-relief than to undertake the entire maintenance of the applicants and their families in the workhouse.

(4) The fear that to refuse out-relief and offer the workhouse where there is great reluctance to accept it, may lead to the occurrence of many cases not merely of extreme hardship but of actual starvation, and

(5) That the workhouse test, as it affects children, infects them with the pauper taint, whereas out-door relief has not the same effect.

As to (1), we have already[1] dwelt upon the absolute necessity of sufficient accommodation for all classes of paupers in the workhouse. The guardians have the remedy in their own hands, and classification is provided for by Articles 98 and 99 of the General Order of 1847.[2] As regards the Metropolis, it is not, perhaps, generally known that the Metropolitan Poor Act, 1867, contemplated classification not *in* workhouses but *by* workhouses. Mr. Longley treats of this at length in his Report on Poor Law Administration in the Metropolis;[3] and explains why the idea was not and for some time could not be fully carried out. Under the Act the Poplar Union Workhouse was set apart for the reception of the able-bodied poor only.[4] The opinion of the Local Government Board on the subject is made very clear:—

"Regarding as we do the recourse by other boards of guardians to the use of the Poplar Workhouse as for the most part a temporary expedient, we regret to state that no great progress has as yet been made towards the permanent classification in separate establishments of the various classes of in-door paupers, other than the sick; with the exceptions of the boards of guardians of the Poplar and Stepney Unions, no boards of guardians in the Metropolis have attempted to combine with each other to avail themselves permanently (otherwise than for the special relief of casual paupers) of the facilities for combination afforded by the Metropolitan Poor Act,

---

[1] *Supra,* pp. 17-20.
[2] See *supra,* p. 17.
[3] 4 L.G.B., pp. 42-49.
[4] This arrangement, however, no longer exists.

1867, section 50, and the amending Act of 1869, section 17. We attach the utmost importance to this improvement of the classification of in-door paupers, which we believe to be a necessary condition of the maintenance of that discipline which lies at the root of an effective administration of in-door relief. This improvement, however, cannot be effected, except at an enormous and almost prohibitory cost, otherwise than by the combination of several boards of guardians for this purpose.

"Their existing workhouses would, in that event, become available for the separate accommodation of various classes of in-door paupers chargeable to the several combined areas. We are advised that in the existing state of the law it is doubtful whether such a combination can be effected otherwise than by the voluntary action of boards of guardians, which we trust may still take place, and the desirableness of which we shall continue to press upon the guardians."[1]

It is satisfactory that much progress has been made since this was written.[2] The state of things in 1867 and in 1884 are contrasted thus :—

"Previous to the legislation of 1867 the classification of inmates of workhouses in London was in very many respects defective. Children of school age had, indeed, for some years before that period, been placed in separate institutions in the neighbourhood of London. But the separation of the sick from the other inmates was in most cases imperfect, and the large class of harmless lunatics were aggregated with the other inmates. Cases of infectious disease also were freely admitted into the sick wards. The establishment of the Metropolitan Infirmaries has remedied the first evil; that of the Metropolitan Asylum District has dealt with the two latter; in the case of the second of these, indeed, providing a machinery applicable far beyond the limits which were originally contemplated. The improved classification of in-door pauperism thus effected has, we believe, counted for much in the diminution of Metropolitan pauperism which has taken place during the last ten years. By the removal of the sick to distinct buildings it became possible to restore due discipline among the able-bodied. Those of the sick who were curable were more rapidly enabled to gain their livelihood; and so far from improved structure of the new infirmaries and the more efficient treatment given in them encouraging the abuse of these buildings, they have acted, it is believed, as a check upon malingering, by the order, control, and the close observation which the new mode of administration has involved. It is true that the number of inmates under medical treatment is double the number so treated in the former period of which we have been speaking.

"This is accounted for, apart from the increase in population, by the large number of cases formerly treated by the district officers at their own

---

[1] 3 L.G.B., p. xxv.
[2] See 10 L.G.B., p. xxx.; 19 L.G.B., p. 106.

homes, and now treated, of course, far more effectively in the infirmary. It is, at least, certain that the diminution in the numbers of out-door paupers receiving medical relief has far more than made up for the increase in the numbers of the in-door sick. In 1873, the earliest period at which accurate reports were kept, the number of orders for out-door medical relief was 144,676. Last year it had fallen to 102,198."[1]

Classification by workhouses can be easily carried out in the Metropolis where the area is so confined, but, as regards the possibility of its being applicable to the country, there is much difference of opinion. Mr. Murray Browne thinks it feasible,[2] while, in the Manchester group of unions, Mr. Henley tells us the idea of some amalgamation between the four unions was broached in 1889,

"and has met with some support, as being calculated to economise space by making the workhouses subservient to the needs of all the group in the matter of classification of in-door poor. This is a subject that requires very close consideration. At present my information in regard to the scheme is unofficial and insufficient to justify me in expressing an opinion upon it."[3]

Mr. Peel, however, is not quite satisfied on the point. He says :—

"Much, too, has been said about the classification of paupers, and the hardships inflicted on respectable old people in forcing them to mix with the less well-conducted ; but, though the poor are seldom backward in speaking of any discomfort, complaints on that score are seldom heard, possibly because there is little or no foundation for them, or maybe they are of opinion that wherever they lived they would come in contact with people whose characters and conversation were not quite to their liking.
"In Northamptonshire, one of the best administered unions in the county appointed a committee to visit all the workhouses, and see if it were possible to suggest a scheme for the appropriation of certain workhouses to separate classes, such as the infirm, the sick, the imbeciles, the able-bodied, or the children, with a view to reduced expenditure and better administration, but the difficulties in the way appear to be almost insuperable. The sick and infirm have a decided dislike to being sent away from that part of the county in which they have been brought up and

---

[1] 13 L.G.B., p. xxxiv.
[2] 22 L.G.B., p. 73.
[3] 19 L.G.B., p. 128.

worked, losing the chance of seeing the few friends who are able to come on market and other days to visit them in the workhouse. The boarding-out system would seem to have rendered a separate establishment for orphans and deserted children almost unnecessary. The withdrawal of the few able-bodied to be found in each workhouse would be attended with obvious disadvantages; but it appears to me that a workhouse in the county might with advantage be set apart for imbeciles."[1]

We entirely agree with him as to the advantage attending the removal of the imbecile paupers from workhouses where there are no means of training and educating them, and where great difficulties attend their being properly looked after.

The arguments 2, 3, and 4, as to the breaking up of the home, the cheapness of out-door relief, the fear that the restriction of out-door relief will cause cases of starvation, are those based upon the grounds of humanity and economy, and have already been dealt with.[2] Cases falling within 2 may be safely left to charity.[3] Further, as to 4, experience has shown starvation never does follow. On the contrary, the returns show, as far as London is concerned, that but few cases of deaths by starvation occur where out-door relief has been refused, and it is a curious fact that, while in 1871 (when out-door relief was freely given) 100 deaths of starvation were noted, in 1891 there were only 30.[4]

Mr. Longley says :—

"The recent Parliamentary returns of the particulars of cases in which a coroner's jury have returned a verdict of death caused altogether, or in part, by starvation during the year 1872 show that in one case only out of 97 had an order for the workhouse, exclusive of other relief, been previously refused by the deceased. I have made inquiries as to the particulars

---

[1] 22 L.G.B., pp. 68, 69.
[2] *Supra*, pp. 73-75, 83-86.
[3] *Supra*, pp. 49-51.
[4] Mr. C. S. Loch has analysed some of the recent "starvation" cases in two letters which appeared in the *Times* of December 19 and 22, 1892. They have been republished in pamphlet form under the title, "Starvation Cases," and the pamphlet can be obtained at the offices of the Charity Organisation Society, 15 Buckingham Street, W.C.

of this case, but can find no trace of it in the records of the union in which the deceased was resident. It is fair, however, to say that these records were at this particular time somewhat imperfectly kept."[1]

Besides which, when they have offered adequate relief in the house, the guardians have done their duty; and if the offer has been refused, and the applicant should suffer, the responsibility is not theirs. A third course, however, is followed in many unions, although the guardians are under no obligation to adopt it. In cases where the workhouse has been offered and refused, the relieving officers are directed to visit the home at short intervals, as often even as three or four times a week, if necessary, and to administer relief *in kind* in all cases which appear to them to require it.[2]

Mr. Longley goes into the question very fully, and points out the objections to this course of procedure. He says:—

"I must not, however, omit to notice a more real difficulty which arises in connection with in-door relief, without a mention of which no examination of the practical administration of relief in London can be considered complete. There is, I will undertake to say, no board of guardians in London which has not from time to time been perplexed by the persistent refusal of an applicant, of whose destitution there is no doubt, to accept the in-door relief, by which alone the guardians all agree in thinking they can effectually and fitly relieve him. But the difficulty of even these cases is, I venture to think, exaggerated, if not actually aggravated, by the course often adopted by the guardians themselves, which is, in many instances, such as to offer a direct encouragement to the applicant to refuse in-door relief. Where the poor learn from their own experience, or that of others, that the guardians are, to adopt the language used in my presence by the chairman of a large union, 'so very pliable,' it is unlikely in the extreme that they will acquiesce in the offer to them of relief in a form less eligible than that in which they may, by importunity, ultimately obtain it.

"In unions where this is the case, it is too frequently the practice merely to advise or to suggest to the applicant that he should go into the workhouse; when he not unnaturally declines to do so, an argument ensues between him and the guardians, in which the latter are almost invariably worsted, and the pauper retires, having practically obtained relief on his own terms, or, at least, having dictated to the guardians, by a curious though not an uncommon inversion of their relative positions, the form in

---

[1] 3 L.G.B., p. 173.
[2] See 3 L.G.B., p. 36.

which he shall receive relief. It is from boards of guardians who adopt this mode of dealing with paupers that the vast majority of complaints of persistent refusals to enter the workhouse arise.

"On the other hand, when it is the practice of a board of guardians, having considered all the circumstances of a case, and having heard the applicant's statement, to make a positive and final order that he shall be relieved only in the workhouse, the paupers soon learn that nothing is to be gained by subsequent remonstrance, and that the guardians mean what they say; while the guardians in turn meet with but little difficulty on account of obstinate refusals to accept the relief given. Still, there is a small residuum of cases, occurring chiefly among the aged, who have been brought up to rely upon out-relief as their right, in which it appears not improbable that paupers may deliberately attempt to carry out their threats of preferring starvation to admission to the workhouse. Under a more sound and uniform administration of the law these cases will probably disappear, but at present they constitute, when they arise, a practical difficulty, which materially embarrasses the work of the guardians. It is, I conceive, clear that the technical responsibility of guardians in respect of an application for relief is discharged by the offer of adequate relief to the applicant, who cannot be said to be destitute if, being physically competent to avail himself of it, he possesses an order of admission to the workhouse. For otherwise, it must be held that guardians are not merely bound to relieve destitution, but to give relief in such a form that the applicant will accept it. In other words, relief is to be eligible and not ineligible, and the applicant, and not the guardians, is to prescribe, as has already been shown, the form in which it shall be given.

"The common practice of boards of guardians in dealing with the class of cases in question seems to be a virtual adoption of the latter alternative. The relieving officer is directed to 'watch the case,' and to supply such need in kind as may be needed to preserve life. This course, which has, I believe, received some encouragement from the board, seems, as I venture to think, to be open to two objections. First, it recognises the continuance of the responsibility of the guardians after adequate relief has been offered; and next, it tends to countenance the erroneous belief that it is for the relieving officer to seek out destitution, and not simply to confine his attention to *applicants* for relief. Further, the grant of out-relief in kind is a concession of the whole point at issue between the guardians and the pauper."[1]

As to the argument—(5)—relating to the pauper taint, statistics do not support the contention. Mr. Lockwood has lately made a careful inquiry into the subject. He says:—

"Many worthy but ill-informed people believe, or at any rate assert, that the great majority of workhouse children become necessarily infected with what is called the pauper taint, and consequently return sooner or later to

---

[1] 3 L.G.B., pp. 172, 173.

the workhouse; the fallacy of this contention is manifested by the return A. of adult inmates of 54 workhouses (with 5,500 adult inmates) on the 15th March, 1892, who during childhood were educated in or from a workhouse, classified under headings giving causes for needing relief. The last column refers to adult female inmates not brought up in any workhouse."[1]

| MALES. | | | | | FEMALES. | | | | | | |
|---|---|---|---|---|---|---|---|---|---|---|---|
| Weak-minded. | Cripples. | Defective eyesight. | Able-bodied, but not in regular employment. | Total. | Weak-minded. | Cripples. | Defective eyesight. | Pregnancy (illegitimate). | Able-bodied, but not in regular employment. | Total. | Unmarried mothers *not* brought up in the workhouse. |
| 23 | 17 | 3 | 24 | 67 | 35 | 11 | 2 | 36 | 17 | 101 | 221 |

The present chairman of the Atcham Union caused a similar inquiry to be made in his own union, with the following result:—

"The number of adult paupers in the workhouse on the date of the inquiry, May 21st, 1890, who were 21 years of age and upwards was, males 157, females 86, total 243. Of these only one male and no females had been brought up in a workhouse, and in this case the training was prior to the formation of the union in 1836. . . . The solitary case referred to is one J. B., who was born in the workhouse of the Atcham incorporation of the poor in the year 1803, and was brought up there. As a boy he was sent to service. He first returned to the workhouse on the 24th May, 1885, when he was 82 years of age and very infirm."[2]

Fortunately the feasibility of applying the workhouse test with success has been proved. In those unions[3] which have adopted the system, pauperism has been almost entirely ex-

---

[1] 22 L.G.B., p. 75.
[2] "Report of the Progress of the Atcham Union," p. 24.
[3] For example Bradfield, Brixworth, Atcham, Whitechapel, Stepney, St. George's-in-the-East.

tinguished; little or no suffering has been caused in the process, while the benefits conferred upon the ratepayers, poor and rich alike, are apparent.[1]

It must be remembered that the workhouse system is founded on practical experience; that it has never failed in times of sudden and extreme pressure of distress among the poor, even although the lax administration of out-relief, en-

---

[1] Mr. Ritchie's return supports this statement. We will take the same unions as on p. 58, showing the effects of the out-door system and in-door system on the amount of their pauperism. "I" signifies "In-door" Union; "O" signifies "Out-door" Union.

| Union. | Day or year. | Paupers receiving medical relief only. | Paupers receiving relief other than medical. | Total. | Proportion of paupers to population. |
|---|---|---|---|---|---|
| I. Bradfield | 1st January, 1892 .. | .. | 136 | 136 | 1 in 132 |
|  | Year ending Lady Day, 1892 .. .. | 52 | 258 | 310 | 1 in 58 |
| O. Hungerford | 1st January, 1892 .. | 106 | 557 | 663 | 1 in 25 |
|  | Year ending Lady Day, 1892 ...... | 533 | 1110 | 1643 | 1 in 10 |
| I. Brixworth | 1st January, 1892 .. | .. | 106 | 106 | 1 in 115 |
|  | Year ending Lady Day, 1892 ...... | 1 | 156 | 157 | 1 in 77 |
| O. Daventry | 1st January, 1892 .. | 48 | 537 | 585 | 1 in 30 |
|  | Year ending Lady Day, 1892 ...... | 98 | 849 | 947 | 1 in 18 |

It will be noticed that the year's pauperism bears much the same ratio to the day's pauperism in the unions compared. In fact in comparing any two unions where the condition of things is much the same, but where the system of administering the Poor Law is different, it will be found that the ratio of the year's pauperism to the day's pauperism will not vary much.

couraging an habitual reliance upon Poor Law relief, has made it more difficult of application at such periods.[1]

By means of the workhouse test *alone* can real destitution be discovered, and fraud, imposition and lying be defeated. Enough has, we think, been said to point out the *pros* and *cons* of *in-door* and *out-door* relief. We would refer those who wish to go further into the subject to the Report of the Committee of the Docking Union, 8 L.G.B., p. 123; and to Mr. Baldwyn Fleming's able reports, 17 L.G.B., pp. 63-65; 19 L.G.B., pp. 116-122; and 20 L.G.B., pp. 220-225.

---

[1] See 3 L.G.B., pp. 138-141, for most interesting remarks on this subject. Also 4 L.G.B., pp. xvii.-xix.; 8 L.G.B., pp. xix.-xxvi.; 14 L.G.B., pp. xxxvi.-xxxviii.

## CHAPTER X.

### MEDICAL RELIEF.

WE are going to consider the question of medical relief in a separate chapter, because although much the same evils attach to the grant of it outside the workhouse as have been described in Chapter V., there is more to be said in favour of it than of other kinds of out-door relief. Still, whenever it is made too easy to obtain, the establishment of provident dispensaries and medical aid societies is greatly hindered, it being contrary to human nature to pay for what can be had for nothing. Still an advance has been made since 1870, and those unions which have reduced their out-door pauperism to a minimum now give very little medical relief, to the great encouragement of medical clubs.

Thus in 1873, Mr. Longley wrote as follows :—

> "There is probably no contingency against which it is less difficult for the poorer classes to make provision than sickness, and that in spite of the numerous and substantial difficulties which at present beset the efforts of the poor towards thrift. The recent extension, too, in practice, of the provident principle to many of the so-called charitable dispensaries in London, has afforded further facilities to the poor for making provision for a time of sickness."[1]

If that was his opinion then, what would it be now that the facilities for insuring against sickness are so much greater than they were twenty years ago? While out-door medical relief is

---

[1] 3 L.G.B., pp. 188, 189.

open to the same objections as out-door relief generally,[1] the main objection to it is that in so many cases it is the beginning of a career of pauperism.

This is, indeed, a matter of such general experience that it is unnecessary to do more than mention the fact.

The recipient of medical relief from the parish is placed in a distinctly better position than the poor person who cannot command such comforts as the pauper gets. The poor person is in consequence tempted to give up subscribing to his club or society and to say, "Why should I pay when the people next door get their medical relief for nothing?" The facility, too, with which medical relief is obtained encourages among the poor the belief that medical aid given at the cost of the poor rate differs in kind and in eligibility from other relief. Guardians are too apt to regard it in the same light. How often are the words, "Oh! it is *only* medical relief," heard in the board rooms and the relief asked for granted as a matter of course.[2]

The facility, also, induces a belief among the poor that there is nothing shameful attaching to the relief, as there is to other forms of out-door relief. In fact, in country districts, "the medical officer is frequently the only practitioner in the neighbourhood, so they see no manifest difference whether they lay by for illness, and then pay the doctor out of their own pocket, or whether they do not do this, and yet are treated by the same person in the same way."[3]

---

[1] See Chapter V.

[2] See 3 L.G.B., pp. 161, 162, 188; 20 L.G.B., p. 237. As in almost every union the doctors are paid by salary only, the guardians are tempted to be lax in granting medical relief because "the relief costs nothing." They are apt to consider the "money" part of the question only, and not the moral effect which the grant of medical relief may have on the recipient of it.

[3] Aschrott's "English Poor Law System," p. 238.

Further, it is evident that malingering must often escape detection. The stringent rules by which clubs are governed are entirely absent from union relief. Neither is there the valuable check of public opinion. If a man cheats his club his fellow-members are against him; but neighbours do not have equally high standards where the cheated party is only the board of guardians. The committee of the Brixworth Board of Guardians reported on this subject as follows:—

"Perhaps no part of the system of out-door relief is more open to abuse than this (*viz.*, medical relief), or requires more care and supervision on the part of the board. A very large proportion of cases now on the out-door relief list obtained relief in the first instance through medical certificates for some illness either feigned or only of a temporary nature, and have now become reduced to a state of almost hopeless pauperism. Your committee would here notice the remark of one of the medical officers belonging to the union, that he is sorry to confess that there is a very strong tendency on the part of the poor to feign disease, and would particularly call the attention of the board to a complaint of the same medical officer, that it is not at all an infrequent thing for his report on a case to be set aside or over-ruled by the applicant for relief procuring an out-patient's letter to the infirmary from some charitable person, on the strength of which he applies again and obtains out-door relief.

"Your committee find that the applications for medical orders generally appear to be on the increase, and particularly in cases of childbirth, and that cases certified as suffering from debility are extremely numerous, and these they think as a rule are suspicious, while in many cases the certificate is obtained by means of a system of 'preparation' which seems now thoroughly understood throughout the union."[1]

But the greatest abuses arise with regard to what are known as *medical extras*.

"I think," says Mr. Sendall, "few persons conversant with Poor Law administration would profess to be content with the system or rather the want of system by which this large item of expenditure is at present governed; certainly many experienced observers regard with grave misgivings" the actual increase to the pauperism of the country arising from this source.[2]

---

[1] 2 L.G.B., p. 73; see also 3 L.G.B., p. 165.
[2] 3 L.G.B., p. 84.

"These abuses," says Mr. Longley, "are notorious to all boards of guardians, who are frequently loud in their complaints, made with much reason, of the inducement to pauperism which is held out by relief given in this form, over which they find themselves too often unable to maintain an efficient control."[1]

He also mentions the following further objections:—

"The issue, by way of relief of articles, which, primarily, and independent of their application to cases of sickness, are regarded by the poor as luxuries, and not mere necessaries, encourages fraudulent applications for medical relief, which is too commonly believed by paupers to carry with it a claim for nourishment; a strong temptation is offered to the families of sick paupers to divert to their own use the relief thus given; the medical officers, as being practically the authors of this relief, are subjected to an undue pressure by applicants for it, which tend to divert their attention from the purely professional aspect of the cases which come before them; and, lastly, persons who would otherwise receive medical aid from the public hospitals are unduly attracted to Poor Law medical relief, because the latter is, while the former is not, commonly accompanied by the grant of nourishment. In some cases, too, I have found that out-patients of the public hospitals are in receipt of relief in the form of nourishment, recommended by medical officers who are not professionally responsible for their treatment. Except, perhaps, in the last case, no direct violation of the orders of the board appears to have contributed to aggravate the misbelief incident to this form of relief; and even there, though in one case it has come to my knowledge that a medical officer has been accustomed to recommend nourishment for patients whom he had not been formally required to attend, it is I believe frequently found that paupers who are out-patients of hospitals, obtain medical orders for the sake of the nourishment which commonly accompanies the attendance of Poor Law medical officers. These persons consequently receive medical attendance and medicine from two sources, and, in practice, they rely upon the hospital medicine and attendance, while they destroy the medicine supplied from the Poor Law dispensary."[2]

He says further:—

"No precautions which the Board[3] or boards of guardians can devise will, I fear, avail to correct the pauperising influence of the grant of meat and stimulants to out-door paupers or to prevent their misuse when given. These considerations, as well as the recent increase of infirmary accommodation just mentioned, all point again to the substitution of in-door for out-relief to the sick. It will probably be deemed impracticable at once to

---

[1] 3 L.G.B., p. 189.
[2] 3 L.G.B., p. 190.
[3] *i.e.* The Local Government Board.

establish a rule to the effect that relief by way of nourishment shall be given to those out-door paupers only who are physically unable to receive it in an infirmary, where, at least, the due use of the stimulants, etc., which may be prescribed for a patient, may be secured with some degree of certainty.  But I would suggest that much of the prevalent mischief in this respect might be obviated, if the guardians would systematically decline to give this relief in these cases for more than a fixed time, e.g., a fortnight or three weeks, the limit of which should be made known before hand to paupers.  In those cases in which it may still be necessary to give out-relief in this form, the misuse of stimulants, though not of course meat, may be effectually prevented by the adoption of a suggestion which has, I believe, already been made to the board, upon medical authority, that wine and spirits issued to sick paupers shall be so prepared for use, in conformity with a practice adopted in some public hospitals, as, without impairing their efficacy, to ensure that they shall not be consumed otherwise than medicinally.  That this suggestion should have been made, is, indeed, in itself a proof of the extent and pressure of the abuses to which I have referred, the occurrence of which is, in fact, so likely that it is scarcely necessary to adduce specific evidence to prove their existence.  I may, however, mention two cases which have been very recently reported to me, one in which brandy, destined for a pauper, was consumed by the nurse in attendance, who was found by the neighbours, who ultimately gained admittance to the room only by forcing open the door, lying in a state of intoxication across the body of the dying patient; the other, in which it was frankly admitted by the head of a family that meat recommended by the medical officer for a sick member of the family habitually furnished a 'good meal' to all its members."[1]

Mr. Courtenay Boyle remarks on this subject as follows :—

" The recommendation by medical officers of extra nourishment is a subject which has attracted considerable attention.  Many guardians who are perfectly ready to admit that the well-doing of the sick poor, and the interests of all who are concerned in their recovery, depend far more upon an adequate and well-regulated provision for diet in sickness than upon the best and most liberal supply of drugs, are forced to believe that extra diet, taking the form usually of meat and porter or meat and brandy, is not unfrequently recommended less upon any certain principle than from a desire to supplement the relief given in individual cases.  Instances are within my experience in which extra nourishment has been recommended on the medical sheet of a district medical officer week after week without any examination whatever of the patient.  One district medical officer substantively stated to me that it was his deliberate intention to 'order' meat and brandy for any case which he was desired to attend.  Guardians are very chary of refusing to act on the recommendation of their medical officers,

---

[1] 3 L.G.B., p. 191.

and it is of great importance that district medical officers, who, as a rule, are most careful of the interests of the sick poor under their charge, should assist the guardians by adhering as much as possible to some uniform principle in recommending extra nourishment."[1]

It is evident, then, that it is most necessary for boards of guardians to grant medical relief most discriminately, and only after the most careful inquiry. The need for this is all the greater because sickness affecting any member of a family brings it within the exception to the Prohibitory and Out-door Relief Regulation Orders.[2]

*Possibility of reducing Medical Relief Pauperism.*

Medical relief can be reduced to a minimum :—

(a) By seeing that the Poor Law Orders are strictly complied with.

(b) By the applicant being obliged to attend the meeting of the guardians.

(c) By granting the relief on loan where possible, and enforcing repayment of monies expended by the guardians on the case.

(d) By the establishment of provident dispensaries and medical aid societies, and

(e) By suitable and adequate provision for the treatment of the sick in the workhouse.

(a) *Compliance with the Poor Law Orders.*

The duties of the district medical officer are set out in Art. 206 of the General Order of 1847, and the duties of the relieving officer in Art. 215 (2-7) of the same order.

---

[1] 8 L.G.B., p. 108.
[2] Prohibitory Order, Art. 1 (2); Out-door Relief Regulation Order, Art. 7 (2).

We have already referred to the good results which follow from medical officers attending the meetings of boards of guardians.[1] As regards the relieving officer we need only draw special attention to one important point, namely, that he should, whenever possible, visit the case before granting the order applied for. He is, indeed, not bound to do this, although he must visit the case as soon as possible after the order has been given.

> "The difference between the practice of relieving officers in dealing with applications for medical and general relief may, in fact, be stated generally thus: On an application for general relief the rule is that the visit to the home shall precede the relief, and it is in exceptionally urgent, and, for the most, in very rare cases, that this order of proceeding is reversed. In dealing with applications for medical relief it is, generally, in special and exceptional cases only that the visit precedes the relief. I believe that in two or three unions only is the former rule observed in both cases. This variance of practice has its origin, no doubt, in a time when the staff of relieving officers was everywhere, as it still is in some unions, so insufficient as to render it impossible for the officers to visit the homes of the applicants before granting medical relief. The majority of these applications are, or are at least represented to be, such as to require immediate attention, and unless a relieving officer is able at once to inquire into these cases (as is the practice in some unions), the order will almost necessarily be granted before a visit is paid. Relieving officers have been led to become chary of any, even the shortest, delay in granting medical orders, by the verdict of coroners' juries, and by the remarks made by police magistrates upon their conduct. It is not for me to sit in judgment upon either tribunal, but the experience derived from the cases which have come to my notice has led me to wish that it might become a matter of wider notoriety that the duties of relieving officers are limited to the relief of destitute applicants, and that it is not incumbent upon them to protect the community generally, and beyond these limits, against the scandal of deaths by starvation, or to seek out recipients of relief."[2]

By the Overseers Order of 1842, any overseer is allowed in cases of urgent *and* sudden necessity to give an order for medical relief. This power is often used in districts with a scattered population, and where the relieving officer's house

---

[1] *Supra*, pp. 23, 24.
[2] 3 L.G.B., p. 154.

may be several miles from the village. It is very open to abuse, and the action of the overseers should be therefore most carefully watched. The law, indeed, obliges him to report *in writing* to the relieving officer of the district or to the board of guardians of the union the fact of his having used his powers;[1] but this obligation is as often as not evaded, and the relief granted never brought to the notice of the guardians. It must be remembered that the power of the overseer is not so extensive as that of the relieving officer in this regard. He can only relieve in case of *sudden and dangerous* illness, whereas the latter can order relief in any case of sickness or accident. The distinction is often forgotten.

#### (b) *The Attendance of the Applicant.*

Mr. Longley remarks on this subject as follows:—

"A ready test of the need of the applicant is furnished by insisting upon his personal attendance, a test which all experience shows to be specially required in dealing with applications for medical relief, while it deters applicants by effectually dissipating the erroneous belief, which too commonly prevails, that *medical*, as distinct from *general*, relief is to be obtained without incurring all the disadvantages of pauperism. A vast reduction in the amount of medical relief, unaccompanied, so far as I can learn, with any hardship, has been the result of the adoption of this practice in a few unions. The guardians of many other unions are ready to admit the efficacy of the practice, but a fear of unduly protracting the time occupied in the administration of the relief has, I believe, prevented in some cases its further extension. Personal experience of the proceedings of those boards of guardians who follow a strict rule in this respect would probably convince other boards of guardians, as it has convinced me, that in this, as in many other points in the administration of relief, a strict practice saves, ultimately, not only time but money, and, what is of far greater moment, prevents injustice. While upon this point, I may add that I believe that the union in which the guardians deal at the same time most expeditiously and efficiently with the administration of relief is that in which the applications for medical relief are most closely scrutinised, and in which personal attendance is most rigidly enforced as a condition of this form of relief. The general importance of a strict system in dealing with applications for

---

[1] Order of 1842, Art. 1.

medical relief is illustrated by the fact that in one union in which the calculation has been made, it is found that the cases in which medical relief alone is given amount to 16 per cent. of the whole number of paupers receiving out-relief."[1]

And further, that,

"In those unions in which the attendance of applicants for medical orders is required by the guardians, numerous cases occurred at the meetings which I attended, in which applicants declined to submit to this test, and preferred to abandon their application, both where it had been refused by the relieving officer, and where, having been granted by him, the confirmation of the guardians was necessary to its continuance."[2]

Mr. Longley's remarks are, of course, more particularly applicable to large towns. In rural unions it must be admitted that there are practical difficulties in the way of enforcing the rule, and in such unions most reliance is to be placed on the loan system, on the medical officer's fee system, and by giving a commission to the relieving officers on monies recovered by them.

### (c) *The Gran of the Relief on Loan.*

This system works well "by enabling guardians to give help where it may be truly needed without putting the whole burden upon the ratepayers. It tends, moreover, to diminish the number of unnecessary applications."[3]

Unfortunately, as we have before said, medical officers are in most unions paid by salary, and in return are under the obligation to give the necessary medicines where they have received an order to attend a pauper case. It is not possible to place any money value on the assistance thus given, and even if it were granted on loan, payment could not be en-

---

[1] 3 L.G.B., pp. 155, 156, and also *ib.*, p. 164, per Mr. Longley.
[2] 3 L.G.B., p. 165.
[3] 8 L.G.B., p. 108.

forced. Where, however, the cost is definitely ascertainable, as, for example, in the case of medical extras, of confinements, etc., the relief should always be granted on loan, the relieving officers receiving a commission in return for the trouble of collection.

In some unions the difficulty attending the recovery of the cost of *all* medical relief granted on loan has been surmounted by *the payment of the district medical officers by case fee, either solely or in addition to a salary.*

Thus in Bradfield (Berks) medical orders have been reduced to a minimum by paying the medical officers, in addition to their salary, 6s. for each medical order granted on loan and recovered by the guardians. This system is quite legal, and has been approved by the Local Government Board.

In the St. Neots Union, where all medical relief is granted on loan, the medical officers are paid 6s. for each case which they are ordered by the relieving officer to attend, and 2s. a quarter for each permanent pauper. The system has been in force for some years in the union, has worked satisfactorily, and has not been found open to any abuse.

The great advantage of the case-fee system is that it shows that medical relief does cost *something*, and has the good effect of curbing the generosity of those guardians who think it costs *nothing*.

The arguments in favour of granting medical relief on loan are well put in the following reply from the Bradfield Board of Guardians to a letter from the Local Government Board, respecting a complaint by a certain individual that free medical relief was not afforded :—

"*21st March*, 1893.

"As the Local Government Board are aware, medical orders are in this union invariably granted, in the first instance, *on loan*, the amount charged to the recipient in respect of each order being six shillings, and the loans being repaid or cancelled according to circumstances.

"It is not the wish, and has never been the practice, of the guardians to exercise undue severity as regards repayment in the small number of instances in which application is made for such orders. Steps are taken to enforce payment only when the guardians are satisfied that there is ability to pay. That this is so, may be gathered from the annual reports, *e.g.*, out of the 49 orders granted in 1892, 22 have been already cancelled.

"At the same time, a long experience has only strengthened their conviction that free medical relief, unless thus carefully guarded, is an open door to pauperism, and is, therefore, in the long run, not a boon but an injury to the poor.

"They are of opinion, moreover, that it is *primâ facie* the duty of heads of families to do their best to provide medical as well as other necessaries both for themselves and their young children, and that anything which may encourage the expectation that such responsibility may be shifted on to the shoulders of the ratepayers will weaken the sense of this duty, and is calculated to hinder the growth of habits of thrift and forethought.

"In this part of the country, from four to five shillings a year for an adult, and two shillings for a child (sometimes limited to a maximum total of twelve shillings,[1] or less than threepence per week), is the 'usual doctor's club' or dispensary subscription, by which medical attendance can be secured, and this sum does not appear to call for excessive self-denial.

"No doubt there may sometimes be exceptional cases in which adherence to the above principles may seem likely to entail hardship; but, while holding themselves free to relax their application of these principles in extraordinary emergencies, the guardians consider that, as a rule, such exceptional cases are best assisted through private channels, inasmuch as (in the words of the Poor Law Commissioners' first report) 'Every exception, every violation of the general rule, to meet a real case of unusual hardship, lets in a whole class of fraudulent cases by which that rule must in time be destroyed. Where cases of real hardship occur the remedy must be applied by individual charity, a virtue for which no system of compulsory relief can be or ought to be a substitute.'"

(*Here follow details as to the particular case in question.*)

"If such cases as this were to obtain free medical relief without the intervention of some test, there would be found great difficulty in distinguishing other more or less similar applications which, with or without *bona fides*, would be almost certain to follow in increasing numbers, and the guardians feel that, if only for the sake of example, they are justified in declining, in the exercise of their discretion, to release . . . . . from the obligation which he has himself knowingly undertaken.

"They have availed themselves of this opportunity of stating their views on this important subject at some length in order to place plainly on record the principle upon which they are endeavouring to act."

[1] NOTE.—Per family.

(*d*) *The Establishment of Provident Dispensaries and Medical Societies.*

**Guardians will find that a strict administration of medical relief will encourage the poor to insure themselves against illness.** They will join the doctor's club, or some medical aid society. It will not take long to wean them from reliance on the relieving officer. Some unions have established medical clubs for the purpose of enabling the poor to become independent of medical relief from the parish, and thereby at the same time reducing pauperism. Thus, for example, in the Milton Union, Kent, a provident club embracing the whole of the union was established in 1857, which now has over 3000 members, and is worked as follows:—[1]

A gentleman (or lady) of position acts as steward in each of the parishes, and receives the subscriptions half-yearly (October and April). These are handed over at the end of each half year to the clerk to the guardians (who is the hon. sec. of the club) with a memorandum as follows:—

| No. of Members | For Dr. A. | £ |
| | ,, ,, B. | £ |
| | ,, ,, C. | £ |
| | | £ |

Each steward obtains copies of the rules and cards from the publisher, for which he pays twopence each, and this is charged to the member as he joins. The hon. sec. makes up the amount for each parish half-yearly, and hands over to each medical man his total proportion of the subscriptions. No collector or relieving officer is employed, so as to avoid all appearance of pauperism. Stewards and secretary being 'honorary,' there are no expenses, and as payments are made in advance there are never any arrears. The ticket for attendance is available for a year, and is drawn up as follows:—

Ticket for attendance for the Sittingbourne and Milton Provident Medical Club

For..............................................

..............................................

To be attended by

.. ..............................................

From April, 18—to October, 18—

...................... .....................Steward.

From October, 18—to April, 18—

..............................................Steward.

The system is thus a very simple one, and is appreciated by

---

[1] From information kindly supplied to the author in November, 1891, by the clerk to the Milton Guardians. See also 20 L.G.B., p. 213.

the doctors, because they are not only certain of their fees, but also are relieved from the trouble of collecting them.

No one is allowed to join the club who might be considered able to pay the doctor's ordinary fees.

The rules of the club are as follows:—

I.—The members shall consist of labourers in agriculture, or working men whose earnings from every source shall not exceed (if married) *thirty shillings* per week, or (if single) *twenty-one shillings* per week, and all agricultural and domestic servants whose wages do not exceed £12 a-year.

II.—The contract entered into with the Society shall be binding on all parties for one year, and the following scale of payments in advance, by half-yearly instalments, payable on the first Saturday after the 11th of October and on the first Saturday in April, shall entitle the members to receive all requisite advice and medicine from any of the medical attendants who may be selected:—

|   |   | S. | D. |
|---|---|---|---|
| 1.—Every individual above fourteen years of age, whether widower, widow, or unmarried, subscribing for himself or herself only, shall pay for the year | | 4 | 0 |
| 2.—A widower having a child or children to subscribe for, shall pay for himself | | 4 | 0 |
| 3.—A widow as above | | 2 | 6 |
| 4.—A man and his wife having a child or children to subscribe for, shall pay for themselves | | 6 | 0 |
| 5.—A man and his wife having no child or children to subscribe for, shall pay for themselves | | 8 | 0 |
| 6.—And for each child under fourteen years of age, in all cases | | 2 | 0 |
| Excepting in the case of widows' children, who shall pay | | 1 | 0 |

III.—A man and his wife, a widower, or widow, having a family, cannot subscribe for themselves only, but must also subscribe for all the children under *fourteen* years of age residing under their roof; but if the man is a member of a Benefit Society his wife shall pay *three shillings*.

IV.—A married female member who has been confined in childbed will not be entitled to benefit from the society till nine days after such confinement unless she has subscribed for attendance in midwifery, in which case the fee shall be *fifteen shillings*, to be paid to the medical attendant whom she has selected one month before the time she expects to be confined.

V.—Persons in health may be admitted at any time, and each member on admission to pay in advance the full subscription for the current half-year, which shall immediately entitle such member to the benefits of the society, but their second payment will become due as stated in Rule II.

VI.—No person above *fourteen* years of age, who is actually ill at the time of his or her application, shall be admitted unless he or she pay an admission fee of *eight shillings* in all cases; or, being a child under *fourteen*, the like fee of *eight shillings* in all surgical cases, and *four shillings* in all medical cases, in addition to the subscription, as a consideration for the attendance, medicine, etc., which such person may require in his or her illness.

VII.—Sick members shall find their own bottles and bandages, and (in case of rupture) trusses, and send for their medicines; and shall attend at the surgery before half-past ten in the morning, except in cases of sudden illness; and in all cases when a visit is required (except in cases of emergency) the message shall be delivered at the house of the medical attendant before half-past ten in the morning.

VIII.—Stewards are appointed for each parish within the Sittingbourne and Milton Districts of the Milton Union.

IX.—The name, age, and residence of each member shall on admission be entered in a book by the stewards, with the name of the medical attendant selected; and no member shall be at liberty to change his or her medical attendant until he or she has made two half-yearly payments.

X.—All subscriptions to be paid to the stewards on the days named in Rule II., and all persons who shall fail to pay their subscriptions for the space of one fortnight after the day on which they shall have become due, shall cease to be members, and shall not be entitled to receive medical aid from the club; but any person thus disqualified may, at the discretion of the stewards, be permitted to renew his or her subscription, and become a member again on payment of a fine of *sixpence* in addition to the subscription for the current half-year, subject to Rule VI. in cases of sickness.

XI.—Habitual drunkards or persons suffering from any of the diseases named in "The Contagious Diseases Act, 1866," shall not be admitted members of this society.

XII.—Persons suffering from chronic or incurable maladies shall be admitted only by the sanction of the medical attendant selected.

XIII.—All surgical operations to be paid for upon the scale of the Consolidated Order of the Local Government Board, except minor operations of surgery, including the extraction of teeth, for which a fee of *one shilling* shall be paid.

XIV.—Each member on joining this society to be furnished with a book of the rules at a charge of *twopence*, and also a card, with their name, date of admission, and name of the medical attendant selected, upon it.

XV.—Any dispute or disagreement which may arise shall be referred to the steward of the parish for arbitration, and his decision shall be final.

The subscriptions are small because the subscribers to the fund are numerous. The pauperism of the union is small, which is in a large measure due to the establishment of the club.

Canon Bury, in reporting on the administration of relief in the Brixworth Union, lays stress on the importance of encouraging medical clubs. He shows how fruitful a source of pauperism medical relief is, and says:—

"I am, however, clearly of opinion that the most effectual remedy for the present state of things is to be found in the direction of the medical clubs, which are already established in many of the villages in the union, by which medicine and medical attendance are secured by a payment so small as to be within the means of the poorest.

"I have been in communication with the chairman of the Uppingham Board of Guardians, who is also secretary to a large medical club, which includes several villages belonging to that union, and I am informed that, although the club is not in any way recognised by the board, the effect it has had in diminishing the number of medical orders, and reducing the expenditure on medical relief, has been remarkable. I have also heard from the medical officer of a club of this description in a large village in a neighbouring union that, since the establishment of the club, there has been a growing disinclination on the part of the poor to apply for medical orders." [1]

He recommends the establishment of a medical club for the whole union.[2]

### (e) *The Proper Provision for the Sick in Workhouses.*

We have already [3] drawn attention to the fact that if the Poor Law is to be well administered there must be proper and sufficient means of treating the sick in the workhouse. In London, and large towns, the infirmary system is now very well carried out, but in the country in many unions the infirmaries and nursing leave much to be desired. Still greater improvements have taken place in providing for the proper treatment of the sick in workhouses during the last twenty years than in any other branch of the Poor Law.

Of late years it has become common for boards of guardians to subscribe to hospitals, convalescent homes, and other institutions, for the relief of the sick and invalided.[4] This is one of the best forms in which out-door relief can be given, and is practically in-door relief, as the pauper is only sent there because the guardians would not be justified in making provision in the workhouse for such exceptional cases.

### *Public Dispensaries.*

Before concluding this chapter we must refer to the public dispensary system. This system has now been working *in*

---

[1] 3 L.G.B., pp. 122, 123.
[2] *Ib.*, p. 123.
[3] See p. 18.
[4] For their powers in this regard, see 14 and 15 Vict., ch. cv., s. 4; and 42 and 43 Vict., ch. liv., s. 10.

*London* for twenty-eight years,[1] and was introduced with the intention of regulating out-door medical relief, and minimising the evils attaching to it. An elaborate report on the system by Dr. Bridges was published in 1887.[2] He shows that, while the number of medical orders issued in 1873 was 143,676, the number had fallen to 111,060 in 1886. He states the cause of diminution to be "undoubtedly connected with the establishment during this period of Poor Law infirmaries in nearly every parish and union in London. To these institutions the district medical officers are in the habit of referring the great majority of serious cases, which, no one who knows how the poor of London are housed can doubt, are treated thus with far more efficiency than heretofore."

Successful as the Poor Law dispensary system has proved,[3] there is no doubt that it must be demoralising to the poor, as it encourages improvidence, and is injurious to provident dispensaries and medical societies. It is open to great abuses,[4] and should not be looked upon as a permanent institution.

Mr. Longley thought that it "should be regarded in common with every improved form of out-relief, not as a final object of Poor Law administration, but merely as a means of administering, with greater efficiency, that legal relief which, as I have attempted to show elsewhere, is most safely and effectually given in the form of in-door relief. It would, of course, be idle, and worse than idle, to stifle all attempts to reform the administration of out-relief, on the ground that it is desirable, and may at some remote period be possible to abolish, or, at least, greatly to curtail, it; and no reform of the practice of relief was probably more urgently needed, or has proved more

---

[1] It was introduced by the Metropolitan Poor Act, 1867 (30 Vict., ch. vi.).
[2] See 16 L.G.B., p. 86.
[3] See 5 L.G.B., p. 30.
[4] *Ib.*

effectual, than that now under consideration. It must not, however, be forgotten that side by side with Poor Law dispensaries has grown up, also under the sanction of the Metropolitan Poor Act, a system to be presently described, which, by encouraging and affording special facilities for the grant of in-door relief to sick paupers, must, if the policy of the Act be unflinchingly carried out, eventually tend, as it has already in at least two instances tended, to the gradual abolition of out-relief to the sick, other than those incapable of removal from their homes. If this be so, Poor Law dispensaries, however valuable during the initiation and progress of this revolution in Poor Law administration, must ultimately be found to have had for the most part a merely temporary place in the system of relief in London. The risk of the perversion of these dispensaries, while under Poor Law control, to the relief of other than pauper patients (of which the Irish dispensary system affords a signal instance), will, I fear, increase in proportion as they are less needed for their legitimate purposes, and it is for this reason that it seems to me that the character of permanence should not be hastily affixed to the system which they represent." [1]

It has often been suggested that the system should be extended to country districts,[2] but the rapid extension of voluntary insurance renders this now unnecessary; and, as its advocates admit, "would have a prejudicial effect upon all medical clubs, and might be calculated, from the additional facilities afforded for obtaining medical relief, to increase pauperism, and discourage habits of independence and self-reliance.[3] The evil done would thus be greater than the good.

---

[1] 4 L.G.B., pp. 41, 42.
[2] *E.g.*, see 23 P.L.B., pp. 175, 180.
[3] *Ib.*, p. 175.

## CHAPTER XI.

### HOW TO DEAL WITH SPECIAL CLASSES OF PAUPERS.

As is well known, out-door relief still continues to be given in all but a very few unions. We shall now proceed to show that in dealing with special classes of paupers the grant of out-door relief should be the exception and not the rule if there is to be good administration.

For the purposes of the official returns paupers (exclusive of lunatics and vagrants) are divided into two great classes, (1) the able-bodied, and (2) the not able-bodied. But as among the able-bodied are classed not only men temporarily disabled from working, but also women and children wholly or partially dependent on them, as well as widows and single women, this classification will not suit our purpose.[1] We must take con-

---

[1] There is no agreement as to what persons are to be considered as able-bodied.

"It is most important to observe in the first instance, with regard to the column headed 'Adult Able-bodied Paupers' in our annual returns, that much misapprehension prevails among persons not practically conversant with the system on which the registers of pauperism are compiled as to the actual character of the paupers classified under this head. The term itself suggests the supposition that all the paupers returned under this head are persons able at the time of receiving relief to earn their own livelihood by labour, whereas in fact the class thus designated contains only a small proportion of such persons.

"The whole of that large proportion of the pauperism of the country which is caused by temporary sickness is included in this class. When persons ordinarily able to earn their livelihood are allowed relief on account of sickness, they are classed as able-bodied. If the sick pauper be the male head of the family, the whole family dependent on him are entered in the able-bodied list. If the relief is given for a sick wife or child of an able-bodied man, he and the member or members of his family who are sick

crete cases, and shall deal with them in the following order:—

(1) The aged and infirm.
(2) Widows with legitimate children.
(3) Children whose parents are dead, or who for any other cause are left chargeable to the rates.
(4) Deserted wives.
(5) Wives of convicted prisoners.
(6) Wives and families of army reserve when called out.
(7) Single women with illegitimate children.
(8) Aged married couples.
(9) Non-resident paupers.
(10) Members of Friendly Societies and Clubs.
(11) Able-bodied paupers generally.

### (1) *The Aged and Infirm.*

There is no class of poor which excites the sympathy of

---

are entered in this list. Widows or deserted wives, able to earn wages, but not enough to maintain their families, are entered as 'able-bodied,' and this class with their children form a very large proportion of the whole. As evidence of prevalent destitution caused by want of employment or depression of trade, the number of the whole class is by no means a true criterion.

"Nor can the classification of paupers as 'able-bodied' and not 'able-bodied' be made in accordance with any strictly defined rule. Official inquiries have at different times been made to ascertain how many really able-bodied persons were in the metropolitan workhouses. The masters do not all adhere to the same definition, many declaring that as regards able-bodied *men*, there were none in the workhouse. A man subject to fits or to any other disease, which only breaks out occasionally, would be classed in some workhouses as able-bodied. Women nursing their children would be always entered as able-bodied if not otherwise sick." (22 P.L.B., pp. xviii., xix.)

See also 3 L.G.B., p. 174. In Mr. Henley's Report on Out-door Relief (23 P.L.B., p. 99), he says, "The term *able-bodied* is widely construed in different unions. In some the age of 60 is sufficient to constitute age, and thus partial infirmity, in others, age without some special infirmity is not deemed sufficient. I latterly saw a man of between 70 and 80 years of age refused out-door relief on the ground that he was able-bodied."

guardians more than this, and which gets out-door relief with greater ease. A man or woman who has worked until he or she can work no more, and who asks, "How could I save out of my scanty wages with a family to bring up?" is almost certain to get relief from the rates in this form. The cruelty of breaking up the "little home" is urged, but it is seldom considered whether the usual weekly pittance affords adequate relief. And yet the fact that the applicant is generally contented with what he gets—indeed he comes expecting no more, knowing as well as, or better than the guardians, the scale of the allowances—is *prima facie* evidence that he has other means of support, very often sufficient to make him independent. The evidence shows that lax administration of out-door relief to this class begets the aged pauper. When it is strictly administered, on the other hand, he is almost unknown. Mr. Murray Browne shows this clearly.

"Special attention," he writes in 1892, "has lately been given to the case of the 'aged paupers' over 60 years old. This is no place for general discussion, but I may perhaps call attention to the remarkable differences upon this point between adjoining unions of the same character. For this purpose I have availed myself of the return as to paupers over 60 years of age obtained for the House of Commons on the motion of Mr. Burt, and dated 9th December, 1890. I have no means of ascertaining the total number of persons over 60 years of age in each union. I have, however, compared the proportion which the total number of paupers of both sexes over 60, as stated in Mr. Burt's return, bears to the total population of certain unions.

"The results are curious. Thus, in the union of Hawarden the total percentage of pauperism over 60 as compared with the population of the union is 1·0, while in the adjoining union of Holywell it is 2·3, or more than double the amount. In the union of Forden the percentage is 1·0, while in the adjoining union of Newtown and Llanidloes it is 2·2. In Wrexham the like percentage is but ·8, while in the adjoining unions of Ruthin and Corwen it is respectively 2·0 and 1·9. I know nothing in the character of the unions named which should cause this enormous difference. But the same contrasts are to be found in other parts of the country. Thus, in the well-known unions of Bradfield and Wallingford the percentages in question are in each case not more than ·4 of the population, while in the adjoining unions of Wantage and Henley they stand at 1·38 and 1·32 respectively. In Aylesbury Union the percentage is 1·3, while in Thame it is 2·6, and so on. The explanation, of course, is that in the unions where the percentages are small, very little out-relief is given; while in those where the percentages are large, out-relief is distributed with a lavish hand. It is noticeable that *in all* the above cases, the percentage of in-door pauperism over 60 to the population is much the same; thus showing that out-door relief does not materially diminish the number of paupers over 60 in the workhouse. It is the *out-door* pauperism which alone makes the great difference in these cases. Out-door relief may or may not be defensible, but, at any rate, it is clear that the rate of pauperism over 60 years of age depends mainly, not on the condition of the poorer classes, but on the administration of relief; in other words upon the comparative ease or otherwise, with which out-door relief can be obtained. It would be perfectly easy to make the pauperism of Hawarden Union, within a year, as great as that of Holywell, and so on. Very few people will refuse a little pension if it can be had (practically) for the asking."

| Unions. | Population, 1891. | In-door paupers over 60. | Percentage on population. | Out-door paupers over 60. | Percentage on population. | Total of in-door and out-door paupers over 60. | Percentage on population. |
|---|---|---|---|---|---|---|---|
| Hawarden...... | 15,802 | 17 | 0·10 | 153 | 0·97 | 170 | 1·07 |
| Holywell ...... | 42,565 | 63 | 0·15 | 925 | 2·17 | 988 | 2·32 |
| Forden ........ | 16,313 | 44 | 0·27 | 121 | 0·74 | 165 | 1·01 |
| Newtown & Llanidloes.... | 21,722 | 31 | 0·14 | 466 | 2·15 | 497 | 2·29 |
| Wrexham ...... | 61,795 | 72 | 0·12 | 427 | 0·69 | 499 | 0·81 |
| Ruthin ........ | 12,929 | 25 | 0·19 | 236 | 1·83 | 261 | 2·02 |
| Corwen ........ | 16,258 | 16 | 0·10 | 297 | 1·82 | 313 | 1·92 |
| Bradfield ...... | 18,017 | 46 | 0·25 | 27 | 0·15 | 73 | 0·40 |
| Wallingford .... | 14,706 | 45 | 0·30 | 23 | 0·16 | 68 | 0·46 |
| Wantage ...... | 16,544 | 30 | 0·18 | 199 | 1·20 | 229 | 1·38 |
| Henley ........ | 22,550 | 24 | 0·11 | 274 | 1·21 | 298 | 1·32 |
| Aylesbury ...... | 25,580 | 50 | 0·19 | 301 | 1·18 | 351 | 1·37 |
| Thame ........ | 13,372 | 28 | 0·21 | 326 | 2·44 | 354 | 2·65 [1] |

If, indeed, we are to rid ourselves of the aged paupers as we are doing so rapidly with regard to able-bodied paupers,

---

[1] 21 L.G.B., p. 172.

we must not depend on such visionary schemes as "Old Age Pensions" (which will only aggravate the evil they are intended to prevent), but upon the more frequent "offer of the house." Mr. Baldwyn Fleming has made some valuable remarks on this subject, which should make us hesitate to deal with the aged poor on a different plan from the able-bodied. He says:—

"Of late years the workhouses have become more and more the refuge of the aged and infirm, whilst the number of able-bodied inmates and of children have continued to decrease. To this cause is no doubt attributable the interest which has been excited with regard to old age pensions. It is a matter of great importance to ascertain whether the present amount of old age pauperism will be permanent or transient. Upon the answer to that question depends the necessity of any scheme of provision for old age at the cost of the rates. Whatever opinion may be formed upon the subject, there can be no doubt that the position of the aged destitute now is the natural consequence of the Poor Law Act of 1834. The problems to be solved by the Poor Law Commissioners were how to deal with the able-bodied pauperism which was terrorising the country, and how to reduce the poor rates which were bringing it to ruin. These problems have been solved. Able-bodied pauperism in the rural districts, at all events, has practically ceased to exist, and the poor rates have been brought down to a very moderate limit. The whole cost of the relief of the poor of this district" (Dorset, Hants, Wilts, and Surrey) "averaged 1s. 4d. in the £ on the rateable value for the year ended Lady Day last" (1891).

"A considerable number of workhouse inmates are returned as able-bodied, but in the country unions very few are so in fact. They are classed as able-bodied because they are under 60, and are not on the workhouse medical relief book, but the large majority of them, for one reason or another, are incapacitated from earning their livelihood by regular work.

"The aged inmates who now fill the workhouses were young in the years when the Poor Law was introduced. Neither they nor their parents and relations had the opportunities which are open to the younger generations of providing for themselves.

"It was inevitable that many of those who survived the wage earning period and their own contemporaries should come upon the rates for support, and find the workhouse the only safe refuge in their old age.

"It by no means follows that the generations to succeed them will be equally wanting in means of support. The available evidence leans strongly in the opposite direction. Able-bodied pauperism has practically ceased in the rural unions. The numbers of children in the workhouses of my district (from Forms A nearest to 1st January, 1893) are 669 less than when I first counted them in April, 1876, notwithstanding that the population of the district has increased since 1871 by 139,610.

|      | Population of District. |
|------|------------------------|
| 1871 | 961,415 |
| 1881 | 1,001,612 |
| 1891 | 1,101,025 |

"There are many other indications that the wage-earners of to-day will maintain their independence in a much larger proportion than has been the case in the past. The greater prudence in regard to marriage (Ages at Marriage, p. vii. of Fifty-Fourth Annual Report of the Registrar-General), the steady increase in the deposits at savings banks, the provision for old age by many of the great employers of labour, and most important of all, the extension and the improved position of provident and benefit societies and unions, together with the growing independence of the working classes, all point in the direction of an immensely greater amount of self-support in the future.

"The proportion of pauperism to population in the country has, although not free from temporary fluctuations, been steadily decreasing in spite of a long-continued depression in agriculture, and in many branches of trade. Any mistaken action now might easily have the effect of perpetuating instead of relieving the old age pauperism which exists, but which if left to itself would pass with the passing of the aged poor whose misfortune it has been to live through the years when the absence of resources in the past, the failure of their own powers, and the loss of the companions of their youth, have left them without other means than the rates for the support of their old age.

"Bearing in mind the extinction of able-bodied, and the large decrease of child pauperism, as well as the other influences above referred to, the probability is that old age paupers will gradually diminish, and that in the comparatively early future few will have to be kept upon the rates except those whose physical ailments will require treatment in the infirmaries and sick wards of the unions."[1]

The figures given in Appendix C., p. 227, show how much adult not-able-bodied out-door pauperism has decreased during the last 25 years, and point to its possible extinction if only out-door relief to this class were very strictly administered.

Many kind-hearted but unwise persons would have our aged paupers dealt with in workhouses as if these institutions were almshouses. Let us hear, then, what the Poor Law Commissioners of 1832 have to say on the subject :—

"With regard to the aged and infirm, however, there is a strong disposi-

---

[1] 22 L.G.B., p. 80.

tion on the part of a portion of the public so to modify the arrangements of these establishments, as to place them on the footing of *almshouses*. The consequences which would flow from this change have only to be pointed out to show its inexpediency and its danger. If the condition of the inmates of a workhouse were to be so regulated as to invite the aged and infirm of the labouring classes to take refuge in it, it would immediately be useless as a test between indigence and indolence or fraud—it would no longer operate as an inducement to the young and healthy to provide support for their later years, or, as a stimulus to them whilst they have the means, to support their aged parents and relatives. The frugality and forethought of a young labourer would be useless if he foresaw the certainty of a better asylum for his old age than he could possibly provide by his own exertions, and the industrious efforts of a son to provide a maintenance for his parents in his own dwelling would be thrown away and would cease to be called forth, if the almshouse of the district offered a refuge for their declining years, in which they might obtain comforts and indulgences which even the most successful of the labouring classes cannot always obtain by their own exertions."[1]

It is well that there should be a dislike on the part of the aged poor to enter the workhouse, but its hardships are much exaggerated. Mr. Peel speaks truly as to this. He says:—

"Much, too, has been said about the classification of paupers and the hardship inflicted upon respectable old people in forcing them to mix with the less well-conducted, but though the poor are seldom backward in speaking of any discomfort, complaints on that score are seldom heard, possibly because there is little or no foundation for them, or maybe they are of opinion that wherever they lived they would come in contact with people whose characters and conversation were not quite to their liking."[2]

Among the advantages attaching to the offer of the house to the class of which we are speaking is, that it often induces the relations of the applicant to contribute towards his or her support.[3]

Mr. C. S. Loch has dealt very fully with this subject in his work, entitled "Old Age Pensions and Pauperism" (Swan Sonnen-

---

[1] Extract from the Report of the Poor Law Commissioners on the Continuance of the Poor Law Commission, etc., 1840, p. 47. See *supra* p. 78.
[2] 22 L.G.B., p. 68.
[3] See *supra*, pp. 88-90.

schein & Co.), pp. 31-39, to which we would refer our readers who are anxious to know more about it.

### (2) *Widows with Legitimate Children.*

This class of able-bodied paupers is that to which the principles we have advocated have been applied most sparingly and with the greatest reluctance, and it is consequently the most numerous. Taking the figures of the 1st January, 1894, we find that widows constitute 65 per cent. of the total number of adult female paupers receiving out-door relief on that date, while the children dependent upon them constitute no less than 58 per cent. of the total numbers of children receiving out-door relief at that date.[1] The difficulty which has been experienced in the administration of relief to

---

[1] See Return (B) for 1st January, 1894. But the figures show a great improvement on what they were on the 1st January, 1873, (see 3 L.G.B., 588), although the percentages are almost the same in both cases.

|  | 1st January, 1873. | 1st January, 1894. |
|---|---|---|
| Wives of able-bodied men | 18,057 | 13,654 |
| *Widows* | *53,502* | *38,599* |
| Single women without children | 4,774 | 2,846 |
| Mothers of illegitimate children | 1,140 | 347 |
| Wives of prisoners, etc., | 1,550 | 871 |
| Wives of soldiers, sailors, etc., | 390 | 125 |
| Wives of other non-resident males | 4,187 | 3,020 |
| Total | 83,600 | 59,462 |
| Children of able-bodied men | 45,285 | 37,880 |
| ,, *dependent on widows* | *140,390* | *111,171* |
| ,, illegitimate | 1,908 | 553 |
| ,, of prisoners, etc. | 4,739 | 2,840 |
| ,, of soldiers, etc. | 892 | 300 |
| ,, of other non-resident males | 11,469 | 8,456 |
| ,, of parents not able-bodied | 32,160 | 20,430 |
| ,, relieved without parents and orphans | 13,363 | 9,971 |
| Total | 250,206 | 191,601 |

this class has arisen partly from their numbers " and partly from a natural inclination towards a lenient dealing with a class whose destitution is caused, as well as aggravated and intensified, by the severest of all bereavements, against the material consequences of which to the families of the poorer classes it is commonly supposed to be specially burdensome, if not impossible, to make provision beforehand. It is felt that however desirable it may be to administer relief so as to encourage provident habits, widows, at any rate, cannot be fairly charged with improvidence, and should not suffer for the fault, if fault there be, of her husband. It is, indeed, frequently urged as an objection to the system of in-door relief that it is generally inapplicable to the class of widows, and for this reason, as well as on account of the intrinsic magnitude of the interest involved, it is of the last importance to vindicate, if possible, the cause of strict Poor Law administration in its dealing with this class. The question at issue appears, when closely examined, to be one of degree and not of kind, for while it is not denied that it is for the general good that in-door relief should be substituted for out-relief, the application of this principle to the class in question is impeded by the special prominence given to those individual interests of the applicants for relief, a too exclusive regard for which, to the prejudice of the general interests of the community, is the adverse influence which persistently and necessarily besets all attempts to place Poor Law administration on a sound basis."[1]

The objections to granting out-door relief to this class may be stated as follows :—

(a) *That it tends to the General Discouragement of Provident Habits.*

The husband relies on the parish to take care of his wife

---

[1] Per Mr. Longley, 3 L.G.B., pp. 179, 180.

and young children if he dies, and his reliance is founded on the fact that he sees out-door relief being given freely to widows. There is thus little inducement to him to provide for the possibility of his death. In answer to the objections that he can never be in a position to insure against death, we will again quote from Mr. Longley's exhaustive report. He says:—

"The suggestion that a man in receipt of regular weekly wages may be fairly called upon to secure his widow (if able to work for her living) against dependence upon Poor Law relief, is not so impracticable as it may at first sight appear. . . . . The cost of making provision for this special contingency need not, it would seem, press unduly upon the husband, while the general adoption of the more stringent rule of relief to widows would, it is to be hoped, encourage him to make the necessary sacrifice. But even a less substantial provision than this would, I believe, in many cases rescue a widow from pauperism. It is frequently found that a widow, willing and able to work, requires some help to make a start, or to take advantage of some special opportunity of obtaining employment. A lump sum of no large amount, secured to be paid to her at her husband's death, would, in these cases, be of the utmost service. Assistance of this kind is supplied to widows, more frequently than is generally known, by subscriptions raised among the fellow-workmen of the husband or among the poorer neighbours. Indeed, I have been led, in the course of these inquiries, to believe that what amounts almost to an interchange of charitable assistance among the poor of London is not uncommon, and that they assist each other in distress to an extent which is little understood, and for which they receive but little credit. It is scarcely possible to conceive a form of charity which combines so completely its highest reciprocal benefits, with the absence of the mischief so frequently incident to alms-giving."[1]

(b) *That it operates as an Inducement to the Recipient to relax her Efforts to obtain an Independent Livelihood.*

"Believing, as I do," says Mr. Longley, "that the present system of relief to widows of this class has largely contributed to deter them from making the special exertions to maintain themselves and their families, which their unfortunate condition calls for, I must protest against the doctrine that their position is to be treated by the dispensers of Poor Law relief as anomalous, even in theory; and this, because the condition of a widow with a large family, however deplorable it undoubtedly is, is one of the ordinary contingencies of human circumstances, which may, in some

---

[1] 3 L.G.B., pp. 185, 186.

degree or other, be provided against, equally with sickness, or accident, or other bereavement. The difference between these contingencies seems to be one of degree rather than of kind, and though, no doubt, the widow's condition is specially hopeless and forlorn, yet, from one point of view, that of the wife of a working man disabled by lingering sickness, and who is prevented by the need of her constant attendance upon him, from exerting herself to support their family, is still more helpless than that of a widow."[1]

(c) *That it tends to encourage a Deceitful Concealment of the Means of the Applicant.*

Mr. Longley, again, speaking of widows, says :—[2]

"There is probably no other class whose earnings boards of guardians and their officers experience such difficulty in ascertaining, and whose applications for relief, when tested, are so frequently found to be groundless, or at least based on untrustworthy statements. A striking proof of this is to be found on a comparison of the rate of wages alleged to be received by these applicants for relief, with that which is given for similar work to persons in independent employment. If the statements made in these cases be true, this difference in the rate of wages must be accounted for, either by the incapacity or the bad character of the person employed, or by the supposition that she is enabled by her receipt of relief to work at a rate below the current rate of remuneration for the class of work which she performs. In either event a strong case would seem to be made for the substitution of in-door for out-relief."

"Relieving officers, I think," says Mr. Sendall,[3] "in many cases fail to give the guardians full and accurate information respecting the present circumstances of widows in receipt of relief. A poor widow is justly the object of universal sympathy, but there is no class (in towns especially) with which the relieving officer has to deal, which requires more careful and unceasing supervision. It is, moreover, of the utmost importance to the community that the relief afforded to widows from the rates should be regulated by an intimate acquaintance with their actual necessities, in order that themselves and their children may be saved from the danger of lapsing into the ranks of fraudulent pauperism. I have before me a list of seven cases, occurring within the last three years, in one relief district of the Headington Union, of widows with from two to five children each, who, being in receipt of out-door relief, have given birth to illegitimate children, and whose relief has been consequently withdrawn, and the workhouse offered. In not one instance was the offer of the workhouse accepted ; nor have any of these women applied again for parish relief.

"Similar cases could be adduced from other unions; and it is to be observed that, notwithstanding the cause of the disqualification for out-relief, it would be altogether a mistake to assume that a career of vice is the usual consequence ; with respect to several of the Headington cases, I am informed that the women are maintaining themselves and their children respectably;

---

[1] 3 L.G.B., p. 183.      [2] *Ib.*, p. 180.      [3] *Ib.*, p. 82.

but the point of the story lies in this, that if these women are able now to maintain themselves without assistance, the relief which they formerly received may have been, and in the case of most of them probably was, to a certain extent superfluous; given, in short, as a matter of course, and without a full knowledge of the real circumstances of the case, with which again the relieving officer, either from press of work or from want of opportunity, failed to make himself thoroughly acquainted. That the labour of able-bodied women may and does often suffice for the maintenance of themselves and children, is further proved by the very numerous cases of women who, having entered the workhouse for the purpose of giving birth to bastard children, discharge themselves at the expiration of a month, and continue thereafter to support themselves and infants, under circumstances far less favourable than those which must ordinarily surround the respectable widow."

*(d) That it has a Tendency to keep down Wages and Earnings.*

How far the price of women's labour is affected by the grant of out-door relief to adult able-bodied females can never be fully ascertained. We have already referred to this point.[1] The Report of the Lady Assistant Commissioners (Royal Commission on Labour) shows that the average wage of 3s. or 3s. 6d. a week paid to the out-workers in the Nottingham hosiery trade is duly supplemented by parish relief, and there cannot be the least doubt that women's earnings are affected whenever out-door relief is laxly administered to the class in question. We do not mean to assert that it is the *exclusive* cause of the inadequacy of the general rate of wages paid for female labour. The above report gives many other causes, but that the grant of this form of relief to over 38,000 persons in the country[2] contributes sensibly to reduce the rate of wages in some branches of female labour is quite certain.

We extract the following passage from the Report of the Progress of the Atcham Union (p. 23) in support of our contention:—

---

[1] *Supra*, pp. 54-62.
[2] See 22 L.G.B., p. 251.

"With reference to the return since the addition of the Shrewsbury parishes it is with satisfaction that I record the fact that, partly as the result of the administration of the guardians, a considerable improvement in the wages of the labouring population in the town of Shrewsbury has taken place, whereby they are able to live in better houses, and habits of cleanliness, thrift and morality have been engendered.

"In 1871 there were a large number of widows with children receiving out-door relief. These supplemented their relief by going out as washerwomen and charwomen; and by being able to undersell other labour of the same class, the wages of charwomen and washerwomen in 1871 were about 9d. per day with food, and they worked from 6 a.m. to 7 p.m. Their children were, in the meantime, much neglected.

"The guardians by discontinuing the out-relief, and taking the children into the workhouse for education, wherever there were no relatives willing to maintain them, freed the widows from being tied down to this branch of work, and many of them became valuable servants and assistants in business, the result being that the wages of charwomen and washerwomen have increased from 1s. 9d. to 2s. per day with food, and the hours of labour are from about 8 a.m. to 5 or 5-30 p.m., both classes being benefited to that extent. . . . Other classes of women have benefited in the same manner."

It is clear that applications for relief by widows with children require the most careful consideration and inquiry before outdoor relief is granted. In well administered unions no outdoor relief is granted to an able-bodied widow with one child. When there is more than one child the offer is made to take some of the children off the mother's hands, and in every case the time for which the relief is granted is limited. In those unions where these rules have been adhered to, it is found that widows eventually cease to apply; and it not unfrequently happens that the widow, appreciating the benefits which her children get by being taken charge of by the guardians, voluntarily comes and asks to have them taken off her hands until she has obtained sufficient work to support them herself. It may appear to be a harsh proceeding to offer the workhouse for the children of a widow, but the reasons for its adoption are weighty:—

(1) It has always been successful.

(2) By it the woman is set free for work and can, if she likes,

become a lodger, and reduce the cost of housekeeping; or if able to maintain herself at home, has thereby the opportunity of making that home a comfortable one for her children when they leave the workhouse, or when she wishes to remove them.

(3) That as regards the children they will be better fed, better disciplined, and better and (to the ratepayer) more cheaply taught; while, in a majority of cases, their uncles, aunts, and other relations, will come forward to take care of them, thus freeing them from becoming paupers.

(4) That a pauper house in the village is avoided.[1]

The Brixworth Report of 1873 answers very forcibly the arguments generally used against this course.

"Your committee are quite aware that there are many objections which can be fairly raised to this plan; as, for instance, that it is a hard thing to separate mother and children, and so no doubt it is, but not they think so hard as to suffer them to exist, for it cannot be called living, on the scanty relief they will receive out of the house, which in such cases cannot be increased without putting a premium upon pauperism, and which, unless increased, must prove the source of future pauperism, laying the seeds of disease and mental weakness. Again the pauperising effect of the workhouse upon the children is further urged against the plan proposed, but your committee believe, and experience in many instances seems to show, that it is not more, perhaps not so pauperising as the constant visit of the relieving officer to the home week by week, which extends its influence beyond the children themselves. Again, it is said, children brought up at the workhouse as a rule do not turn out so well as others; possibly not, when compared with children brought up at a respectable home, but when compared with those brought up at a pauper's home such as is contemplated, your committee think it more than probable that they will turn out better. Further, it is said that this course will diminish the supply of labour in the union (children from the workhouse being usually put out to service), to which your committee would reply that so it ought to do; and if by this means pauperism, and consequently the rates, are reduced, the object of guardians in relation to the poor and the ratepayers is at once attained; and once more it is said that supposing the woman refuse the offer of the house for her children and no out-relief be granted, she may be driven to

---

[1] See Report of the Committee of the Brixworth Union on Out-door Relief, 2 L.G.B., p. 70; and the Report of the Progress of the Atcham Union, p. 42.

immorality in order to maintain herself; but your committee think that first of all, if the adoption of the plan proposed be found generally successful, the guardians ought not to be deterred by the fear of particular consequences, and secondly, that the evil anticipated might be guarded against in a great measure by enlisting the help and co-operation of the landlord of the cottage, together with that of the clergyman and other charitably-disposed persons in the place."[1]

The system we are discussing has been successfully adopted in the Bradfield Union among others. This is what the late Mr. Bland Garland has to say upon it.

"In regard to the out-door relief to widows—and for this I beg the particular attention of the ladies, who, no doubt, have already thought me very hard-hearted—the number of widows since 1876, who have applied for out-door relief—and there are many of them who have never applied for it—is 55, with 213 children. The number that have accepted our offer to go into the workhouse is one widow and eleven children. I think I ought to have said—I do not think I did say—that when we stopped out-door relief to widows, we agreed to offer them all, when destitute, a refuge in the workhouse with their children, or, if they preferred it, to take in most of their children, and leave them out. This is the result. We have one widow in who has been turned out of her house for misconduct, or she would not be there, and eleven children. Now the remaining 54 widows and 202 children who declined to go into the workhouse are far better off than similar widows and children were when they got out-door relief. As a matter of course the children of widows in receipt of out-relief are brought up as beggars, and pauperised from their infancy, and the pauperism hangs to them. I have no doubt that you may consider that hereditary pauperism. I do not think that we ought to have an hereditary pauperism. The widows, it is very easy to see, are improved. They are free from the incubus of pauperism. They can demand full remuneration for their labour. They could not do that when they were receiving the pauper dole. They only got a pittance then from their employers. Those that require assistance from their relations get it far more readily than they did when they received the pauper dole. I would say from my heart that one of the happiest circumstances of my life is that we refused to give any more out-door relief to widows, because I see plainly, all over the union, that they are far better off and far happier than ever they were before."[2]

On the 1st January, 1893, the Bradford Union had no female

---

[1] 2 L.G.B., p. 70; see also 3 L.G.B., p. 185 (per Mr. Longley).
[2] "From Pauperism to Manliness" (Occasional Paper, No. 21, of the Charity Organisation Society's series).

able-bodied out-door paupers, and only eight in-door. Brixworth had none out, and only one in.

There is then no reason for differentiating widows from other classes of the poor. But without entirely abolishing outdoor relief, boards of guardians can do a great deal towards making married people more provident, by restricting it and making it difficult to obtain.

"It is notorious that large numbers of widows of the poorer class do maintain and bring up large families independently of Poor Law relief. Again, it has invariably been found that where, as of late has frequently been the case, out-relief has, from one cause or another, been refused to widows with families, a large proportion of them have under this pressure found it possible to obtain an independent livelihood. The special classes of cases which have been thus dealt with in those unions in which the law is more strictly administered, are these: (1) Widows in receipt of regular weekly wages. In this case the interference with the labour market occasioned by out-relief, is more distinct and prominent than where the widow's income is made up of intermittent earnings. (2) Widows whose earnings are distinctly below the market value of their labour, or who are considered to withhold from the guardians information as to their income. (3) Widows of bad character, or whose home is insufficient for their wants, or is improperly kept. (4) Another class of widows has, within the last few months, been found capable of maintaining themselves and their families: I allude to the steps taken by some boards of guardians, acting in concert with the Charity Organisation Society, to offer work in the manufacturing districts to able-bodied widows with families receiving out-relief. In these cases the widows have been carefully selected by the officers of the society, with special reference to the fitness of themselves and their families for the employment in question. The guardians have then offered them the alternative of accepting either this employment or relief in the workhouse. Much reluctance to emigrate to the North has been evinced by many of these women, who have, nevertheless, refused in-door relief, and are now maintaining themselves and their children. It has been suggested, but the suggestion has not as yet, I believe, been put in practice, that able-bodied widows, if receiving out-relief at all, should, at the end of a given duration of relief, be systematically required to come into the workhouse. Some such rule as this would certainly operate as an incentive to exertion." [1]

In all cases where out-door relief *is* given to widows with children, special care should be taken to see that the children are sent to school. If not, the relief should be discontinued, and the house offered. (See 39 and 40 Vict., ch. 79, s. 40.) In many unions little or no attention is paid to this important point.

We have quoted at length from Mr. Longley's valuable report, but to those who wish to have a grasp of the subject we would recommend the perusal of all that he has to say about it.[2] His comments are as applicable to the circumstances of to-day as to those of twenty years ago. There is no doubt that his report has greatly influenced the administration of the Poor Law, and the figures that we have given on p. 138 (note 1) show what an improvement has, since it was written, been effected in dealing with the class under consideration.

(3) *Children whose Parents are dead, or who for any other Cause are left chargeable to the Rates.*

There are three good ways of dealing with these children—

---

[1] 3 L.G.B., p. 183.
[2] 3 L.G.B., pp. 179-86.

(1) by keeping them in the workhouse and sending them to the village or board school, (2) by sending them to a district school and (3) by boarding them out.[1]

### (a) *The Village School System.*

With regard to the first course there is a universal agreement that if the children are educated *outside* the workhouse, the system answers very well, and as they can now obtain free education, it is perhaps the most economical system.

The system is in force in some of the best administered unions in the country, and is found to answer very satisfactorily.

Mr. Courtenay Boyle approves of it.

> "There are in my opinion," he says, "many advantages in the plan. The children learn a great deal of the outer world. They mix with others not of the pauper class. The very going to and from the school is, if properly managed, a benefit. They gain an expansion of ideas which is not obtainable in a workhouse."[2]

He points out the only disadvantage to it, namely, the difficulty in taking proper care of the children out of school hours.

> "Children if left alone do not perhaps get into mischief, but they remain uncultivated and untrained. If education means anything more than the teaching of a modicum beyond the three R's, it is important that workhouse children should not be left alone out of school hours.
>
> "A good master or mistress can exercise as much beneficial influence out of school hours as in them. It is sometimes believed that the ordinary officers of the house can 'give an eye' to the children when school is over. But I strongly doubt the expediency of trusting to the ordinary officers.

---

[1] The workhouse school is rapidly becoming a thing of the past. At Lady Day, 1892, there were in England and Wales 148 workhouse schools, 66 detached workhouse schools, 29 district schools, while 378 unions and parishes used the public elementary schools, and 27 the schools of other unions. At Lady Day, 1872, there were over 450 unions and parishes which educated their children in the workhouse itself. Mr. Peel, however, says that children in the workhouse schools in his district still bear favourable comparison with other children, and that there is a great demand for them when fit for service. (See 23 L.G.B., p. 100.)

[2] 8 L.G.B., p. 117.

Their proper discharge of their own duties is incompatible with any attempt at efficient care of children. The officer entrusted with the supervision of the children may, indeed, occasionally look into their ward to see that they are not in actual mischief, but the watchful care which a conscientious master or mistress can bestow must be wholly absent. The following story displays, probably, an exceptional state of things, but it affords an instance of what may happen :—In one of the workhouses whence children are sent to a neighbouring public elementary school, I asked under what supervision the girls were out of school hours. The answer was that the nurse took charge of them. I asked where they sat, and the answer was that they were kept in their day-room and the nurse sat with them. Turning to a little girl of about thirteen, I asked her where she had spent the afternoon of the previous day, which was a half-holiday. 'In the lying-in ward,' then occupied by two or three single women. 'Oh! did you ; who was there with you?' 'Oh, only the woman going to be confined.' In some cases a pauper inmate is employed to take charge of the children. I am far from thinking that it is impossible that a pauper inmate should be a proper person to do this. In the Billericay workhouse is a woman of unfortunate physique, who is, as far as I can judge by what I am told of her, and what I can see of her management, thoroughly qualified by both moral power and by discretion to take charge of the girls, and to wield that beneficial influence over the girls which I hold important. She reads to them, aids them in their play, keeps them usefully employed, and in a word educates them. In Colchester there is an aged inmate of good character, who is nearly as useful in looking after the boys. But such a state of things is wholly exceptional. Far oftener the person employed is one whose failure in life is greatly attributable to subjective causes. The master of the workhouse usually selects the best he can find ; but very rarely indeed is that best anything but bad. Nothing can be less calculated to develop the character of workhouse boys, whose nature is *ex-hypothesi* such as needs most careful handling, than that they should have to spend the hours of the afternoon and evening in the society of a man of no resources, no cultivation, no aptitude for anything except dull stagnation. I have seen workhouse boys sitting over the fire with their pauper attendant in a listless, helpless, motionless attitude, which is most depressing. The difficulty for providing for the non-school hours is equally apparent in the twelve unions where there is a mixed school under a schoolmistress. .... But when they leave the school the old question arises, Who is to look after the boys? If the guardians are urged to appoint an industrial trainer they not unusually say, We might as well pay a little more and have a schoolmaster at once.

"The temptation to trust to an officer already sufficiently occupied, or to a pauper, is very great, but I venture to urge that it should be strongly resisted."

He refers to an exceptional system obtaining in Norwich in 1878.

---

[1] 8 L.G.B., pp. 117, 118.

"Part of the boys are kept in the workhouse under a schoolmaster. Part, averaging about thirty, are sent to a building in another part of the town where they are trained in service. Here they are divided into schoolboys, half-timers, and house boys. The last two classes are sent out for either half or all the day as errand boys, shop boys, house boys. They sleep in the house and have, according to their employment, some or all their meals in the house. Their earnings, which amount to five, six, and seven shillings a week, go to pay for their maintenance, with the exception of a small sum put by for themselves. In the numerous conferences which I have had with the guardians on this home, I have pointed out the doubt which I entertained as to the legality of this system, and the objections which might be taken to it on the score that rate-supported children were competing in the open labour market. In answer to which the guardians have dwelt with great emphasis on the immense advantage of gradually accustoming pauper boys to the battle of life, and of slowly and carefully merging them in the outer world instead of thrusting them out to trust to their own undeveloped resources. The institution has now been going on for many years and has done considerable good to the boys themselves, while there has been no complaint whatever, as far as I am informed, of interference with the labour market, or undue competition with independent boys. The system, if sound, should be extended to all the boys in the workhouse; and I am glad that the guardians have passed a resolution to this effect."[1]

Mr. Lockwood approves of the system. He says :—

"I am not one of those who hold that relief in the workhouse during childhood has as its main result the manufacture of paupers; indeed, seeing that universal boarding out is impracticable, I have the temerity to express the opinion that relief in the workhouse, combined with education at an elementary school outside, is in its operation and results as successful a manner of dealing with pauper children as any yet devised."[2]

Mr. Baldwyn Fleming also sees no harm in it so long as due provision is made for the supervision of the children by paid officers; but it acts harmfully, he thinks, where the children are placed under the care of paupers out of school hours.[3]

*(b) The District School System.*

With regard to the system of district schools, it is certainly

---

[1] 8 L.G.B., p. 118. The system which Mr. Courtenay Boyle describes is still in force in Norwich.
[2] 22 L.G.B., p. 75.
[3] 22 L.G.B., p. 83.

not so economical as the other two plans, but it works very satisfactorily. The disadvantage attaching to it is that the children are herded together in a large barrack-like building, and cannot have the practical training in housework which the children of the poor can get at home. This disadvantage, of course, does not exist when the district school is managed on the cottage home system. At the same time it must not be forgotten that the objections to it apply equally to the best managed orphan asylums supported by the charitable public.

### (c) *Boarding Out.*

The third plan is that which is most popular at the present time, not only on account of its being economical, but on account of the benefit the children get from it. They have, in fact, all the advantages attaching to a free life. The foster-parents very often get fond of the children boarded out with them, and treat them as their own. Unless, however, the visiting committee are very attentive to their duties, the system is liable to abuse. Miss Mason's annual reports on the boarding out of pauper children [1] give instances where the foster-parents have been cruel to, or neglectful of, the children under their charge. The system is much more beneficial to very young children than to older ones, because the latter come with habits, and often bad habits, already formed.

To go fully into the respective merits of the three systems would fill a volume, especially as it is now the subject of so much controversy. It will suffice to say that the success of each system depends entirely on vigilant supervision by the responsible authorities.[2]

---

[1] See reports beginning with that printed in 15 L.G.B., and which have since been annually made by her.

[2] As to the Sheffield experiment of hiring small houses in various parts of the town for the care of selected children by paid foster-mothers, see 23 L.G.B., p. 138.

### (4) *Deserted Wives.*

There is no doubt that in every case of a wife deserted by the husband the relief should only be given in the workhouse. Mr. Wodehouse's remarks on this subject, made in 1871, are as applicable now as when they were written. He says:—

"It is extremely difficult, especially in town unions, to obtain any very satisfactory evidence that there is no collusion between the husband and wife, and that the latter is not receiving remittances from her husband at the same time that she is in receipt of parochial relief. Such remittances are easily made through the post without the knowledge of the relieving officer, who is driven to rely upon the gossip of the neighbours, as to the mode in which the woman has been living, as the only available evidence on the subject. It is clear that this is a practice to which it is very undesirable to resort, and one which cannot be adopted without bringing with it many evil consequences. At Plymouth, where deserted wives are as a rule given out-relief, and the husbands are very rarely prosecuted, one of the relieving officers informed me that he had found cases 'in which a wife had for several weeks been receiving relief while her husband had never been out of the town, and many other cases in which the wife, while in receipt of relief, had been receiving remittances from her husband.' In several unions the general practice is to give out-relief in these cases, unless there is some positive reason to suspect collusion, while in many others, in which the rule is said to be to offer the workhouse, the exceptions to the rule are as numerous as the cases in which it is followed. In the Farringdon Union, which is exceptionally well managed, out-relief in these cases is never given, when the wife is able-bodied, a rule which might with great advantage be generally followed. The cost of maintaining the wives and children in the workhouse, and of instituting legal proceedings against the husband, which the guardians in many unions are somewhat reluctant to undertake, would to a great extent be counterbalanced by the diminished frequency with which, if such a system were uniformly adopted, such cases would occur."[1]

Mr. Longley says:—

"There is, I believe, little difference of opinion among boards of guardians as to the necessity of stringent administration of relief to deserted wives. The habitual grant of out-relief to applicants of this class, especially among the Irish residents in London, is very generally believed to encourage and facilitate the desertion of their wives and families by husbands. And in the

---

[1] 1 L.G.B., pp. 97, 98.

majority of unions, as has already been stated, it is now the rule to refuse out-relief in these cases." [1]

Mr. Knollys, reporting in 1889 on the pauperism of his district,[2] says :—

"In all the larger unions of the district the practice has been almost universally adopted of refusing to give relief, except in the workhouse, to persons representing themselves as wives deserted by their husbands, or who represent that their husbands have emigrated to America or the colonies. Constant imposture has led the guardians to consider the adoption of such a measure of self-protection imperative." [3]

Without the workhouse test in these cases it is quite impossible to tell whether or no there is collusion between man and wife. Mr. Wodehouse mentions a practice adopted by the Poplar Board of Guardians at the time he wrote (1871). "They allow the husband to be away for two or three weeks, giving the wife out-relief, but generally in kind only, for that period. At the end of it the wife is brought into the workhouse, and the husband is prosecuted." [4]

### (5) *Wives of Convicted Prisoners.*

In these cases again the workhouse should be offered. If there is any good in the man, and he is fond of his family, it will be an inducement to him in future to preserve a good character so that they shall not suffer for his fault. If the man is of a bad character, and does not care for his family or what becomes of them, it is very possible that he treats his wife cruelly. Out-door relief to the wife in such cases only pre-

---

[1] 3 L.G.B., p. 187.
[2] Comprising the counties of Durham and Northumberland, and parts of Cumberland and the North Riding.
[3] 18 L.G.B., p. 134.
[4] 23 P.L.B., p. 37.

vents her from taking the right course by getting a separation order, and by so doing enabling her to support herself and her children by her own efforts.

(6) *Wives and Families of Army Reserves when called out.*

They should be dealt with in the same way as widows.[1] The last time the reserves were called out was in 1878, and the Local Government Board report as follows:—[2]

"In consequence of the calling out of the reserve forces on the 3rd of April 1878, we were applied to by the boards of guardians of several unions for advice as to the course which they should adopt in dealing with applications for relief from the wives of men who had been called out to serve in the army and militia reserves. We pointed out that under the regulations relating to the administration of relief it was competent for the guardians, in the exercise of their discretion, to determine whether out-relief should be allowed in such cases, or whether the applicants should be required to enter the workhouse: that the first question upon which the guardians should satisfy themselves was, whether the applicants were destitute to such an extent as to require relief: and that if their destitution was clearly established, the next question to be determined was, what kind and amount of relief should be given in the case. We recommended the guardians in deciding upon the applications made to them to bear in mind that an allowance was made by the Government for the wives and children of the men of the army and militia reserves at the rate of sixpence a day for each woman and twopence a day for each child under fourteen years of age, and that the Secretary of State for War had made an order for the payment of these amounts monthly in advance. We also furnished particulars as to the amount which each man in the first class army reserve was entitled to receive before being called out. With respect to the kind of relief to be given, we stated our opinion that where the applications were made for the first time, and the guardians were satisfied that some assistance was necessary, out-relief might not improperly be given for a short period, in order to enable the applicants to make such arrangements for their support as their altered circumstances might require."

(7) *Single Women with Illegitimate Children.*

It is almost unnecessary to say that relief should always be

---

[1] *Supra*, p. 138.
[2] 8 L.G.B., xlv.

given in the workhouse in these cases. There it is possible through ladies' visiting committees to bring such influences to bear upon this unfortunate class that they may be stopped in their downward career, and led to amend their lives. Besides which there will be a chance of getting them situations which will give them a fresh start in life.

### (8) *Aged Married Couples.*

Boards of guardians are very apt to be lax in granting outdoor relief to this class, and this because it is considered a very harsh proceeding to take them into the workhouse where they may be separated, although the law says that this shall not be done against their wish. In the majority of cases the workhouse test will be found to answer well; and, if the house be offered, it is extraordinary how seldom the offer is accepted, showing that there cannot be the destitution alleged to exist, or that their children and relations have simply looked to the rates to relieve their own pockets. Many workhouses have one or two rooms set apart for aged couples, so that they can live together if they want to; almost all can provide the necessary accommodation; and the wants of an old couple can be provided for much more adequately inside the workhouse than outside.

Mr. Fleming says, speaking of his own district:—

"There are few workhouses at present where old married couples cannot be provided for much more comfortably than in any home of their own which could be kept going by the 4s. or 5s. and a loaf or two which would be given as out-relief. Married couples in the workhouse need not be separated in sickness for any ordinary ailment. If serious illness requiring special nursing had to be dealt with, one or other would no doubt have to go to the sick ward. There must be a separation of the sexes in a sick ward of a workhouse, as in the sick wards of a hospital, but even where this is the case the married couple in the workhouse would have facilities for daily visiting to an extent which would be impracticable in any other public institution. There is much more reason to fear that the kindness with which the aged and the sick are treated will interfere with proper discipline than that any hardship or suffering will be permitted by the guardians. It is indeed remarkable how few cases of improper treatment occur, and the severity with which they are regarded in the rare instances in which they are substantiated is quite sufficient to protect the inmates against any danger on this score. As a matter of fact, married couples seldom care to live together in the workhouse, no matter how good the accommodation for them may be.

"I have had a somewhat amusing experience of this in the Poole Union. There used to be no married couples' quarters in the Poole workhouse, and out-relief was given almost as a matter of course to all old married applicants, the alleged necessity for such relief being that in-door relief could not be offered without hardship, as married couples would have to be separated in the workhouse. This appeared to me to be open to very considerable abuse. The guardians agreed with me, and consequently erected a small building with good accommodation for two married couples. This happened several years since, but I believe that the rooms have never been occupied. The provision of this accommodation has enabled the guardians to test the cases in which relief was previously given as a matter of course, but in that sense only has it been of service."[1]

Mr. Dansey's experience is similar. Commenting on the improved administration of relief in the Wellington Union (Salop), he says:—

"It was objected here some time ago that it was cruel to offer the workhouse to married couples, because they would have to be separated. To meet this objection two rooms were last summer set apart at the workhouse for married couples, but they have never been occupied, and this is quite in accordance with my general experience throughout the district."[2]

The complaint of being separated in the workhouse is frequently made merely for the purpose of obtaining out-door relief, but when it has been pointed out to the applicants that the law permits them to be together in the workhouse, and that they will have a room to themselves, thus removing the grievance, no more is heard of the case.

"There does not seem to be any reason to suppose that the knowledge that aged married couples are in certain cases allowed to live together has had any prejudicial effect in impairing the efficacy of the workhouse test, nor has any case been brought under the notice of the Board in which the

---

[1] 17 L.G.B., p. 65.
[2] 18 L.G.B., p. 123.

arrangement has interfered with the discipline of the establishment. On the other hand the arrangement is of considerable advantage in removing an objection which might be raised to the system of in-door relief if aged married couples were compelled to live apart from one another in workhouses."[1]

### (9) *Non-resident Paupers.*

In the best administered unions, when a person who has been in receipt of out-door relief leaves the union and goes to reside in another, the relief is at once stopped. There is no doubt that this is the right course to adopt. It is quite impossible to be certain, when the pauper is removed from the observation of the relieving officer, that the relief will be properly applied.

### (10) *Members of Friendly Societies and Clubs.*

Ever since the establishment of these institutions there has always been a dispute as to how this class should be relieved, in case they should have the misfortune to be obliged to apply for relief from the rates. In a most elaborate minute[2] of the Poor Law Commissioners of the 27th March, 1840, on this subject, they point out the objections attending the grant of out-door relief to members of benefit societies. The Poor Law Board took the same view, and gave it as their opinion, that to take the club money at less than its full value was quite illegal.[3] In the best administered unions out-door relief is not given to members of friendly societies, because it encourages the establishment and continued existence of societies whose benefits are inadequate, *i.e.*, when the member is ill; the weekly payment he receives from his club is not sufficient to support him

---

[1] 10 L.G.B., p. xxix.
[2] 6 P.L.C., p. 93.
[3] See 22 P.L.B., p. 108. The letter of the Poor Law Board is printed *infra* in the Appendix, p. 238.

and his family. The societies we are referring to are generally financially unsound, and sooner or later come to grief, causing extreme distress.

If out-door relief is given at all (and in an union granting out-relief to what are considered deserving cases, such relief could not well be refused to members of clubs), the club money should be taken *at its full value*.

Mr. Culley says :—

"The usual practice of boards of guardians in dealing with members of friendly societies who apply for relief, is to take the club allowance at half its value, in assessing the income of the applicant. In taking this course, as it appears to me, guardians are not only acting illegally, but missing the mark at which they aim. In the first place, their business is only to meet the necessities of a case without any regard to the character of the applicant, except in so far as they are entitled to offer out-relief to a good character, and the workhouse to a bad one. In the second place, they are encouraging a class of societies many of which are doing infinite mischief. Members of such societies as the 'Manchester Unity of Odd Fellows' and 'Ancient Foresters' seldom apply for poor's relief, and it does not appear to me that any benefit society is worth encouraging which does not provide for its members a more eligible maintenance than boards of guardians have any right to bestow. I do not for a moment, however, wonder at the line of action adopted by most guardians. They know that the labouring class mean well by these societies, and that the troubles they have fallen into are the result of ignorance."[1]

So also Mr. Wodehouse says :—

"The usual mode in which guardians deal with applicants who are receiving money from a benefit club is to give them the benefit of one half the money which they receive from their club, and to take the other half only into account in determining the amount of relief, while in many other unions in which the guardians have laid down no fixed rule upon this point, yet in practice they look upon money received from a benefit club more favourably than upon income derived from any other source. I found very few unions in which club money was taken into account at its full value in determining the amount of relief, but it struck me as remarkable, that in one of these unions, *viz.*, Farringdon, in which in this as well as in other respects

---

[1] 3 L.G.B., p. 75.

the law is very strictly administered, although the guardians show no favour to applicants who are receiving money from a club, yet the amount of subscriptions to benefit clubs within the limits of the union has of late years been decidedly on the increase."[1]

Mr. Bury, in his report on out-door relief in the Brixworth Union,[2] thinks that the system of taking the club allowance at its full value must conduce ultimately to the formation of clubs which are self-supporting. The committee of his board found that in the union of Farringdon, where this plan had been adopted, the clubs at once began to raise their subscription.[3]

We can only hope that the Out-door Relief (Friendly Societies) Act, 1894, will not induce boards of guardians to deviate from the rule so clearly laid down and supported by such forcible arguments in the letter of the Poor Law Board. (See Appendix I., p. 238.)

(11) *The Able-bodied.*

As this subject introduces the questions of relief works, stone yards, etc., etc., we propose to deal with it in a separate chapter.

---

[1] 1 L.G.B., p. 98.
[2] 3 L.G.B., p. 120.
[3] 2 L.G.B., p. 72.

## CHAPTER XII.

### THE RELIEF OF THE ABLE-BODIED.

OWING to the different conditions of life of the poor in large urban unions and in country unions, guardians have a much larger discretion in granting out-door relief to the able-bodied in the former class of unions than in the latter. Under the Prohibitory Order of 1844, which applies to country and small urban unions, no out-door relief, unless with the consent of the Local Government Board,[1] can be given to the able-bodied of either sex, subject to certain exceptions;[2] whereas the Out-door Relief Regulation Order of 1852, applying to large urban unions, permits out-door relief to be given to the able-bodied of both sexes. If, however, such relief is given to a male person, half, at least, of it "must be given in food or fuel, or in other articles of absolute necessity," in return for which he must do the work set him by the guardians, *and under their direction and superintendence.* Nor can such relief be given to him "while he is employed for wages, or other hire, or remuneration, by any person."[3] We will deal with the orders separately.

(1) *The Out-door Relief Regulation Order, 1852.*

It is scarcely necessary to say that applications by the able-

---

[1] Art. vi.
[2] Art. i.
[3] Order of 1852, Arts. i., v., vi., vii.

bodied for relief should always be treated by the offer of the house, and we need not again repeat the arguments we have used in favour of this course. Unfortunately, the workhouse test cannot always be applied on account of insufficient accommodation. This is especially the case in times of exceptional distress, and of strikes. The best managed unions have, therefore, provided for such times of pressure by the establishment of "Test Houses." Most unions, however, employ the out-door labour test. This test is applied by means of stone-yards, labour-yards, agricultural employment, etc., but it is attended by many drawbacks. Thus :—

(a) *The Out-door Labour Test is no Deterrent.*

It is found in practice that men will accept work in this form who would not go into the house if it was offered.

It is looked upon as more eligible than in-door relief.

"Some boards of guardians have been so strongly impressed with the mischievous effects of the 'stone-yard system' that, though by no means favourably disposed towards the alternative test of the workhouse, they have closed their labour-yards, and have thus, in fact, voluntarily placed themselves, as regards relief to able-bodied males, under the Prohibitory Order. Stories are rife in these unions of paupers who have formerly remained at work in the stone-yard for two or three years consecutively, and in one of them a relieving officer assured me that there were then 100 men in the union, formerly employed in the stone-yard, but now earning their own living, who would infallibly have been still receiving relief in the stone-yard if it had remained open. Such cases as these are not wholly matter of history, for I found in the labour-yard of one union a man who had been there with the exception of a few weeks for two years.

"A more stringent discipline and a systematic offer of in-door relief to paupers receiving relief beyond a certain time in the labour-yard, would probably be found to prevent many of the abuses which have thus occurred, but in any case an out-door labour test can never, even under the most favourable conditions, be but an inefficient substitute for in-door relief."[1]

---

[1] 3 L.G.B., pp. 175, 176 (per Mr. Longley).

Mr. Wodehouse says that at Southampton

"Some men now in the labour-yard have been working there for five years, and in some cases have not been absent for an entire week during the whole of that period. There were 50 men in the yard on the day of my visit, and of these not six would in the opinion of two of the relieving officers accept the offer of the workhouse.

"The other relieving officer thought that the offer of the workhouse would be accepted by more than six, but less than ten."[1]

(b) *The Out-door Labour Test causes the Poor to think the State should find Work for them.*

The experience of Mr. Wodehouse convinced him that the out-door labour test, unless used with the utmost caution, was productive of very injurious consequences, by creating in the minds of the poor a belief that they had not merely a right to claim at the hands of the guardians that which the English Poor Law confers as a right upon all destitute persons, namely, relief, but that they were further entitled to demand that the guardians should provide them with work.[2]

Mr. Henley also says:—

"I have in previous reports called the attention of the board to what I considered to be an abuse of the provisions of the out-door labour test order in some Lancashire unions, the idea having been produced that the guardians were empowered to provide the wages of labour out of the rates, instead of only relieving certain classes of destitute persons by providing a labour test according to law."[3]

(c) *The Out-door Labour Test is demoralising.*

Mr. Longley tells us that,

"It has been found in London that a large class of paupers too indolent to seek for, or too dissipated to obtain employment, have been encouraged by this system of relief to rely upon it as a regular means of subsistence."[4]

And Mr. Murray Browne says:—

"Stone-yards are understood by too many as a sort of advertisement for starving people. And it may be safely assumed that if starving

---

[1] 1 L.G.B., p. 91.
[2] 1 L.G.B., p. 92. See also 23 L.G.B., p. 109.
[3] 17 L.G.B., p. 71.
[4] 3 L.G.B., p. 175.

people are advertised for, the supply will always equal the demand. The large towns of England are unhappily full of a class of low loafing tipsy people, very different from the *élite* of the artisan and labouring classes, though shading gradually into them. People of this class, being utterly thriftless, and bad workmen, are always on the brink of pauperism. By them, and not by them alone, any public recognition of the existence of unusual distress is treated as giving a sort of sanction to begging, and sponging upon others in every possible way, whether through the medium of the Poor Law or otherwise. This opening of the flood-gates of mendicity may at times be inevitable; but the certainty of its occurrence should not be left out of sight when the question is considered. The class described forms unhappily one of the largest factors in the sum total of our population; and its existence should never be forgotten. How to deal with it, is perhaps the most important social problem of the day."[1]

Writing in 1892, and speaking of the action of the guardians in the Cockermouth Union, he says:—

"Desiring to alleviate the distress in Workington they have opened a stone-yard, in other words have distributed out-door relief to able-bodied men, requiring the performance of a task of stone-breaking as a test of destitution. The objections which attend this mode of relief have often been pointed out, and are too numerous to be recounted here. The experiment has not proved more successful at Workington than elsewhere. The cost has been very large, the difficulties of management have been considerable, and the moral effect upon the men thus relieved has, I fear, been bad. Such, at least, is my own personal opinion of the matter."[2]

*(d) The Out-door Labour Test makes the Preservation of Discipline Impossible.*

Men assemble in unmanageable numbers; adequate supervision is impossible; the space is too crowded; and there is a want of method in gauging day by day the work performed by each man.[3]

Mr. Longe says:—

"In most unions where guardians have met applications from the ablebodied by 'opening the stone-yard,' this provision has been much abused by

---

[1] 16 L.G.B., p. 84.
[2] 21 L.G.B., p. 172. See also 23 L.G.B., pp. 109, 116, 143.
[3] See 15 L.G.B., p. 36.

the claims of a number of persons whose idle habits or bad character disentitle them to such assistance, and by others who, although out of work, are not in extreme destitution. The guardians of the Wolverhampton Union opened yards in Wolverhampton and Bilston in the second week of March for the employment of destitute able-bodied men in stone-breaking.

"The number of able-bodied men thus relieved on the 10th April, was 2,951. There were as many as 946 of this class in the yards on the 3rd of May, when the guardians found themselves compelled to close them."[1]

#### (e) *The Out-door Labour Test causes Discontent.*

Mr. Murray Browne says :—

"I have made it my business to talk with the men at work in the various stone-yards whenever I have had opportunity. I have always found them very discontented; anxious to have alterations made in the several rates of pay, sometimes in one way, sometimes in another; and generally persuaded that the guardians made money out of the stone-yard; and were paying them, the workmen, grossly inadequate wages. On one occasion, I chanced to stand within hearing of the hammers both of the vagrants in the workhouse wards, and of the men employed under the labour test. Both were breaking stones; but while the hammers of the vagrants, who worked by the piece, went pretty briskly, those of the others, who were paid by the day, told a very different story. There are, moreover, inferior men of the loafing class, who would like very well to stay at work in the stone-yard all the year, if they were allowed; and who, while so employed, will make no real effort to obtain work elsewhere."[2]

#### (f) *Advantages of the Workhouse Test over the Out-door Labour Test.*

Boards of guardians then should be very loath to open their yards. They should be prepared beforehand where their workhouse accommodation is insufficient, by making "temporary provision in the workhouse for receiving applicants for relief; as when the paupers see that guardians are in earnest, and do not intend to be hustled into giving out-relief, the rush soon ceases."[3]

If they are obliged to have recourse to the labour-yard they

---

[1] 16 L.G.B., p. 68.
[2] 16 L.G.B., p. 83.
[3] Per Mr. Davy, 8 L.G.B., p. 147.

should not allow the men to remain in it beyond a limited time, and should then offer the house. It will be found that few will accept the offer. Another mode of ridding themselves of these out-door paupers, or of diminishing their numbers, is to increase the task of work. In the West Bromwich Union (in 1887), in consequence of some 700 men and boys being thrown out of employment owing to the closing of the Bromford Ironworks,

> "The guardians had recourse to the labour test order. The task of work imposed in the first instance was very slight, being only the picking of two lbs. of oakum instead of the usual task of four lbs. With this light task the number of able-bodied men receiving out-relief, including several men who had not been employed at the Bromford works, was about 120 during the months of July and August. In September the task was increased to three lbs., and, in consequence of the refusal of the men to perform this task, the guardians stopped this mode of relief. This step was not followed by any material increase in the number of able-bodied men accepting in-door relief. The better class appear to have got employment in other works in the district."[1]

A change from stone-breaking to oakum-picking has also had a good effect in causing the men to seek an independent livelihood.[2]

But the out-door labour test can never, even under the most favourable conditions, be anything but an inefficient substitute for in-door relief, as the following examples show.

Mr. Stevens, writing in 1890, refers to the great decrease in the number of out-door paupers in the Nottingham Union in one year only.

> "This large decrease was on the out-door list, and due to the action of the guardians in closing their stone-yard at the workhouse, a measure which, as elsewhere on other occasions, was found not to materially swell the workhouse numbers."[3]

---

[1] 17 L.G.B., p. 68. See also 23 L.G.B., p. 116 (Walsall), p. 129 (Prescot).
[2] 17 L.G.B., p. 69.
[3] 20 L.G.B., p. 241.

Mr. Jenner-Fust, speaking of an increase of pauperism in the Kendal Union in 1892, attributes it to the opening of the stone-yard.

"It was thought necessary in this union, on account of the number of men out of work, to open a stone-yard, and the numbers in receipt of out-relief which had, up to the opening of the stone-yard on 10th December, been only slightly higher than in the corresponding period of 1891, at once sprang up from 553 in the week ending December 16th to 726 in the following week, and rose quickly in the course of the next three weeks to 1051, the highest number reached. The yard was closed on 28th January, 1893."[1]

As an example of good administration, Birmingham may be quoted.

Mr. Henley writing in 1886 says :—

"The guardians of that parish have, for some time," (*i.e.*, since 1880) "steadily refused to open their stone-yard to able-bodied men applying for relief, but have dealt with all such cases by giving an order for the workhouse, with the result of a steady diminution of pauperism."[2]

It was the dissatisfaction, indeed, with the system of the open stone-yard which led the Birmingham guardians to establish their test-house. We believe that this was the first union which adopted this plan, and it has been most successful.

Mr. Henley tells us why it was adopted.

"During a time of exceptional pressure there was a very large number of men employed upon the out-door labour-test order; but it was found in practice to be one of the most demoralising forms of relief that could possibly be adopted. It was impossible to keep the men closely to work to perform their task of work; it was also impossible to know what they were doing during the night-time after they received their relief; and it was also found that it was really reverting back very much to the old gravel-pit system, under which men considered that they had a right to receive either relief or work from the guardians; and the guardians determined during the summer of 1884, I think, to put an end to this system

---

[1] 22 L.G.B., p. 92.    [2] 15 L.G.B., p. 33.

altogether. They quite admitted that in time of very exceptional pressure, when the workhouse was full, it might be necessary to revert again to the out-door labour-test system; but they thought that under ordinary circumstances they might meet the cases, either by giving ordinary out-door relief, or by giving in exceptional cases short relief; but that, as a general rule, they would offer the workhouse to all able-bodied men that went before them."[1]

For this purpose the guardians, with the consent of the Local Government Board, proceeded to erect a test-house. Until it was ready for occupation they borrowed from the corporation a large disused factory, and fitted it up rapidly as a branch workhouse. But the test-house was soon ready.

"They do things very rapidly in Birmingham. They built a three-storied building of brick and slate in six weeks, and it was then opened."

It was first opened on the 15th November, 1880, and for men only. Upon the 27th January, 1881, the Birmingham Guardians obtained the consent of the Board to receive a limited number of able-bodied men from the West Bromwich workhouse. The following extract from a letter addressed by the clerk to the guardians to the inspector of the district testifies to the success of the experiment. " Return from week ended 20th November, 1880, to week ended 26th February, 1881. Test-house—number of orders given by relieving officers, 276; number of such orders used, 274; sent direct from Birmingham workhouse or West Bromwich workhouse, 110. Total admitted, 384; discharged, 340; remaining on 26th February, 1881, 44; average length of stay in the test-house about one week. Strict discipline has been maintained, all refractory paupers being taken before the magistrates and summarily dealt with. The test-house has had an immensely deterrent effect upon idle, dissolute, and worthless fellows.

---

[1] House of Lords Committee on Poor Law Relief, 1888, pp. 44, 45.

Its success is far beyond the most sanguine expectations of the guardians." During the week ended 1st January, 1881, no persons were set to work in the stone-yard under the provisions of the out-door labour test order, whereas in the corresponding week of 1880 the number of cases so relieved was 706.[1]

> "During the whole of the last two or three winters, when there has been the greatest possible pressure upon other parts of the workhouse, the test house has been, I may say, nearly empty; there have never been more than between 30 or 40 people in the test house, and I have a return this morning from Birmingham showing that there are only 11 men and 5 women in it at the present time."[2]

The example set by Birmingham was followed in 1887 by the three unions of Liverpool, Toxteth and West Derby acting jointly in the matter, and a separate test-house somewhat after the Birmingham system was established. The results were equally satisfactory.

> "The numbers of persons so relieved during the last week of 1886 were:—Liverpool 59, Toxteth Park 72, West Derby Union 127 (exclusive of wives and children, which in the West Derby Union alone raised their total to 508); total in the group 258. The numbers so relieved during the last week of 1887 were:—Liverpool 12, Toxteth Park 0, West Derby 0; total 12.
> "This, including wives and children in the same proportion as in West Derby, would be equivalent to a reduction, in numbers receiving out-door relief, of about 984."[3]

The greatest difficulty in dealing with the able-bodied is in regard to the work to be set them, as that work must not in any way compete with free labour.[4]

---

[1] House of Lords Committee's Report, 1888, p. 47.
[2] *Ib.*, p. 48.
[3] 17 L.G.B., p. 72. The appendix to Mr. Henley's report contains the regulations in force in the test house. (See p. 75.)
[4] See circular letter of L.G.B.; 18 L.G.B., p. 104, relating to wood-chopping.

Stone-breaking and oakum-picking are not suitable for those whose hands require to be kept fine, and who are merely temporarily out of work.

"The work of tying up bundles of wood has often been used as a test for such people, the able-bodied men cutting up the wood into small pieces, and the old men and those other men who are not used to hard labour, tying up the bundles for the purpose of sale in the town or use in the workhouse."[1]

In some test-houses they have corn-grinding, *e.g.*, in the Kensington test-house. Mr. Knollys goes very fully into the whole question.

"In some of the workhouses in the district questions have arisen with regard to the mode of the employment of male pauper inmates. At the beginning of the year it was my duty to call attention to their employment in three workhouses in teasing hair. This work was shown to be objectionable on many grounds. It was exceedingly distasteful to the old men engaged in it; was accompanied by the danger of the introduction of disease into the workhouse through the medium of the hair brought in to be teased; and was liable to injuriously affect the health of those engaged in it.

"There was in one instance some reluctance to relinquish this work; and Dr. Downes, the medical inspector of workhouses, visited this workhouse with me, carefully investigated the process of hair teasing, examined the men who had been employed in it, obtained specimens of the hair they had to deal with, and took samples of the air from the workshop in which the work was going on. As soon as it was made clear from his report that the employment was accompanied by the dangers I have stated, a majority of the guardians at once decided that it should be discontinued; and I am happy to say that this work no longer exists as an employment for paupers in the district.

"Questions have also arisen as to wood-chopping and the sale of firewood, both as to the way in which it was carried on in some workhouses and the price at which the firewood was being sold. These rendered it practically impossible for the independent labourer in that branch of employment to earn a living in the neighbourhood. The custom prevailed of employing inmates in delivering the firewood to purchasers and collecting the money to be paid for it. The objections to thus employing paupers hardly need demonstration. Instances, unfortunately, have not been wanting to prove that they are not merely theoretical. Apart from the evil on general grounds of allowing inmates of workhouses to be constantly

---

[1] House of Lords Committee's Report, 1888, p. 47.

employed in work away from the workhouse premises, there is the danger to the inmates themselves from the temptations connected with their employment. These arise, not only when they are allowed to collect the money, but also when they deliver the wood only and a paid servant is employed to collect the money. In both cases, I am obliged to say, I think they have been often increased by the absence of any adequate check as to the quantity of the firewood made and its disposal. The pauper inmates employed have not only delivered the firewood at the doors of purchasers, but have been instructed to carry it into their houses and store it for them; for doing this they have frequently received small gratuities, which have taken different shapes, but often that of money or stimulants. The results at times have been most regrettable. At one workhouse I was told that the men frequently came back showing signs of 'having had liquor,' and one of the men once returned helplessly drunk. The master of another workhouse told me that, although for two years he had had no fault to find, before that three men who had been employed in this work had all at different times returned to the workhouse drunk, and had had to be superseded. Within the last few weeks the inmate employed at another workhouse to deliver the wood and collect the money, failed to return at the time expected, and was subsequently found in a public-house drunk, having spent the greater part of the money he had collected. The plea constantly urged by those who are anxious that this arrangement should continue is, that it is a great convenience to the ratepayers; but if this is examined a little more closely, I have always found it really amounts to this, that a few ratepayers in the town in which the workhouse is situated or its neighbourhood, get work done at the expense of the rates for which they would otherwise have to pay. At Richmond workhouse, where inmates formerly delivered firewood, since Michaelmas, all persons requiring it have to send to the workhouse for it. The result, I am told, has been, that those who have not the means themselves of sending for it have had to pay men and boys to fetch it for them, and an increase has thus arisen to the earnings of partially disabled men. Although the changes which it appears indispensable should be introduced in carrying on this employment by inmates of workhouses do not always commend themselves to boards of guardians, and there may be some little difficulty in arriving at a just conclusion as to the price that should be charged to enable the independent labourer to compete with pauper labour, I have good hope that no long time will elapse before the matter will be placed on a proper footing, and, when it is thus placed, there is not probably any employment for the old or infirm inmates of workhouses which could be suggested which would be more suitable for its purpose and compete less with independent labour than wood-chopping." [1]

In the Whitechapel workhouse no difficulty is found in finding all kinds of work suited to the inmates;

"Men being variously employed at corn or coffee grinding, wood-chop-

[1] 20 L.G.B., pp. 245-247.

ping, flour dressing, bread making, tin work, smith's work, carpentering, coffin and furniture making, matting-weaving, mat making, bricklaying, whitewashing, painting, glazing, chimney sweeping, shoemaking, tailoring, gardening, etc. . . . In the female department some idea of the extent of work done—much of the lighter work by the aged women—will be formed by a reference to the following figures in relation to the past year, *viz.* :—136,059 articles passed through the laundry, 34,015 articles were repaired, and 974 articles of clothing made. These figures are additional to those representing work done for the Bakers' Row Infirmary during the year, *viz.*:—2,116 articles of clothing and bedding made, 2,068 blankets and quilts washed, and 731 beds and 414 pillows washed—the flocks contained in them being fumigated and repicked before being replaced."[1]

### (2) *Prohibitory Relief Order*, 1844.

In unions to which this order applies, the conditions which render the application of the out-door labour test sometimes necessary, harmful though it be, do not exist, and it is very seldom that boards of guardians have to ask the consent of the Local Government Board for the relaxation of the order.

### (3) *Evasion of the Orders.*

In advocating the Poor Law provisions of the Local Government Bill, 1893, Mr. Henry Fowler argued that the orders would prevent any great abuses of administration. But we think he must have been blind to the fact that they are often evaded now. Thus with regard to the Out-door Relief Regulation Order the following evidence shows how it was evaded more than twenty years ago:—

"In many of the Metropolitan unions the provisions of the Out-door Relief Regulation Order are more or less frequently infringed. Thus in many unions money is occasionally given to costermongers and others to enable them to set themselves up with a basket of fish or vegetables; in others, relief is given for a week or fortnight to able-bodied men to enable them to

---

[1] Report of Whitechapel Union for the year ending Lady Day, 1890, p. xviii.

seek for work. In the Greenwich Union the relieving officer is directed to redeem from pawn the goods of persons whom the guardians assist to emigrate. In the Clerkenwell district of the Holborn Union I saw a case in which money was given practically, though not ostensibly, to enable a carpenter to redeem tools from pawn." . . . . . . . . . . . . . . . . . .

"In some unions it was acknowledged to me that a practice prevailed, which cannot be too strongly reprehended. I mean the practice of granting a sum of money, such as ten shillings, for a purpose prohibited by the Out-door Relief Regulation Order, and entering it in the accounts as though it were ordinary relief to the amount of two and sixpence a week granted for four weeks. The evils resulting from the practice are too apparent to require comment. Not only is the system of audit rendered to a great extent nugatory, but an example is thereby afforded to the relieving officers, upon whose integrity the proper administration of out-relief so largely depends, which cannot fail to be most injurious. The names of the unions in which this practice was acknowledged to exist will be found in the annexed reports, and I do not repeat them here because I think it more than probable that a more searching investigation would show that it prevailed to a greater or less extent in several other unions."[1]

Mr. T. Mackay, who speaks on all questions connected with the Poor Law with great authority, shows that the practice still exists.

"I am credibly informed," he says, "of one East London Board where a long list of interim relief given to the able-bodied is brought up and passed without comment at every relief meeting of the board."[2]

Mr. Longley relates the following amusing experience :—

"The following case, while it throws some light on the mode in which the provisions of the out-relief regulations are evaded by boards of guardians, affords also an amusing illustration of the attitude assumed (I am bound to say with perfect good temper) by some boards of guardians in London, towards the central authority.

"A man who was classed as an able-bodied inmate of the workhouse, and who was on the point of leaving it, applied to the guardians for a sum of money to enable him on his discharge to buy brushes, etc., in order to set himself up as a shoeblack. As the grant of this relief would involve a violation of Arts. 1, 3 and 6 of the Out-relief Regulation Order, my attention was at once attracted to the case, upon which the following conversation ensued :—

---

[1] 23 P.L.B., p. 39.
[2] "The Unemployed," *Charity Organisation Review*, January, 1894.

"The chairman—'Here is a knotty point.'
"A guardian—'The inspector is here.'
"The chairman—'I don't care a pin for the inspector.'

"Upon this I represented to the guardians that whatever my opinion of the case might be, I could give no practical effect to it, but that the relief, if given by them, would in all probability be disallowed by the auditor.

"Chairman—'I don't care a pin for the auditor either.'
"A guardian—'We should give the relief if the inspector were not here, and I hope we shall not make any difference now.'

"On making further inquiry, the guardians found that the man was subject to fits, and they therefore decided that they would not encourage him, by the grant of the relief asked for, to leave the workhouse."[1]

---

[1] 3 L.G.B., p. 196.

## CHAPTER XIII.

### THE UNEMPLOYED.

How to deal with the unemployed is one of the great questions of to-day. There are no reliable statistics to show whether or not their numbers have increased of late years. A great strike or lock-out always swells their ranks, and when these occur during times of depression of trade a considerable increase must be expected, although the increase will only be temporary. But if we go by the Returns of Pauperism we find that the number of adult male paupers has greatly decreased, in proportion to the increase of population; and as the majority of the unemployed come under that head, we may assume that there has been a decrease in their numbers also.

The following table shows the number of *male* adult paupers, excluding lunatics and vagrants, relieved on the 1st January and 1st July in each year, from 1871 to 1894.[1]

---

[1] The figures are calculated from 23 L.G.B., pp. 320-323, 331, and from the B Returns. The effect of the restriction of out-door relief to able-bodied males is most marked, the mean in-door and out-door male adult paupers for the year ending Lady Day, 1871, and Lady Day, 1894, being as follows:—

|      | In-door. | Out-door. | Total. |
|------|----------|-----------|--------|
| 1871 | 9,773    | 37,654    | 47,427 |
| 1894 | 16,853   | 15,466    | 32,319 |

It will also be noticed that an increase or decrease in the number of vagrants is quite independent of the amount of adult male pauperism (see especially the years 1876, 1878, 1881, 1887, 1889, 1891 and 1892).

| Year ending at Lady Day. | 1st July | | 1st January. | | Mean number. | | Mean total. | Mean number of vagrants (including men, women and children). | Population. | Proportion to population. | |
|---|---|---|---|---|---|---|---|---|---|---|---|
| | Able-bodied. | Not able-bodied. | Able-bodied. | Not able-bodied. | Able-bodied. | Not able-bodied. | | | | Adults. | Vagrants. |
| 1871 | 38,029 | 146,752 | 56,826 | 159,260 | 47,428 | 153,006 | 200,434 | 5183 | 22,712,266 (Census 1871) | 1 in 116 | 1 in 4382 |
| 1872 | 35,078 | 146,172 | 39,512 | 150,787 | 37,295 | 148,480 | 185,775 | 3836 | | | |
| 1873 | 26,058 | 134,996 | 30,043 | 149,473 | 28,051 | 137,735 | 165,786 | 2700 | | | |
| 1874 | 22,238 | 126,954 | 25,568 | 131,698 | 23,903 | 129,326 | 153,229 | 2787 | | | |
| 1875 | 20,474 | 123,249 | 28,455 | 130,437 | 24,465 | 126,343 | 150,808 | 2767 | | | |
| 1876 | 18,943 | 115,395 | 21,585 | 121,722 | 20,264 | 118,559 | 138,823 | 3248 | | | |
| 1877 | 16,811 | 110,949 | 20,886 | 119,323 | 18,849 | 115,136 | 133,985 | 3770 | | | |
| 1878 | 17,380 | 111,454 | 23,024 | 119,734 | 20,202 | 115,594 | 135,796 | 4216 | | | |
| 1879 | 18,992 | 111,768 | 23,635 | 125,215 | 26,314 | 118,492 | 144,806 | 4143 | | | |
| 1880 | 25,210 | 116,869 | 33,206 | 131,449 | 39,708 | 124,159 | 154,867 | 6790 | 25,974,439 (Census 1881) | 1 in 172 | 1 in 3722 |
| 1881 | 21,593 | 120,031 | 28,968 | 130,543 | 25,281 | 125,287 | 150,568 | 6979 | | | |
| 1882 | 21,092 | 120,976 | 26,452 | 130,665 | 23,772 | 125,821 | 149,593 | 6114 | | | |
| 1883 | 19,396 | 120,871 | 26,534 | 132,141 | 22,965 | 126,506 | 149,471 | 4790 | | | |
| 1884 | 18,819 | 119,343 | 23,582 | 128,555 | 21,201 | 123,949 | 145,150 | 4097 | | | |
| 1885 | 18,692 | 119,564 | 26,800 | 130,143 | 22,746 | 124,854 | 147,600 | 4483 | | | |
| 1886 | 19,543 | 120,105 | 31,125 | 133,807 | 25,334 | 126,956 | 152,290 | 5094 | | | |
| 1887 | 21,896 | 123,960 | 31,619 | 138,399 | 26,758 | 131,180 | 157,938 | 4833 | | | |
| 1888 | 21,498 | 126,533 | 33,558 | 141,242 | 27,528 | 133,888 | 161,416 | 5265 | | | |
| 1889 | 21,774 | 128,907 | 29,784 | 141,125 | 25,779 | 135,016 | 160,795 | 6504 | | | |
| 1890 | 19,505 | 127,807 | 27,094 | 140,487 | 23,300 | 134,147 | 157,447 | 4929 | 29,001,018 (Census 1891) | 1 in 188 | 1 in 5223 |
| 1891 | 18,518 | 125,328 | 26,672 | 136,961 | 22,595 | 131,145 | 153,740 | 5552 | | | |
| 1892 | 20,667 | 120,649 | 29,979 | 129,539 | 25,323 | 125,094 | 150,417 | 6498 | 29,403,346 [1] | 1 in 191 | 1 in 4269 |
| 1893 | 24,878 | 116,823 | 34,210 | 131,516 | 29,544 | 124,170 | 153,714 | 6888 | 29,731,100 [2] | 1 in 182 | 1 in 3327 |
| 1894 | 25,621 | 123,265 | 39,019 | 137,640 | 32,320 | 130,453 | 162,773 | 8935 | | | |

[1] Estimated population in middle of 1892.   [2] Estimated population in middle of 1893.

We shall divide the subject into two parts ; (1) dealing with the permanently unemployed, and (2) dealing with the temporarily unemployed.

(1) *The Permanently Unemployed, or the " Misfits " (as they have been happily termed).*

They include that class of persons " who, without being wholly bad, are unsteady and unreliable, and are usually of low character, and more or less given to tippling, etc. These men constitute the mass of the unemployed. When work is plentiful they obtain it. But when the demand for labour (of whatever kind) diminishes, they are naturally the first to lose work and the last to regain it." [1]

It is a sad thing to confess, but we can do nothing for this class, except by emigrating the most active and capable of them. Labour colonies have proved no cure, nor have public relief works. Those who are not fitted to do work for the private employer cannot be fitted to do work for the " State " employer ; nor, indeed, is it the duty of the latter to find work for them. Boards of guardians and vestries ought to be the last bodies to give them work, because, by so doing, they must be taking work away from others, who could do it much more quickly and economically. It is well known that Mr. Chamberlain's Circular of 1886 [2] was never meant to be generally acted upon, re-issued though it has been more than once since that date. It is, indeed, quite impossible for public bodies to provide work on a large scale (and if the unemployed are to be relieved adequately this must be done) " which will not involve the stigma of pauperism ; which all can perform whatever may

---

[1] Per Mr. Murray Browne, 17 L.G.B., p. 87.
[2] 16 L.G.B., p. 5. See Appendix, p. 241.

have been their previous avocations; which does not compete with that of other labourers at present in employment; and which is not likely to interfere with the resumption of regular employment in their own trade by those who seek it."

Public relief works have been tried and found wanting.

Mr. Lockwood says that,

"In no instance during 1886 was it found necessary by boards of guardians in the Eastern District to adopt exceptional measures for dealing with relief, though in Norwich, Ipswich, Yarmouth, and King's Lynn, relief funds were raised by public subscription and relief works instituted by the urban authorities, which continued in operation for several weeks. It is, however, the unanimous opinion of those best qualified to judge, that the mischief indirectly done by this method of dealing with distress, greatly discounted any temporary good results that may have been achieved.

"Looking to the many facts promotive of distress, bad seasons, slackness of business, and so forth, it is somewhat surprising that there has been comparatively little increase in pauperism, but it must not be forgotten that, whereas the rate of wages has in most branches of business risen during recent years, the purchasing power of money has appreciably increased, the very competition which has tended to cripple the manufacturer having greatly cheapened all the necessaries of life. All due credit, too, must be given to the beneficial operation of greater thrift and more temperate habits among the working classes ordinarily so called; it is not, however, among that class that the results of a decade of trade depression have been most severely felt, but rather among small householders, petty traders, farmers, and the like, who have had to pay augmented rates out of greatly diminished profits, and if the increase and diminution continue in a similar ratio to that of the past few years, many of these will be reduced themselves to seek relief from the rates to which they have now so great a struggle to contribute what is demanded of them."[1]

Even Mr. Murray Browne's lukewarm support is absolutely condemnatory of relief works to those who can read between the following lines:—

"I have hitherto," he says, "said nothing of the efforts made by municipalities, and other local authorities (not being boards of guardians) to afford work to those out of employment, by putting in hand public works of different kinds. This was done largely, and in many places. The works

---

[1] 16 L.G.B., p. 59.

in question included street improvements, footways, the laying out of parks and public gardens, preparation of land for building, and a variety of other matters. The relief afforded was no doubt considerable. The carrying out of such operations at such a time possesses obvious advantages. The work is possibly done somewhat more cheaply than when labour is in demand; and the wages are received at a time when they are peculiarly acceptable. Unfortunately in many places it is almost impossible to find any useful work which can be done by rough labour, and with little previous preparation. Unless it can be done mainly by rough labour, it is not available. And unless the work when done is really useful it has no advantage over stone-breaking; where the broken stone is at any rate good for the roads. Bearing in mind the probable recurrence of periods of like distress, it would perhaps be well if public bodies were to reserve suitable works of this character (if they can be postponed without injury) to be done at such periods; or at any rate in the winter, when work is always slack."[1]

Relief works are, in fact, only a palliative, and probably do much more harm than good by leading the poor to lean upon State aid instead of on their own exertions and providence.

### (2) *The Temporarily Unemployed.*

These can best be dealt with by well organised charity, and by distinguishing by means of careful inquiries between those who have a claim from their general good character and provident habits to be relieved in this way, and those who have not. Strikes, lock-outs, depression of trade, and a prolonged severe winter are the main causes of the existence of the class. There is a great deal of evidence in the reports of the Poor Law inspectors to guide us as to modes of dealing with exceptional distress. As regards strikes, we may mention the strike of cotton operatives at Bolton, which began on September 1st, 1877, and lasted over eight weeks.[2] By the action of 1,800 men striking, 12,500 persons, including about 5,000 women, were thrown out of work.

---

[1] 16 L.G.B., p. 84. Mr. Murray Browne reverts to the subject again in 23 L.G.B., at p. 107.

[2] See Mr. Davy's report on the strike, 7 L.G.B., p. 233.

"The vast majority of these received no 'strike pay,' and were left dependent on their own resources and on charity." . . . . . . . . . . . .

"There is hardly a town in Lancashire with more resources for meeting such a crisis than Bolton, which is exceedingly rich and prosperous, and which has enjoyed a large share of the good trade that immediately preceded the present depression. There are many thriving industries not dependent on the cotton trade at all: and further, no notice of reduction had been given at several mills which kept running throughout the strike, and in which about 3,000 persons were employed. At no time during the strike was there the least risk that there would be any difficulty in relieving the destitute. The real danger was that the relief might be given in a form which would be a source of permanent demoralisation to the inhabitants."

The great difficulty in dealing with the distress arose from the fact that the workhouse accommodation was insufficient; consequently the out-door relief labour test had to be used. A table appended to the report shows this conclusively, no material increase occurring in the number of in-door paupers on the corresponding number in the previous year. In the last week of the strike 1,000 more persons were receiving relief than during the corresponding week of 1876 (2,831 as against 1,839), while the number of in-door paupers was much the same (875 as against 840).

A large proportion of the increase of in-door paupers (which, as we have seen, was very small) arose from wife desertions, and the wives were invariably relieved by an order for the workhouse.

"The able-bodied men who received out-relief from the guardians were for the most part set to break stones or pick oakum in the cells of the new vagrant wards. This was a sufficiently stringent test, and in my opinion it worked admirably. Some of the men were also employed in the lighter work of stripping the land and excavating the foundations for the new schools which are being built by the guardians. On the whole, I think the work given to the male out-door paupers had a sufficiently deterrent effect, and was about as good a test as any form of work outside the workhouse can be. With the women the case was different. A great deal of sympathy was felt for them on account of their sex and because they had been thrown out of work through no fault of their own, and, consequently, as far as I observed, no test work was exacted from them. I suggested that all the able-bodied women should be set to pick cotton in the vagrant wards at the workhouse; or should at all events be detained there in the separate cells for a few hours in each week. But the guardians seemed to be unwilling to do more than institute careful inquiries with respect to each case, and then give relief to those who appeared to need it without requiring any work from the recipients. Had the strike continued I think the guardians would have found it necessary to appoint additional officers to investigate the circumstances of these women. It is noteworthy that only one case was reported by the guardians to the Local Government Board in which relief had been given contrary to the provisions of the Out-relief Regulation Order."

As to the work done by charitable associations, "The Poor Protection Society" and the "Toilet Weavers' Association," partly from their own resources and partly from specially collected funds, distributed a considerable amount of relief in money and kind. In addition to these charities some of the employers gave a weekly allowance to those of their hands who were not in receipt of strike pay to keep them from applying to the relieving officers: others opened reading-rooms for the hands, provided entertainments for them, and even took them excursions to the seaside. Many of the card-room hands were employed in cleaning the mills, and occupation for others was found in running the machinery occasionally to keep it in working order.

There was no general starvation or anything like it existing at any time during the strike in the union.

"Although the workpeople out of employ in Bolton were considerably impoverished and distressed, yet there was nothing like wide-spread destitution among them. I do not think the strike lasted long enough to exhaust the credit which was given by the shopkeepers or to expend the money which many of the people were able to raise on their furniture. Certainly the resources of the Poor Law were sufficient, in spite of the deficiency of workhouse accommodation, fully and amply to provide for all distress within the union."

It was estimated that over £100,000 in wages was lost to the artisans by the strike, and yet the men yielded to all intent and purposes unconditionally. "It is an ill wind which blows nobody any good," and it is worth remarking that the charges of drunkenness before the magistrates decreased no less than thirty per cent. during the strike.

Mr. Davy's comments on the strike are valuable, and serve as a warning. He says :—

"In this particular instance no obvious evil from a Poor Law point of view has resulted from the cessation of work, except perhaps that some of the lower classes were taught to look for indiscriminate relief from charitable associations. Yet it was impossible to watch the course of events without seriously reflecting on the adequacy of the present Poor Law machinery and of the present Poor Law policy for meeting a crisis of a similar nature. In the first place, the difficulty—I had almost said the impossibility—of setting large numbers of able-bodied women to work was very clearly shown. To provide an adequate test for this class when the workhouse accommodation is inadequate, rooms for cotton or oakum-picking under very careful supervision are necessary, or means must be taken for isolating each woman for a certain number of hours in each week. If the women are really destitute such tests are no hardship, but it is nearly impossible to induce guardians to provide the necessary machinery beforehand; and during a period of destitution, however firm the guardians may be disposed to be with regard to the men, they are inclined to relieve the women quite indiscriminately, rather than risk the appearance of being hard with those whose appearance appeals to the sympathies of everyone, and who are in distress through no fault of their own. Another point to be noticed is, that during periods of distress caused by strikes and lock-outs, there is always a considerable risk that the Poor Law may be used to promote private interests. In this particular case I saw nothing which led me to believe that this was done by anybody; but attention can hardly be too often called to a matter of such importance to the administration of the Poor Laws generally, though it is by no means easy to suggest an adequate remedy for the evil. If out-door relief is given lavishly from mere ignorance and thoughtlessness, the poor are demoralised and the ratepayers are wronged. But if the relief is given with the deliberate purpose, either expressed or implied, of preventing men from leaving the town, and thus producing a scarcity of labour when the strike is over, the breach of trust on the part of the guardians would constitute a still greater evil. The desire to 'keep the men together,' as it is called, will always, in times of trade depression, expose the administrators of public relief to the temptation of applying the funds with which they are entrusted to uses which may seem to be for the benefit of the locality, but which can only result in the demoralisation of everyone concerned.

"A still more important point is the use which trades unions are able to make of Poor Law relief as a subsidiary resource to assist them in prolonging a struggle with the employers. They are to a certain extent assisted by a fund mainly levied from the employers themselves. The guardians can only refuse all relief to persons who are destitute from being out of employment in cases where it can be shown specifically that the applicant for relief could obtain work at a certain place and time. When the want of employment results from a lock-out this is of course impracticable ; and, when dealing with individuals, it is not always possible even in the case of a strike. The guardians are not discharged from their responsibility by merely pointing out in general terms that employment can be obtained somewhere. But even if it were possible to absolutely refuse relief to all persons who are destitute from their own deliberate choice, still as long as any out-door relief at all is given, it is quite certain that some portion of it will go either directly or indirectly to aid the men by supporting their relatives and friends, and by sustaining the credit given by the shopkeepers. The evil is very great, and I fear that as yet we have only seen the beginning of it. As it is inherent in the sound fundamental principle of the English Poor Law that a person must be relieved according to his need, irrespective of his antecedents or character, I do not see how it can be met, except by the provision of a large surplus of workhouse accommodation."

The Northumberland coal strike commenced at the end of January, 1887, and lasted until the end of May (4 months).[1]

"The full meaning of the strike to the working classes of the district may be appreciated when the number of the collieries affected by the strike is considered, and it is stated that, when the Northumberland collieries are all working, the coal owners pay about £20,000 a week in wages alone. In their appeal to the trade unions of the country on February 7th made by the Northumberland Miners' Union, it is stated that 16,000 men and boys were then out of work in the county, resisting a reduction of wages, of whom 12,000 were members of their association, and that £8,000 per week was required to afford adequate support to these latter. This statement, and the facts of the speedy exhaustion of the deposits of the miners at the co-operative stores, and the almost total cessation for the time being of any contributions from Northumberland to the Miners' Permanent Relief Fund, which included amongst its members no less than 12,022 men working at the principal collieries in Northumberland, speak for themselves as to the effect of the strike on the savings of the working classes. It was, however, amongst the 4,000 non-unionist miners and their families that the destitution caused by the strike was felt with all its force. The evidence of those living in their midst can leave no doubt as to the reality of the dire distress that existed amongst them. This was met by subscriptions from their fellow-workmen elsewhere, and from the general public in Northumberland and the neighbouring county of Durham, and by the aid of charitable relief committees, soup kitchens, and so forth."[2]

Mr. Knollys' comment on the result of the strike is that

---

[1] See Mr. Knollys' report on the strike, 17 L.G.B., p. 76.
[2] See also 23 L.G.B., p. 116 (Bedminster); and p. 128, 130 (Prescot).

"It must be a matter of continuing regret that a settlement resulting in so small an ultimate difference between the proposals of the owners and the terms accepted by the men could not have been brought about by less disastrous means."[1]

It is an interesting fact that in the two unions principally affected by the strike, *viz.*, Morpeth and Tynemouth, there was no appreciable increase in the number of out-door paupers. Therefore, again the Poor Law proved itself adequate to deal with exceptional distress.

At the beginning of 1879 symptoms of approaching distress of a serious character began to appear in Birmingham after about three weeks of snow and frost.

"The number of applications for relief rapidly increased, and the difficulty in meeting the pressure was intensified by the crowded state of the workhouse, which already contained 2,500 inmates, and was at the time undergoing extensive alterations and additions. The guardians at once decided to adopt the following measures:—

1. To provide means to set the able-bodied to work.
2. To erect sheds upon ground adjoining the workhouse capable of containing altogether 400 men, and to divide the men into working gangs of moderate size.
3. To set apart oakum workrooms for able-bodied women.
4. To provide, fit up, and furnish a large disused factory in Floodgate Street for the purpose of a temporary workhouse, and also to afford the means of setting to work a certain number of the out-door poor.

"The guardians also made considerable additions to their staff of officers with a view to meet the pressure upon them. It required much energy on the part of the committee appointed by the guardians to enforce these regulations, and it is owing to their exertions that a period of pressure, which might have been marked by confusion and disorder, was surmounted without any serious departure from the ordinary principles of Poor Law relief.

"The following is a statement of the number relieved in the stone-yard during the week ending—

| | |
|---|---|
| 4th January, number relieved, | 1,363 |
| 11th ,, ,, ,, ,, | 2,587 |
| 18th ,, ,, ,, ,, | 3,471 |
| 25th ,, ,, ,, ,, | 4,962 |
| 1st February, ,, ,, | 5,688 |

[1] As to the evil effects of strikes see 23 L.G.B., 128, 143.

"In January 1879 the board issued an order enabling the guardians to provide the temporary workhouse above referred to (guardians' proposal No. 4), and owing to the untiring energy of the committee the building was in a condition to receive inmates by the 8th February. On that day orders of admission were given to 90 able-bodied men, 30 of whom availed themselves of the relief, and of these 14 gave notice of discharge. Up to the middle of February 154 orders were given, 98 only were used, and 52 of these discharged themselves."

Mr. Henley endeavoured to ascertain the trades or occupations of the persons who were relieved under the provisions of the Out-door Labour Test Order with the view of finding out how far their distress depended upon slackness of trade or on severity of weather. The following table shows the occupation of 100 men taken as a fair sample:—

| | | | |
|---|---|---|---|
| Bricklayers ...... 3 | Butcher ............ 1 | Strikers ............ 6 | Porter ............ 1 |
| Labourers ........ 28 | Grinder ............ 1 | Slaters ............ 4 | Chaser ............ 1 |
| Gun trade ........ 2 | Filer ............... 1 | Strip caster ........ 1 | Clerk ............. 1 |
| Stamper .......... 1 | Glass gilder ........ 1 | Carters ............ 3 | Ostler ............ 1 |
| Buttonmakers .... 2 | Charwomen ........ 2 | Wire drawer ...... 1 | Bedsteadmaker.... 1 |
| Brassfounders .... 7 | Plasterers .......... 3 | Nail cutter ........ 1 | Printer ............ 1 |
| Painters .......... 3 | Spectaclemaker .... 1 | Japanner .......... 1 | Billposter.......... 1 |
| Brushmaker ...... 1 | Metal rollers ...... 2 | Burnisher ........ 1 | Machinist ........ 1 |
| Bedfitter .......... 1 | Glass cutters ...... 2 | Jeweller .......... 1 | Nail feeder........ 1 |
| Cabinetmaker .... 1 | Harnessmaker ...... 1 | Casters ............ 3 | Storer............. 1 |
| Carpenters ........ 2 | Umbrellamaker .... 1 | Brazier ............ 1 | |

It will be seen that not half of those seeking relief could be said to have lost their employment by stress of weather. Moreover it is a significant fact that during the frost the number of vagrants, not only in Warwickshire but in other parts in my district, considerably diminished, and it would not be unfair to assume that a proportion of this class tended to swell the pauper roll of Birmingham. It would not be right, in describing the mode of relief at Birmingham, to pass over the great amount of public charity administered under the guidance of the Mayor.[1]

Birmingham is generally ahead of other unions in its business-

---

[1] 8 L.G.B., p. 138.

like and depauperising mode of action during periods of exceptional distress. Mr. Jenner-Fust, jun., described as follows what was done there to meet the exceptional distress arising at the beginning of 1887:—

"I abstract an account from the report of the committee which administered the relief fund, and which was headed by the Mayor, and included several members of the board of guardians; for I venture to think that the action of the committee tended to minimise the evils inseparable from the administration of relief funds, and as such is valuable for future guidance. The appeal for funds was not made until 26th February, when a sum of £3075 was raised. The borough was divided into eight districts, corresponding generally with the districts of the relieving officers. Sub-committees were appointed to work each district, and were authorised to add to their number such gentlemen connected with each district as were willing to help, such as local clergymen, representatives of trade associations, and other relief agencies. No person was eligible for relief who had not resided in the borough for the previous six months, or who had recently been in receipt of poor relief, and all relief was given in kind.

"Personal application was not received by any of the sub-committees, but forms of recommendation were issued to the agencies referred to above, and others. On these forms were supplied the fullest details as to the condition, character, and circumstances of the applicant and his family, and, before relief was granted, the particulars were verified by a member of the sub-committee from which the recommendation forms were issued, and by this means the committee believe that the fund of 1886 was distributed to deserving persons, and that the least possible amount of imposition existed.

"When a case was approved, tickets to the value of 1s. each were issued to the applicant bearing the names of tradesmen who had undertaken to supply articles of good quality at the lowest possible prices. By arrangement with the gas committee of the corporation, tickets were issued for small quantities of coke at very low prices; individual gifts of milk, peas, and clothing were also received. By the middle of April the committee were able to discontinue their work. The visiting officers of the School Board, the relieving officers, and the police rendered valuable assistance in the verification of applications for relief.

"I may add that some very terrible cases of distress were met with, and it should be recorded that after the sub-committees had been at work a short time they frequently received expressions of gratitude for the help that had been afforded, with an intimation that work had been obtained and further relief would not be required."[1]

As an example of how exceptional distress should *not* be

---

[1] 16 L.G.B., p. 58.

dealt with, we may mention the case of the Mansion-House Fund of 1886.

The fund was hastily collected and hastily distributed, and no one would, we think, venture to assert that it did any permanent good. On the contrary, it undoubtedly tended to create more " unemployed," and so increased the number of persons chargeable to the poor rate.[1]

As Mr. Henley says in commenting on it :—

"It is certain that there is no day throughout the year when numbers could not easily be got together, who might truthfully represent themselves as unemployed, as not knowing with certainty how the wants of the morrow would be supplied."[2]

The following year the unemployed naturally came into full view again, choosing Trafalgar Square as their meeting place. Again mistaken philanthropy only accentuated the evil.

Mr. Henley's description is as follows :—

" As the weather grew colder the attention of the public was drawn to them, and well intentioned, perhaps, but mistaken philanthropy introduced hot coffee on the scene; the effect was an immediate and large increase of numbers, and the accommodation in the casual wards of the central parts of the Metropolis became insufficient. Trafalgar Square is situated in the Strand Union, which is one of the few unions unprovided within its own area with any vagrant wards, those in Macklin Street in the union of St. Giles and St. George Bloomsbury being within easy reach and having hitherto proved amply sufficient for both unions. Under these circumstances numbers of vagrants applied late at night to the Strand relieving officer, who had no alternative but to give free tickets of admission to the common lodging-houses of the neighbourhood. Free lodging without a task of work was naturally

---

[1] 16 L.G.B., p. 54.   [2] 16 L.G.B., p. 57.   See also 22 L.G.B., p. 67.

attractive, particularly in such a neighbourhood as that of the Strand and Covent Garden, where the theatres at night and the market in the morning always bring together numbers of casual labourers and loafers. At one time as many as 500 free tickets to lodging-houses were being issued nightly, and this number would soon no doubt have grown to a much higher figure but for the prompt action taken by the Strand guardians in providing temporary wards in Hart Street, when the issue of lodging-house tickets was discontinued. Additional vagrant wards were at the same time provided by the Holborn guardians in Old Street, and the women's wards in Macklin Street were temporarily used for men, the female vagrants being accommodated in St. Giles's Workhouse.

"During the winter and spring of the year, distress of an exceptional character was said to exist among the working-classes of the Metropolis, but I am inclined to doubt the applicability of the term exceptional.

"When during the American War the great distress amongst the cotton operatives arose in Lancashire, such distress was undoubtedly exceptional, being due to a temporary cause, *viz.*, the failure of supply of the one article of raw material which provided the means of livelihood to a large population. No such temporary cause has existed in London, where the distress is, as I believe, rather of a permanent and chronic character. Much of it is, I fear, due to improvidence. Provisions never were cheaper than they are now, but the standard of diet of the working-classes of London is far higher and more expensive than that of the same classes in any other capital of Europe. The great evil from which the poor in this crowded Metropolis suffer is the difficulty of obtaining house accommodation at a rent at all in proportion to their income, and an improvement in this direction ought to be the great aim of legislators and philanthropists.

"I attended in October at the Mansion-House, under the presidency of the Lord Mayor, a meeting of the Mansion-House Committee on Metropolitan poverty. There was then a general agreement of opinion that no such distress existed as to call for any special measures, but that existing charitable societies should be liberally supported."[1]

The Mansion-House had by this time learnt their lesson.[2]

The way then to deal with the class in question so that the evil may not increase is (1) to provide adequate in-door accommodation for the able-bodied, *i.e.*, accommodation above and beyond what is ordinarily required, (2) a wise and careful dispensation of charity, and (3) close co-operation between the Poor Law and charity. Mr. Henley gives instances of the good effect of the workhouse test used in 1878-79 in three unions in his district.

"As regards Reading, the Board, on the application of the guardians, issued the Out-door Labour Test Order to the union to enable them to deal with the numerous applications for relief they expected to receive during the severe weather. It is, however, important to note that it has not been necessary to put the provisions of the order in force. In this union 61 able-bodied men, on applying for relief, were offered the workhouse, and 9 only accepted the offer.

"The pressure in the Uxbridge Union has been rather severe, and, for a time, while the workhouse was full, the guardians were compelled to grant out-relief to able-bodied applicants, chiefly brickmakers, deprived of work by the frost. About the middle of January there was some spare accommodation in the workhouse, and the guardians gave workhouse orders to 40 of the applicants. No admission took place under these orders. One or two of the men came to the workhouse, and having ascertained that there was accommodation for them went away and returned no more. Men with large families received relief by way of loan.

"At the commencement of any period of pressure the guardians require

---

[1] 17 L.G.B., p. 53.
[2] Most interesting evidence as to how the exceptional distress of 1886 was dealt with is contained in the report of a special committee of the London Charity Organisation Society, published in 1886 by Cassell & Co., together with suggestions as to how exceptional distress may best be dealt with. We would also refer our readers to Mr. C. S. Loch's paper read at the Central Poor Law Conference of 1886 on "Exceptional Distress."

the support of the Board in administering relief, as they are certain to be urged by members of their own body to depart from the principles of the law, and to give out-relief to able-bodied men with families.

"I may instance the case of the Aston Union. The guardians passed a resolution to depart from the principles of the Out-door Relief Prohibitory Order, but, through the action of the Board, they were induced to return to their usual mode of administering relief."[1]

### Experience in dealing with exceptional distress teaches two lessons.

"1st. That in times of prosperity it is a dangerous policy to limit the accommodation in workhouses for able-bodied men in order to provide additional accommodation for the aged and infirm; and 2nd, That any departure from the principles of the Prohibitory Order should lead to a thorough investigation of the circumstances of the union and the mode of administering relief, and, if necessary, the guardians should provide additional accommodation."[2]

It is most important that charity and the Poor Law should co operate in dealing with exceptional distress. Charity helps the Poor Law to a great extent, and the guardians should make a return for such help. Mr. Cane, reporting in 1879 on the distress of his district (containing the counties of Lancaster, Cumberland, Derby, Westmoreland, and part of the West Riding of York), says:—

"Nor have the guardians been content to receive and avail themselves of the incidental benefits conferred on them by voluntary associations and charitable societies without making any return. The guardians have seen the importance of keeping up the distinction between charity and pauperism—they have been fully aware of the danger to which the benevolent committees were exposed by attempts of paupers to obtain unnecessary and unmerited aid from the committees as well as from the union. By sending lists of paupers and by giving other information, and by directing their relieving officers to be present at the sittings of the committees when applicants appeared before them, the guardians have enabled the committees to reject large numbers of unfounded claims.

"Moreover, the sight of, and even the knowledge that the union officers were in attendance, has caused the sudden disappearance of many who

---

[1] 8 L.G.B., p. 139. See also *ib.*, pp. 142, 147.
[2] *Ib.*, p. 140.

were waiting to attempt to take improper advantage of the liberality of the committees, and who would not have scrupled to obtain from the committees, as well as from the guardians, any contributions which they could fraudulently secure."[1]

In Norwich, experience has shown the value and absolute necessity of such co-operation. We must set out Mr. Lockwood's report in full.

"The only instance of an approach to the adoption of exceptional measures by a board of guardians for dealing with relief occurred at Norwich in January, 1889, when some 300 of the unemployed presented themselves at the relief offices and demanded relief. The relief committee, who were sitting at the time, in no way disconcerted by the unusual number of applicants, at once undertook to give relief to the extent and under the conditions which by the law and the regulations they are empowered to do. It is hardly too much to say that the firmness and judgment displayed by the relief committee under these exceptional and difficult circumstances gave an opportune and salutary check to a movement which, if unwisely or weakly dealt with at this juncture, might have had serious developments; but with respect to the details of this incident and as bearing on the unemployed question generally, I cannot do better than quote from a memorandum issued, and published in the local press in December last. The memorandum, after referring to what has been done in past winters in Norwich for the relief of distress, continues as follows:—

1. It is a very grave question whether the annual provision of special funds for the unemployed has not tended to increase pauperism and to discourage the invaluable habit of thrift.
2. The existence of such funds having become known, labourers from other districts have been attracted to the city in hope of getting help by joining 'The unemployed.'
3. The most serious evil, however, of the present administration of these funds is the extreme difficulty of distinguishing those who have deserved relief from the idle and undeserving. The local committees generally are dissatisfied with the present system, while two of them have intimated to the general committee that they must decline any further distribution of the funds unless adequate means can be adopted to sift the deserving from the undeserving cases. In illustration and proof of the imposition that has been practised, it may be stated that many of the cases dealt with by the local committees have, after subsequent investigation, been found totally undeserving of help.

"This experience of the District Visiting Society is also corroborated by that of the Board of Guardians. (See *Daily Press* report, January 15th, 1889.)

---

[1] 8 L.G.B., p. 135.

"On January 14th, 1889, a procession of the unemployed marched down to the guardians' office in St. Andrews, to seek the aid of the relief committee of the board; and a deputation from the main body was received by the committee, who were then sitting.

"They were told that as many as chose could come to work in the woodshop the next morning, and those who preferred to go to the workhouse could do so at once. Names were taken of all who were willing to do either, with the result that of the crowd, variously estimated to be from 200 to 400, only 88 were willing to accept either offer, 29 electing to go to the workhouse, and 59 to come to work. Of those who went to the house (nearly all single men), the whole, or nearly the whole, discharged themselves the next day. Of the 59 who should have come to chop wood, 48 came on Tuesday morning, 6 of whom did not return after the first day, 5 more worked two days, 5 others three days, and 8 only four days, so that by Saturday only 24 remained.

"Under these circumstances the committee of the District Visiting Society has anxiously and carefully considered afresh the whole question of the relief of the unemployed during the winter months, and it has been aided in its deliberations by deputations from the Board of Guardians and Labour Bureau.

"'The two objects which should be the sole aim of any system of temporary relief are:—

"'1. That no deserving case should be left without relief.
"'2. That no undeserving case should receive relief.

"'After prolonged deliberations we have come to the following resolutions, and we lay them at once before the public of Norwich as the principles on which alone we are prepared for the future to undertake the distribution of any fund intrusted to us:—

"'Lists of applicants, whose cases are not fully known to members of the local committees, shall be sent to the relief committee of the Board of Guardians, whilst the Labour Bureau will endeavour to procure work for those out of work.

"'By this arrangement we are sanguine that any funds which may be contributed for the unemployed shall reach their proper destination, and that the really necessitous and deserving poor shall neither be deprived of the relief they need and ought to obtain, nor shall the sum given in relief be lessened by the imposition of those who are unwilling to work for their living.

"'Knowing, as we do, the evils attending the indiscriminate distribution of charity, we respectively urge the public to intrust any monies intended for the relief of the poor in times of exceptional distress to the administration of the District Visiting Society and the Labour Bureau, who are now fully prepared to undertake such administration.'

"The memorandum quoted is signed by representatives of the Labour Bureau, the District Visiting Committee, and the Board of Guardians, and the opinion thus unanimously expressed by three independent bodies as the result of the work and experience of a succession of winters is a valuable addition to the evidence already to hand from other parts of the country of the evils likely to accrue from hasty appeals to the public for funds to meet occasional depression in the labour market and the difficulty attending the proper application of funds so contributed." [1]

Sometimes the guardians have themselves acted as almoners with advantage. In such cases the left hand knows what the right hand does, and the danger of over-lapping of relief is lessened. Thus :—

"In the Newcastle Union the charitable fund opened by the guardians in the winter months at the beginning of 1887 was found to have answered its purpose admirably in enabling them to meet deserving cases of distress, after strict inquiry, without pauperising the recipient; and a similar fund has been opened during the present winter" (1888). [2]

The following plan has been adopted with a certain amount of success by the Whitechapel Guardians. The board obtained in 1887 from the Local Government Board a modified workhouse test order. The effect of this was to permit the guardians to relieve the man in the workhouse, and to give out-door relief to the family while he was there; and afterwards to give an out-door allowance for a short period to the man and his family, to enable the man to look for and obtain work. We understand, however, that the board has not found it necessary to make any considerable use of the order. [3]

In the report of the Whitechapel Board of Guardians for the year ending Lady Day 1893, the opinion is expressed that "the system which seems adequately to meet the necessities of out-of-work cases, and to be at the same time conducive to the interests of the community, is in-door relief to the head of a family coupled with charitable aid to the wife and children, so as to keep a decent home intact. There would of course re-

---

[1] 19 L.G.B., pp. 113, 114.
[2] 17 L.G.B., p. 78.
[3] See "The Unemployed," *Charity Organisation Review*, January, 1894, p. 5.

main a further legitimate work for private charity in saving the more deserving from the Poor Law, and encouraging them in their efforts to achieve independence."[1] This course is followed in the St. George's-in-the-East Union. There, in cases which, after thorough inquiry and investigation, are found to be deserving of assistance in this way, charity keeps the home together while the husband is relieved in the workhouse.

Finally, we must draw attention to the valuable paper of Mr. George Macdonald, the clerk to the Manchester Board of Guardians, on Poor Relief during Depression of Trade, a paper which was read at the North-Western Poor Law Conference in 1879. His conclusions were drawn from the experiences of different large urban unions in dealing with the exceptional distress which occurred in the winter of 1878-79, and are absolutely in favour of the application of the workhouse test, and against the out-door labour test for the able-bodied, leaving *organised* charity working in close co-operation with the guardians to do the rest. He summarises his suggestions as follows:—

"1. That in times of pressure the cases of all applicants should be investigated with even greater care than in ordinary times, and that with that view prompt and efficient assistance should, where necessary, be provided for the relieving officers.

"2. That relief in the workhouse only should be given in all doubtful cases, as well as in those where there is no prospect of the applicant becoming self-supporting within a reasonable time.

"3. That no out-door relief be given to single able-bodied men.

"(In making this recommendation, Mr. Macdonald assumes that the inmates of the workhouse are properly classified, that strict discipline is maintained amongst them, and that a sufficient labour test is stringently enforced. Where these conditions do not exist the workhouse will in some cases fail to operate as a test.)

"4. That out-door relief be refused, as a rule, to able-bodied married couples without children, or having only one child.

"5. That out-door relief be not granted to single able-bodied women, except in special circumstances.

---

[1] Pp. xii., xiii.

"6. That the labour test be stringently enforced both for men and women; that a sufficient number of officers be engaged to superintend them while at work, and that, where necessary, sheds be erected in which the men could be set to work in inclement weather.

"7. That when temporary relief is given by a relieving officer to an able-bodied man the applicant be immediately set to work.

"8. That where the workhouse accommodation is insufficient, temporary arrangements should be made to extend it, or, at least, to make room for able-bodied inmates.

"9. That relief to the able-bodied should not, in any case, be given by the guardians in the form of wages.

"10. That the relief to able-bodied men be given in daily portions, and only on those days they have been at work, and that as large a proportion of it as possible be given in kind.

"11. That no able-bodied man be allowed to remain in the continuous receipt of out-door relief for a longer period than from two to three months.

"12. That should any charitable relief fund be raised in the union, the guardians should co-operate with the distributors of the fund, with the view to prevent imposition.

"13. That the distributors of the relief fund be recommended—

"(a) Only to give relief after careful investigation of the applicant's case;
"(b) Not to assist any person who is in receipt of relief from the guardians;
"(c) To refer all doubtful cases to the Board of Guardians;
"(d) To adopt measures for setting able-bodied recipients of the charity to work."

## CHAPTER XIV.

CAUSES AFFECTING INCREASE OR DECREASE OF PAUPERISM.

WHILE the amount of pauperism in an union depends so much on the mode of administering the Poor Law, we cannot deny that it may be affected to a considerable extent by strikes, epidemics of disease, commercial depression, severe weather, or other causes of exceptional distress. But it is easy to prove that these causes swell the number of paupers to a much greater extent in an union where out-door relief is laxly administered than in one where it is made the exception and not the rule.[1] In unions where out-door relief is lavishly given, the poor become dependent on it, and provident habits are discouraged. The contrary is the case in those unions where the difficulty of getting out-door relief has taught the poor to rely on themselves, and to make provision against times of difficulty and distress. If we examine the tables of the mean pauperism of the country for each year ending Lady Day,[2] we find that since 1870 the general improvement in Poor Law administration has been accompanied by a marked decrease of pauperism. This is entirely owing to a decrease in the number of outdoor paupers (from 880,730 in 1871 to 566,264 in 1893), for it has been accompanied by a comparatively small in-

---

[1] See Tables A, B, C, and D, *infra*, pp. 196, 197.
[2] See 22 L.G.B., pp. 264-269.

crease of 36,178 (from 156,178 to 192,512) in the number of in-door paupers.[1]

[1] *Cf.* Table A. The decrease of out-door pauperism since 1870 has been 35·7 per cent., and the increase of in-door pauperism 23 per cent. During the same period the population has also increased nearly 30 per cent. Thus there is no relative increase in-door pauperism.

The following figures show how the increase of 36,178 in in-door pauperism is distributed among the different classs of paupers :—

| Classes of Paupers. | Mean Pauperism for Year ending Lady Day, 1871. | | Mean Pauperism for Year ending Lady Day, 1893. | | Increase. | | Decrease. | | Total Increase. |
|---|---|---|---|---|---|---|---|---|---|
| | Able-bodied. | Not Able-bodied. | Able-bodied. | Not Able-bodied. | Able-bodied. | Not Able-bodied. | Able-bodied. | Not Able-bodied. | |
| Males (Adult) | 9,774 | 37,924 | 14,841 | 52,283 | 5,067 | 14,359 | — | — | 19,426 |
| Females (Adult) | 14,939 | 25,396 | 15,362 | 36,434 | 423 | 11,038 | — | — | 11,461 |
| Children under 16 | 17,994 | 34,442 | 13,203 | 37,034 | | 2,592 | 4,791 | — | [Dec. 2,199] |
| Totals | 42,707 | 97,762 | 43,406 | 125,751 | 5,490 | 27,989 | 4,791 | — | 28,688 |
| | 140,469 | | 169,157 | | 33,479 | | 4,791 | | 28,688 |
| Vagrants | 4,149 | | 6,561 | | 2,412 | | — | | 2,412 |
| Insane, viz. : | | | | | | | | | |
| Males | 4,848 | | 6,768 | | 1,920 | | — | | 1,920 |
| Females | 6,405 | | 8,793 | | 2,388 | | — | | 2,388 |
| Children | 466 | | 1,236 | | 770 | | — | | 770 |
| Grand Totals | 156,337 | | 192,515 | | 40,969 | | 4,791 | | 36,178 |

[NOTE.—The figures for the mean in-door pauperism of 1871 is given in 22 L.G.B., p. 264, as 156,430. This does not quite tally with the figures for July, 1870, and January, 1871, which are given on p. 260 as 144,594 and 168,073, the sum of these being 312,667, which, divided by 2, gives the correct mean number as 156,334. The mean in-door pauperism of 1893 is given correctly as 192,512. The slight difference between the true figures and those given in the table above is accounted for by the fact that in dividing a total by 2 in order to get the average of two numbers added together, the last numeral of the total when an odd figure has been raised to an even figure.]

The above table shows that the great increase in in-door pauperism has occurred in the numbers of the not-able-bodied, vagrants, and lunatics.

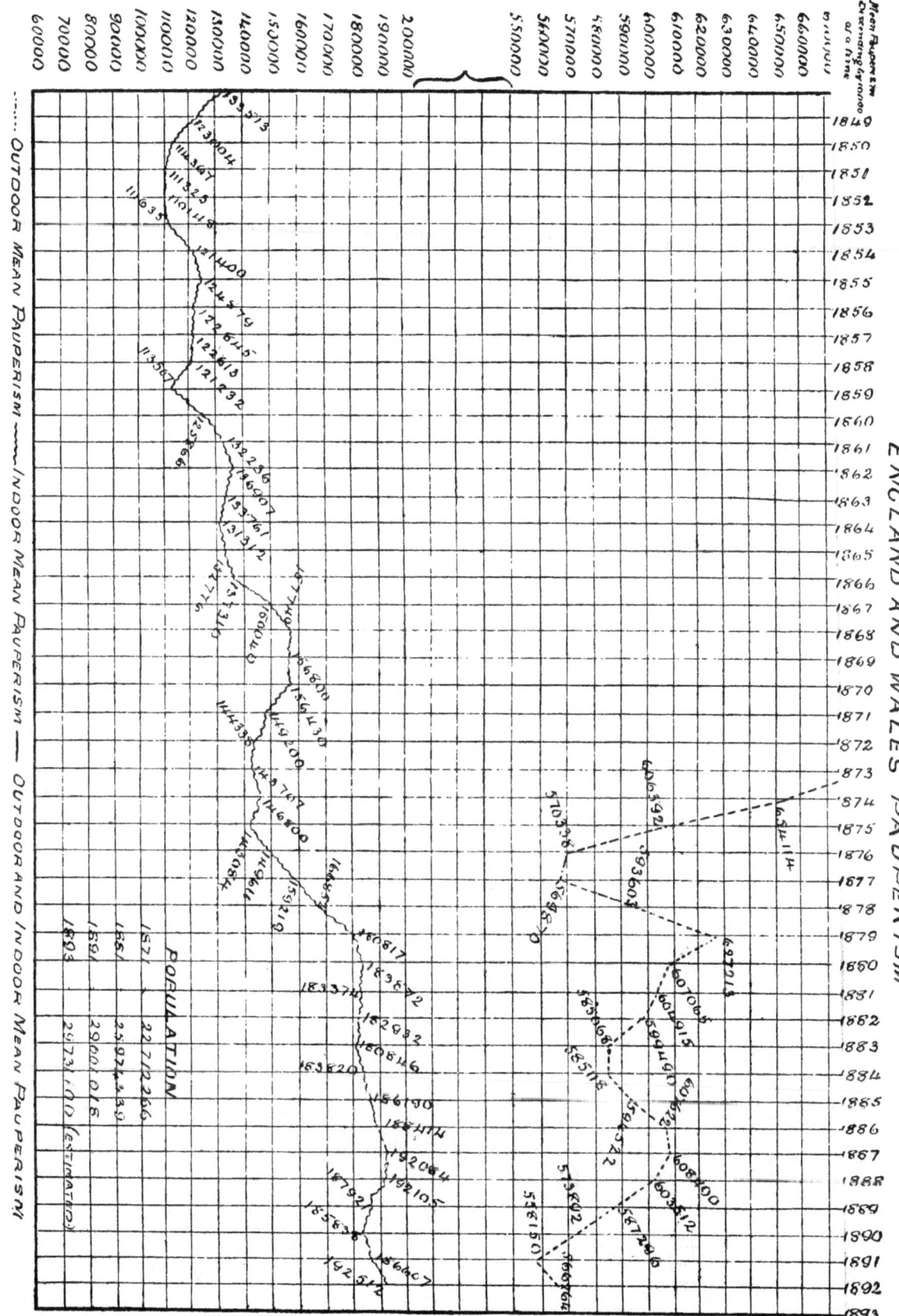

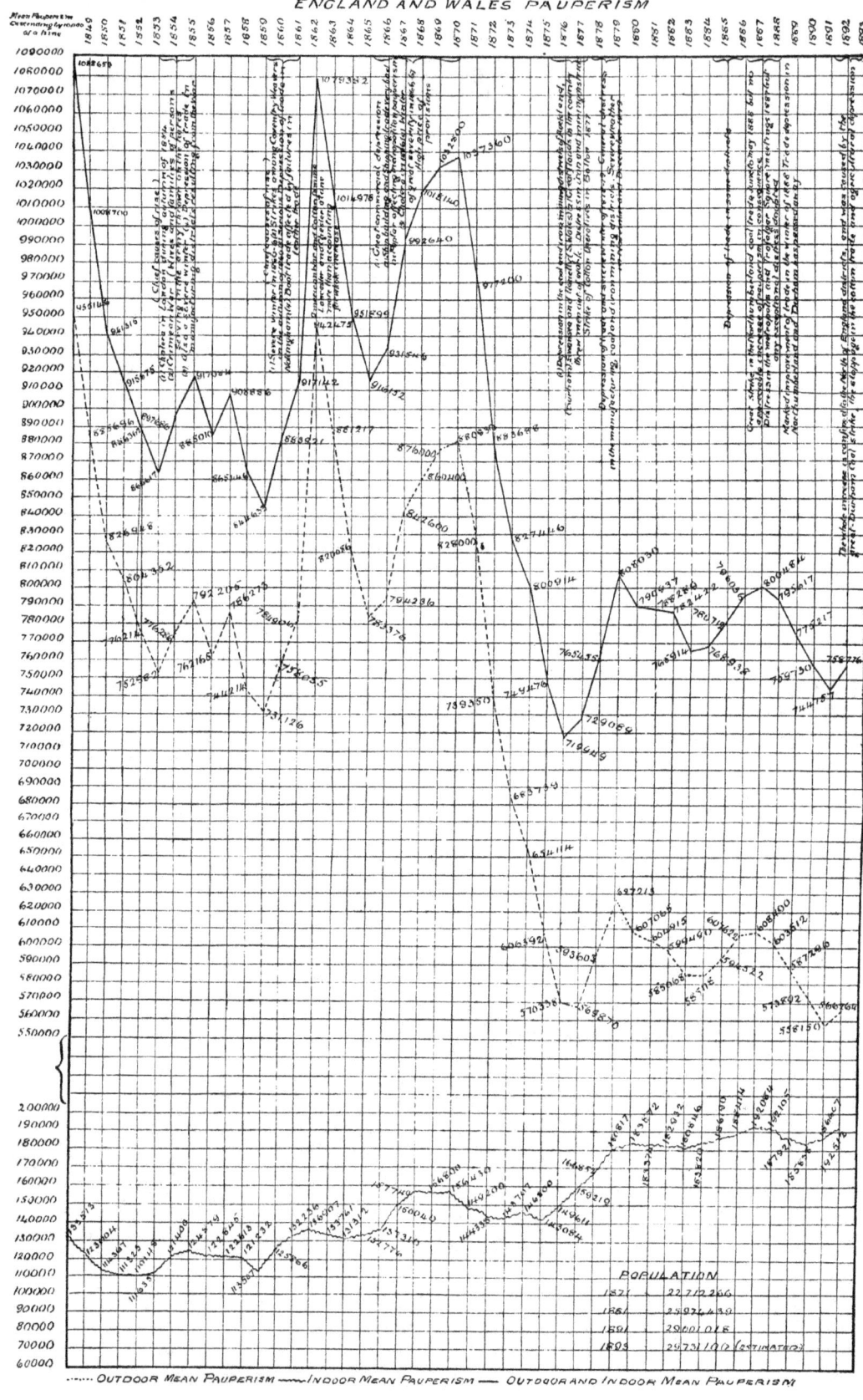

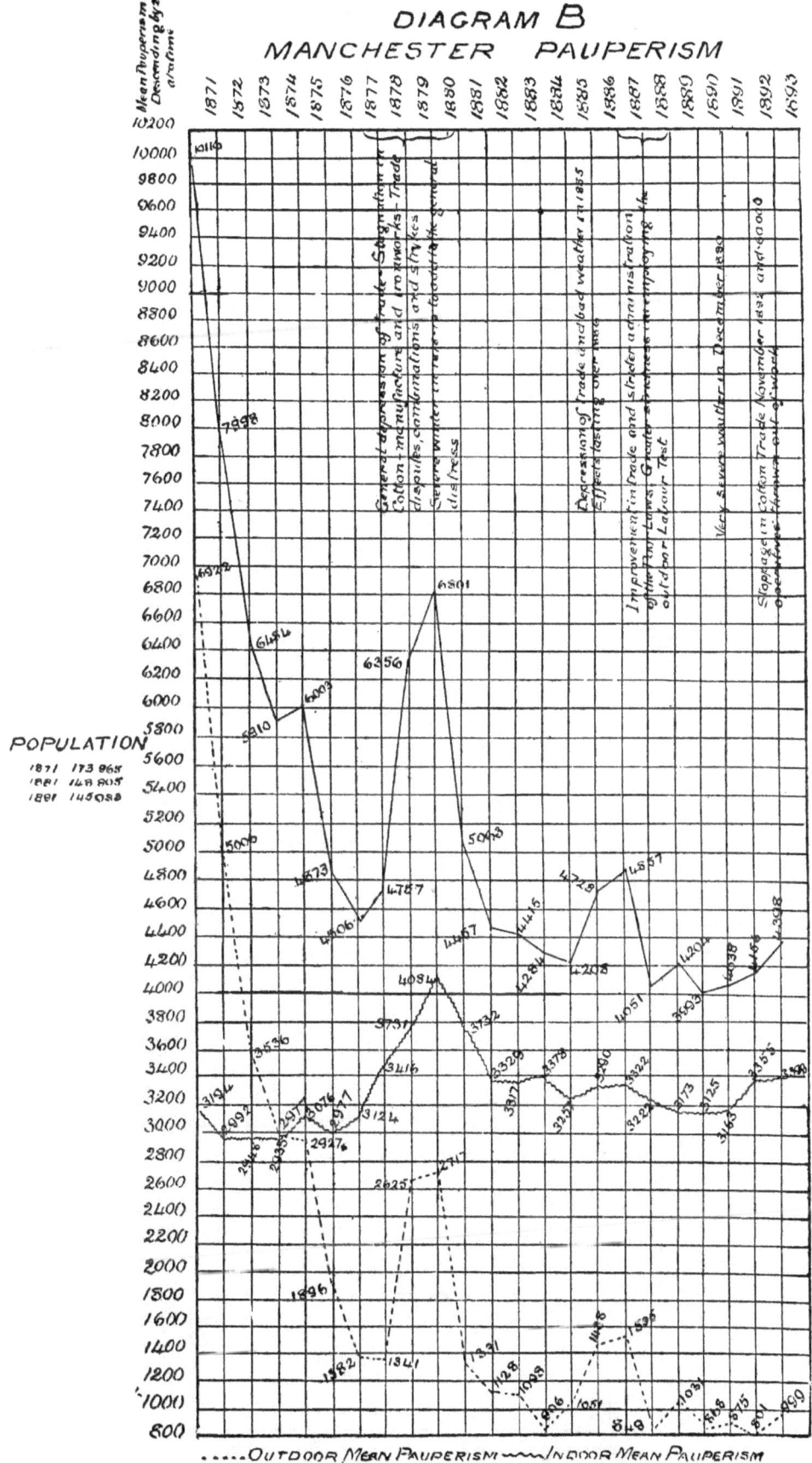

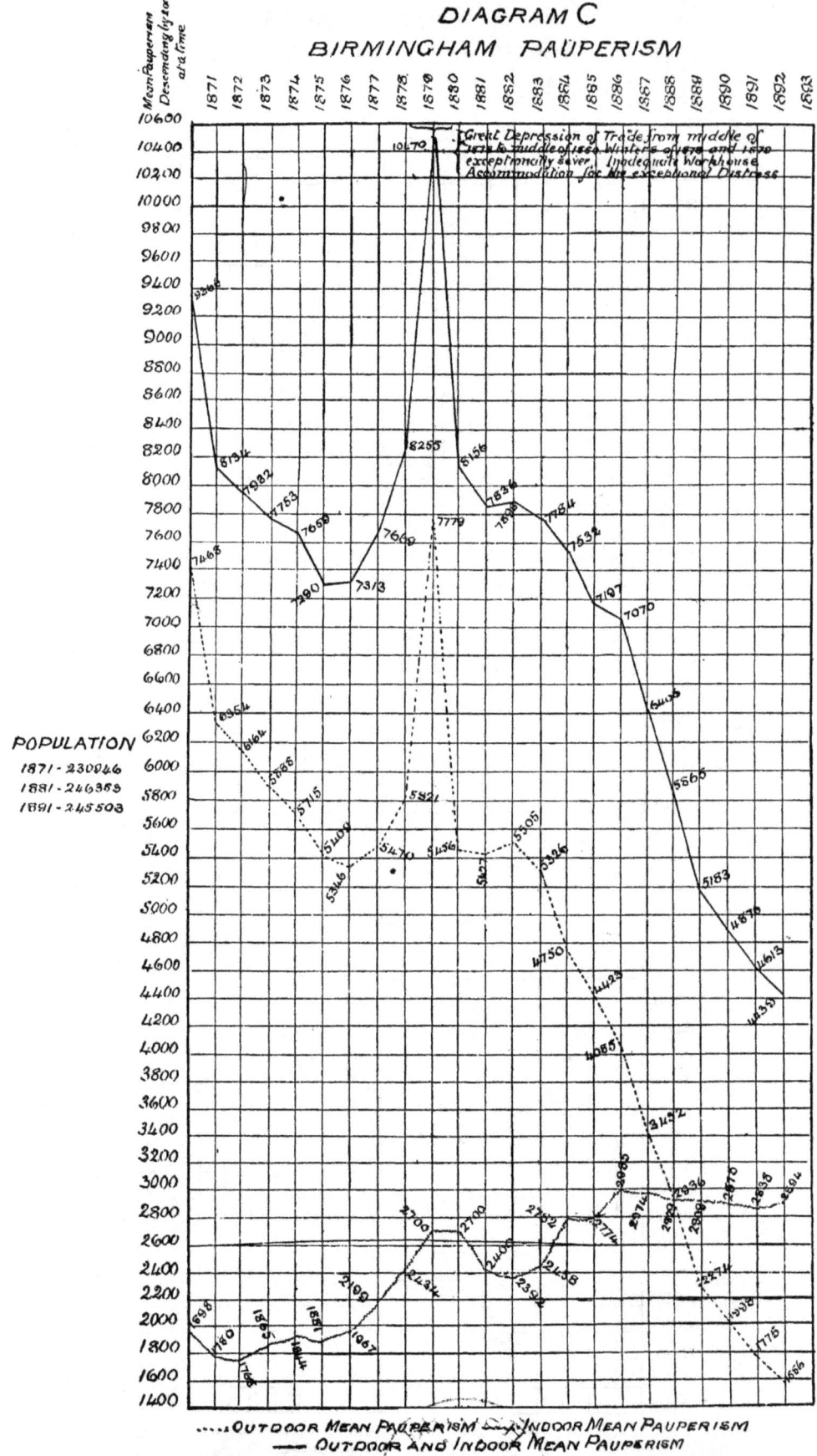

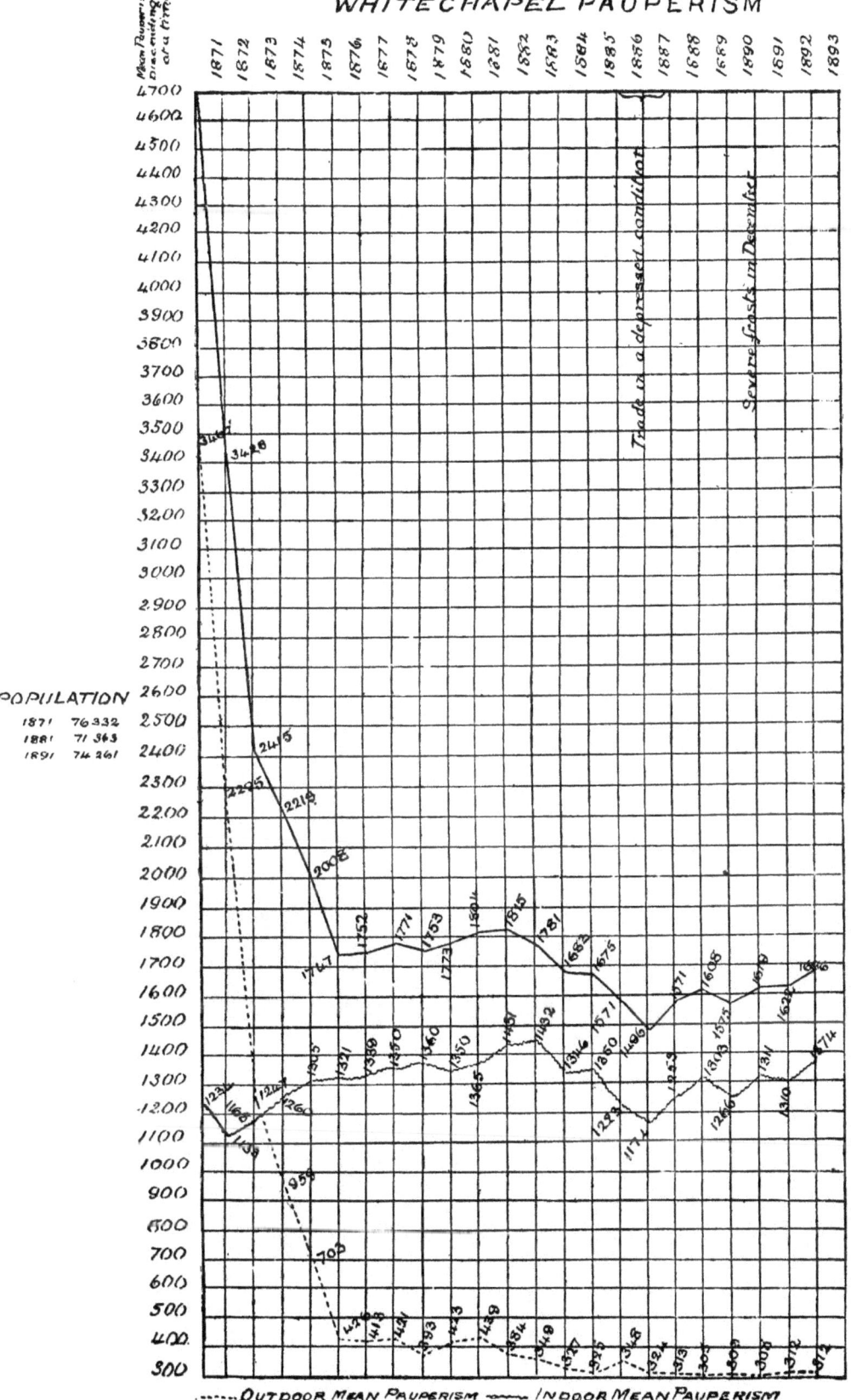

But in considering this increase of in-door pauperism, we have to take into account the attraction which the better management and greater comforts of the workhouse infirmaries offer to the sick poor. Unfortunately, the Returns do not give the increase in the number of this class, which, for the reason given, must be very large, and which must by no means be left out of account when a comparison has to be made between the present in-door pauperism and that of former years.

We have said that the amount of pauperism depends entirely on whether out-door relief is freely given or not. The statistical Tables show this most clearly. Table A shows the mean pauperism of England and Wales from 1849; Tables B, C, and D, show that of Manchester, Birmingham, and Whitechapel since 1870.

We have taken these three unions as typical ones, because their pauperism would be certain to be affected in times of depression of trade. We have also selected them because their boards of guardians have, since they reformed their method of administration, granted out-door relief very sparingly, and have used the workhouse test very freely.

Whitechapel altered its policy in 1870; Manchester adopted their out-door relief regulations in 1875, although its guardians were working more or less on the reformed method for about two years before that time; and Birmingham adopted its rules in 1885, but established its test house (see *supra*, p. 183) in 1880.

An examination of the four tables will show the following facts :—

(1) That the pauperism of the whole country and of particular unions depends upon the number of its out-door and not of its in-door paupers, in-door pauperism maintaining its level, or showing a slight and quite unimportant increase.

(2) That since Lady Day, 1887 (the year 1886-87 being

the first whole year since the rules came in force), the out-door pauperism of Birmingham has decreased 61 per cent., and the in-door pauperism 3 per cent., while the population remains stationary.

(3) That since 1873, Manchester has reduced its out-door pauperism by 72 per cent., as against an increase of in-door pauperism of only 15 per cent., and a decrease of population of 17 per cent.[1]

(4) That since 1871 Whitechapel has reduced its out-door pauperism by 91 per cent., increased its in-door pauperism by 11 per cent., while its population has only decreased 3 per cent. Since 1881, while there was an increase of population of 4 per cent., in-door pauperism has decreased 7 per cent., and out-door pauperism 18 per cent.

(5) That since 1870 (taking the estimated population in 1892) while the population of England and Wales has increased nearly 30 per cent., the out-door pauperism has decreased nearly 36 per cent., against an increase of in-door pauperism of only 23 per cent.; and that while since 1881 the population has increased by 13 per cent., out-door pauperism has decreased 6 per cent., against an increase of in-door pauperism of 5 per cent.

(6) That the restriction of out-door relief (as instanced by these three unions) does not materially increase the number of in-door paupers.

(7) That depression of trade, severe winters, strikes and lock-outs, do affect the amount of pauperism, but not nearly so much in unions where out-door relief is restricted, and where there is sufficient accommodation so as to employ the

---

[1] The township of Manchester contains a population almost entirely composed of the labouring class and a very large common lodging-house population, and the decrease in population has been caused by the emigration of the more respectable and better portion of the former. It thus contains a much poorer population than in 1881. (See First Annual Report of the Out-relief Department for the year ending March 25th, 1891.)

workhouse test, and not have to fall back on the stone or labour-yard.

And (8) That in consequence of all these facts, the policy of Poor Law administration should be to restrict the grant of out-door relief, and provide proper workhouse accommodation against times of distress.[1]

Mr. Lockwood has some interesting figures of the pauperism of his district, showing how the amount of it depends on out-relief being given with discrimination, and how "prosperity and depression are not necessarily directly reflected in the returns of pauperism."[2]

Referring to Table A, and taking the decade 1871-1881, we know that its earlier years were prosperous, while the others were seasons of great depression, and yet the number of out-door paupers mounts up very little. The expenditure, too, on out-door relief shows a steady decrease over the whole decade.[3] These two facts are evidence of much more careful administration.

But the amount of pauperism no doubt depends to a certain extent on other causes.

Thus severe weather has much to do with the rise and fall of the pauper barometer.[4]

Then the effect of depression of trade is to increase the number of applications for relief in cases of sickness, where the head of the family has hitherto been able to manage without recourse to the rates. It obliges a great number of aged

---

[1] If the numbers of lunatics and vagrants were not included in the returns of mean pauperism, the three unions in question would show up much better as compared with the whole of the country.

[2] 17 L.G.B., p. 61. See also Table D., *supra*.

[3] See 22 L.G.B., p. 327. The expenditure on out-relief was £3,663,970 and £2,660,022 for the years ending Lady Day 1871 and 1881 respectively.

[4] 21 L.G.B., p. 146. See also 8 L.G.B, p. 148, 23 L.G.B., p. 109, and Tables, *supra*, pp. 196, 197.

men and their families to come upon the rates for subsistence, and on which they are likely to remain a permanent charge. Such men, though scarcely able-bodied, can get their living in prosperous times, but there is naturally no chance of their being employed where there is a surplus of able-bodied labour.

Strikes and lock-outs, too, naturally affect pauperism.[1]

Thus Mr. Dansey says that owing to the great coal strike of 1893 the pauperism of his district (which includes Cheshire and part of Staffordshire) showed at the end of 1893 an increase of 1692—in-door 618, out-door 1074—as compared with the previous year.[2]

The counties of Durham and Northumberland, however, which did not take part in the strike, benefited by it. Thus Mr. Dawson tells us that:—

"The coal trade, which was at a very low ebb in the early part of the year, experienced an unexpected revival in the latter half in consequence of the great coal strike in other parts of England, the stoppage of work in Yorkshire and the Midland counties having at once created an immense demand for Durham and Northumberland coal. In the county of Durham, where the depression was the greatest, some pits had been temporarily closed, and many men thrown out of employment; but in consequence of the increased demand for coal the pits were re-opened and the men re-engaged."[3]

The strike in the Lancashire cotton trade began on the 5th November, 1892, and did not end until the 25th March, 1893.

"Beginning with the strike of some 45,000 hands, the stoppage gradually extended until ultimately it was estimated that no less than 125,000 hands were involved, while the loss of wages was considered to have been from £60,000 to £70,000 per week. No wonder that the dispute was described as the most costly that has ever taken place in the cotton trade of Lancashire. Inquiries addressed to several unions where the increase was most

---

[1] There was a great increase of pauperism in the North Riding of Yorkshire in the summer of 1892, entirely caused by the distress in Middlesborough which followed upon the Durham coal strike. See a review of the Twenty-second Report of the Local Government Board, which appeared in the February number of the *Charity Organisation Review*, 1894; also Mr. Dawson's report, 22 L.G.B., p. 97.

[2] 23 L.G.B., p. 117. See also *ib.*, pp. 116, 120, 122, 136, 143.

[3] *Ib.*, pp. 139, 140.

marked showed that this disastrous stoppage was the chief cause of the increased pauperism, though not the only one." ...... "At Ashton-under-Lyne the large increase of pauperism is attributed to the dispute in the cotton trade, which is assigned as the primary cause of increase in Barton-upon-Irwell."[1]

Mr. Murray Browne draws attention to the evil effects of strikes; owing to which old people, entirely dependant on able-bodied sons and relations, find their means of subsistence suddenly withdrawn.

"It would be well," he says, "if those responsible for strikes, at all events those of an unnecessary and unwarrantable kind, could come and see for themselves at the guardians' table the widespread misery that is inflicted by the stoppage of an industry like that of coal producing; they would see there how the blows which they intend for each other fall far more heavily on helpless and innocent people, on the old and the infirm, the sick and the disabled."[2]

The action of trades unions may also increase pauperism since their rules prevent men from working for anything under the full trade wage; and employers under the fair wages clause, now common in contracts, must protect themselves by employing none but men who are at their best.[3]

Another cause is undoubtedly the improvidence of so large a number of the poor, who never look beyond the "To-day."

This improvidence has been encouraged by the ease with which out-door relief can be obtained in most unions in cases of old age and sickness. But, as regards the able-bodied, the law forbidding them out-door relief has in a large measure contributed to the great increase in the membership of Friendly Societies since 1834.

We give the figures showing the increase in the membership of three great Friendly Societies, *viz.*, the Hearts of Oak, the Oddfellows, and the Foresters.

---

[1] 23 L.G.B., p. 128 (per Mr. Jenner-Fust.)    [2] *Ib.*, p. 143.
[3] 21 L.G.B., p. 146 (per Mr. Henley).

| Hearts of Oak (Established 1842). | | Oddfellows Manchester Unity (Established 1822). | | Ancient Order of Foresters (Re-organised 1834).[1] | |
|---|---|---|---|---|---|
| Date. | Members. | Date. | Members. | Date. | Members. |
| 31st Dec., 1852 | 2,180 | 1st Jan., 1852 | 225,194 | 1st Jan., 1852 | 88,687 |
| ,, ,, 1862 | 9,040 | ,, ,, 1862 | 335,145 | ,, ,, 1862 | 202,734 |
| ,, ,, 1872 | 32,837 | ,, ,, 1872 | 458,159 | 1st Dec., 1872 | 388,872 |
| ,, ,, 1882 | 98,873 | ,, ,, 1882 | 547,909 | 31st ,, 1882 | 501,883 |
| ,, ,, 1893 | 184,006 | ,, ,, 1894 | 722,725 | ,, ,, 1893 | 611,018 |

How much the Friendly Societies owe to the Poor Law, and how much the Poor Law owes to the Friendly Societies, it is impossible to say. The account probably balances.

Among the causes which have contributed to the *decrease* of pauperism besides improved administration, we must not omit to mention the low price of necessaries.

Mr. Bircham says :—

"I am confident that hundreds of families, the heads of which receive but very scanty wages, still manage to subsist without applying for relief owing to the low prices at which they can obtain the chief necessaries of life. Bread, bacon, cheese, and butter are cheaper than they have been for years, and the importation of the last three articles from America has had an effect very beneficial to the poorer classes of South Wales and Monmouthshire, as I have no doubt it has also had in other parts of the kingdom."[2]

Mr. Davy, writing in 1886, says :—

"The extraordinary low price of provisions is no doubt one of the main causes which explain the fact that pauperism has not materially increased in the rural unions."[3]

---

[1] The numbers given for the Foresters are only those of members resident in England and Wales. As regards the other two societies, the vast majority of the members are so resident, but we have not been able to get at the figures for the different nationalities. At the annual meeting of the A.M.C. at Northampton, it was stated that there were 84,869 members in the colonies in 1893.

[2] 8 L.G.B., p. 149.

[3] 15 L.G.B., p. 33.

## CHAPTER XV.

### SUGGESTED REFORMS.

(1) *As to restricting the Powers attaching to the Grant of Outdoor Relief.*

THE evils attaching to out-door relief are so apparent that it is no wonder that it has been often proposed to limit the present powers of boards of guardians with regard to the grant of it, and consequently to oblige them to apply the workhouse test more frequently. Thus, at the Central Poor Law Conference of 1876, the following resolution was passed :—

"That the conference requests the Local Government Board to make such further regulations for the administration of out-relief, and to introduce such legislative changes as they think conducive to the proper working of the Poor Law Amendment Act of 1834." [1]

A deputation subsequently waited on Mr. Sclater Booth, the then President of the Local Government Board, and made the following proposals :—

"1. That, in order to give better effect to the principle of the Poor Law, boards of guardians be empowered to frame by-laws, which, when duly approved by the Local Government Board, should have the force of orders until revoked by authority.

"2. That the liability for the maintenance of a pauper be extended to the grandsons of the pauper.

---

[1] 6 L.G.B., p. xxvi.

"3. That all relief be recoverable at the discretion of the guardians within a certain limit of time after the stopping of the relief.

"4. That a money value should be put on all medical relief in order that it may be recoverable.

"5. That power should be given to the justices in petty sessions, on the certificate of the medical officer of the district, to order the removal of an applicant, who is without lodging or accommodation, to the workhouse of the union.

"6. That no out-relief should be given for a longer period than thirteen weeks without fresh application.

"7. That boards of guardians be empowered, if they have not the power already under Section 13 of the Poor Law Amendment Act of 1876, to subscribe to the publication of the reports of the conferences held in the various Poor Law districts."[1]

As to 1, it was objected that by-laws connoted penalties which it would be difficult to enforce, and, further, if the power were granted, "it would inevitably tend to introduce variety and exceptional practices in the administration of relief, and in this manner would prevent the attainment of that uniformity which it was the object of the Poor Law Amendment Act to establish."[2]

As to 2, the President saw no objection to the proposal, and, in fact, a Bill has recently been introduced into Parliament to give effect to it.

As to 3, the President objected to it. Boards of guardians had already power to grant relief on loan, and it would be at variance with the policy of the existing law "if every recipient of relief were to feel that, after he again succeeded in obtaining employment, any savings he might be able to put by would be liable for the repayment of the relief which he might have received."

As to 4, the President did not think it feasible so long as

---

[1] 7 L.G.B., p. 52.

[2] Whether, however, there would be any less uniformity under the proposed system than there is at present is very doubtful, and the argument of the L.G.B. is rather a weak one. There could hardly, we think, be less uniformity of administration than there is under the existing Acts and Orders.

medical officers were paid by salary; and as to medical officers being paid by a separate fee for each case, so as to put a money value on the relief given, that practice had, "owing to the abuses and inconvenience with which it was attended, been generally abandoned."[1]

As to 5, the President thought the change contemplated would be beneficial in the case of "sick and infirm paupers or applicants for relief, who are without proper lodging or accommodation, and who refuse to go into the workhouse," but he was not prepared to go further than this.

*Note.*—It is astonishing that this reform should not have been made. There is an almost universal consensus of opinion in favour of it. In 1870, Mr. Goodlake, Chairman of the Farringdon Board of Guardians (Farringdon being at that time one of the best administered unions in the country), stated his views as follows:—

> "The great defect, in my opinion, of the present administration of the Poor Law is that there exists no power to compel paupers, on a certificate from the medical officer, to receive relief in the workhouse. I have known scores of cases of semi-idiotic helpless creatures, living alone in wretched filthy hovels, absolutely refuse the comforts of our infirmary, and, for the want of the power I speak of, dragging out an existence which we are incapable of mitigating."[2]

Mr. Longley's opinion is that,

> "The only absolutely certain and universal solution of the difficulty in question, is probably to be found in the compulsory admission to the work-

---

[1] But see *ante*, p. 123, as to the system in force in Bradfield. As regards the Metropolis, Mr. Henley suggests, "that a scale of salary to be paid to the several officers of Poor Law establishments out of the Metropolitan Common Poor Fund, should be fixed by the board, as is now the case with relieving officers, and that guardians should have power, with the sanction of the board, to give any further remuneration as the reward of merit or long service out of the funds of their own union. I believe what is now frequently the cause of a considerable amount of friction between the central and the local authority would be thereby avoided." (See 16 L.G.B., p. 56.)

[2] 23 P.L.B., p. 100.

house of applicants, whose refusal to enter it voluntarily is likely to be suicidal, or destructive of the life and health of their families.

"This suggestion, novel and somewhat startling as it may appear, has been made to me on several occasions by individual guardians, and has been mentioned with favour at meetings of boards of guardians which I have attended. I was disposed, in the first instance, to regard the object proposed by it as unattainable, however desirable it might on some grounds appear to be. On further consideration, however, I am inclined to think that, though at present such a step in the direction of compulsory admission to and detention in a workhouse would be neither practicable nor altogether expedient, some such modification of in-door relief may, perhaps, be anticipated, as a specific result in the future of the mutual effect on each other of public opinion and a strict administration of the Poor Law.

"For a sound and, consequently, a successful administration of the law tends to conciliate public opinion, which in turn is found to strengthen the hands of those who administer the law in their further progress. Some such progress as this has rendered it possible to confer upon guardians the powers of compulsory detention of casual paupers lately entrusted to them by the Pauper Inmates Discharge and Regulation Act. A few years ago, and before the successful results of a more stringent course of dealing with paupers of this class had become notorious, no such proposal could, probably, have been made with any prospect of success.

"The precedent thus set applies closely to the suggested extension of the principle of compulsory residence in a workhouse, and if the poor be gradually induced by a course of strict administration of the law to rely, as a matter of right, upon none but in-door relief, and if the dispensers of private charity will exercise their peculiar function of mitigating the necessary severity of the Poor Law, by coming to the aid of deserving applicants for relief, who are unwilling to receive it in a workhouse :—If by such means as these, the number of cases to be further dealt with be, as no doubt it will be, reduced to a minimum, it may be found practicable to provide that in certain cases an application for relief should be taken to be a constructive self-commitment to the workhouse for, at least, a prescribed time, or until the pauper can show that he has a reasonable prospect of procuring a maintenance elsewhere. The system under which able-bodied applicants for relief in the city of New York are said to 'commit themselves' to the workhouse for a period of three months, which has been described in a report of my visit to some of the American pauper institutions, may be cited as illustrating this suggestion."[1]

As to 6, the President entirely approved of the suggestion, but no legislative action has resulted.

As to 7, the Poor Law Conference Act, 1883, permits the subscription.

The same deputation further suggested certain alterations to

---

[1] 3 L.G.B., pp. 173, 174.

be made in the Out-door Relief Prohibitory Order of 1844, and that the Order should be made universal.[1]

"Art. 1. That a proviso be added that relief, if granted under Exception 2, which relates to relief in cases of sickness, accident, or bodily or mental infirmity, should not be granted for a longer period than one month at a time.

"Art. 1., Exception 3. That where relief is given to defray the expenses of burial, the funeral should be wholly undertaken by the guardians, or not at all.

"That Exception 4, which allows out-door relief to a widow during the first six months of her widowhood, should be omitted.

"That Exception 5, allowing out-door relief to a widow with a legitimate child or children dependent upon her, and incapable of earning their livelihood, and having no illegitimate child born after the commencement of her widowhood, should be restricted; and that the Local Government Board should, by instructional letter or otherwise, recommend, instead of giving out-relief, the plan of relieving widows with dependent children by taking some of the children into the workhouse or district school, stating the conditions and securities under which this course is desirable.

"That Exceptions 6, 7, and 8, which allow out-door relief to the wives and children of persons in gaol, or serving as soldiers or sailors, or being non-resident within the union, should be omitted.

"Art. 3. That no relief be given to non-residents, and that all exceptions to the article be rescinded, excepting 3 and 6, relating to suspended orders of removal and education."

As to Art. 1, a fear was expressed "that to impose any such restriction upon sick relief as that proposed would be attended with considerable danger. It cannot be foreseen how long sickness may last, and the relief might be discontinued at a time of the utmost importance, such as a critical moment or when an operation was urgent, because the appointed time had arrived;" and for these reasons the President could not agree with the suggestion.

As to Art. 1., Exception 3 : Section 31 of the 7 and 8 Vict., ch. 101, was an obstacle, and it would probably over-ride the proposed order. "Besides, it is impossible to allow a pauper to remain unburied, however unreasonable the relatives may be. If the guardians were more strict in their inquiries before

---

[1] 7 L.G.B., p. 52.

making allowances for funeral expenses, they would probably be able to effect to a considerable extent the object of this proposal." [1]

As to Art. 1, Exception 5, the President considered the proposal impracticable.

"A widow, with or without children, could not, on the death of her husband, in all cases be required to go into the workhouse, and if an absolute regulation was made to this effect, it could not fail to excite very strong feelings of hostility and opposition.

"It may be that the period of six months now allowed is too long, but the President as at present advised is not prepared to shorten it, preferring that the guardians should exercise their discretion in dealing with each case according to its merits.

"The President will not object to recommend that in certain cases where widows with children apply for relief, an offer should be made to take some of the children into the workhouse; but it must be borne in mind that since the passing of the Elementary Education Acts, this offer as a test of destitution has not the same effect as previously, inasmuch as the children being required to attend school, the mothers cannot have the benefit of any earnings which otherwise their children might obtain."

As to Art. 1, Exceptions 6, 7, and 8, the President agreed that it was

"inexpedient to allow out-door relief to the wives and children of persons who are in gaol, especially those who are under sentence; but the law has provided that regulations prescribed in regard to widows shall apply to the wives in these cases, and for this reason it would not be practicable to lay down the absolute rule suggested; and as regards the withdrawal of Exception 6, it must be observed that it affects the general subject of the military and naval service of the country, and cannot be dealt with without the concurrence of those departments of the State.

"Exception 7 is only a technical provision, which deals with legal liability, and if repealed might cause some embarrassment in regard to the legal liabilities of the husbands of paupers."

[*Note.*—Mr. Courtenay Boyle, speaking of his own district, says that there no difficulties would arise " by forbidding all non-resident out-relief, all out-relief to able-bodied widows with one child dependent, and all out-relief to wives of militiamen on duty, and of persons in custody of the law." [2]]

---

[1] See *supra*, p. 95, as to the practice in the Atcham Union.
[2] 8 L.G.B., p. 110.

As to Art. 3, the President quite concurred in the suggestion.

With regard to making the Prohibitory Order universal, the President thought that this proposal could not be safely or properly adopted.

"The Order is now in force in all the rural unions of the country, and in many urban unions also, and the Board continue to apply its provisions from time to time to other unions as often as the circumstances enable them to do so, but it has never been attempted to apply the provisions of the Order to the Metropolis, or those centres of manufacturing industry where large numbers of persons are periodically thrown out of employment by sudden and extensive depressions of trade.

"It is obvious that if the Order were extended to these places, it would be necessary to suspend it whenever the periods referred to might happen to recur, and there is nothing more calculated to weaken the force of the regulations of the Board than to be obliged to abrogate them whenever a period of pressure arises.

"The President has the less hesitation in adhering to the policy which the Board have hitherto pursued in this respect, as he finds that both in the Metropolis and some of the unions in the manufacturing districts, such for instance as Manchester, the administration of relief is ordinarily conducted upon principles quite as stringent as those laid down in the Order in question, and in a manner which would serve as an example for many of those unions in which the Order has long been in force."

[*Note.*—The difficulty, of course, in the way of applying the Prohibitory Order to large towns is that their workhouse accommodation is generally insufficient, so that in times of exceptional distress they are unable to apply the workhouse test.]

Mr. Longley deals with the question with his usual acumen and force,[1] and his arguments apply to large towns as well as to the Metropolis.

He thinks that the difficulty arising from insufficient accommodation might be met by the issuing of a new Order

"Which shall combine the prohibitory clauses of that Order[2] (extended perhaps to the case of a widow, having no more than one legitimate child, applying for relief after the first six months of widowhood)

---

[1] 3 L.G.B., pp. 178-179.   [2] *i.e.*, The Prohibitory Order.

with the provisions of the Supplemental Labour Test Order, and in which some provisions of the Out-relief Regulation Order (which should be rescinded) shall be embodied (*e.g.*, Art. 3)."

He rests this recommendation on the broad grounds that

"Inasmuch as at the instigation of the Board individual boards of guardians, aided by the expression of public opinion, have voluntarily made substantial progress, by the abandonment of the out-door labour test, towards a formal and decided advance in Poor Law administration, it is for the Board, in the exercise of its exclusive and most important function, not only to embody and to realise for general dissemination the scattered results of individual experience, and to constitute the successful efforts of one board of guardians the standard and measure of the practice of their neighbours, but, further, to register and to give permanence to the progress which has been already made, and to secure it, as a step towards a further advance against the fluctuations of opinion and of constitution incident to local bodies, by means of an Order which shall nevertheless have been suggested by their independent action.

"This no board of guardians, however firmly they may adhere to sound principles, can do for themselves; they are unable to impose a binding rule of practice upon themselves, much less upon their successors, and I cannot but think that the intervention of the Board in such a case is aptly characterised in the pregnant remark recently made in my hearing at a Poor Law conference by an active guardian, 'We look to the Local Government Board to save us from ourselves.'"

A reform which has been for a long time advocated is that of granting boards of guardians greater powers as to detaining paupers in the workhouse.

Mr. Henley says:—

"The discharge of workhouse inmates is at present regulated by the provisions of 34 and 35 Vict., ch. cviii., s. 4. For the words 'twenty-four hours,' 'forty-eight hours,' 'seventy-two hours' in that section I would substitute the words, 'seven days,' 'fourteen days,' 'twenty-one days.' There is a considerable, and, I fear, an increasing number of paupers who are in the habit of constantly going in and out of the workhouse, thereby giving a great deal of trouble to the officials, and causing a large amount of extra book-keeping. They are, for the most part, undeserving characters. I see no reason why it should not be made a condition of in-door relief that a person should not be entitled to claim his discharge under a week."[1]

And further:—

"I must again refer to the vast amount of labour and trouble given to

---

[1] 16 L.G.B., p. 56.

workhouse masters and other officials by the practice on the part of certain inmates, chiefly of the so-called able-bodied class, of constantly discharging themselves and again seeking re-admission, often on the evening of the day of their discharge. At the workhouse of St. George's Union, Fulham Road, there have been 17,309 discharges and 17,381 admissions during the year. One man discharged himself no fewer than ninety-three times, being nearly always re-admitted on the evening of the day of his discharge. His only lengthened absence from the workhouse was when he was undergoing 21 days' imprisonment. I cannot but think that this is an abuse of Poor Law Relief."[1]

Another reform advocated is that there should be other means of compelling children to support their destitute parents without necessarily making the latter chargeable to the parish, and we are glad to see that a Bill has been introduced into Parliament with this intention.[2] Mr. Baldwyn Fleming draws attention to the subject. He says:—

"The 43 Eliz. places upon certain members of a family the duty of maintaining 'at their own charges' their impotent relations in that manner and according to that rate as by the justices shall be assessed. In practice, however, it is now necessary that a person must be actually chargeable before an order of justices can be made. In other words, supposing a father have several rich sons who will not support him, he cannot himself obtain an order for them to do so, but he must apply to the union authorities to make him a pauper, in order that the guardians may be able to put the law in motion. And further, supposing this to be done, the liability upon the sons determines directly the father ceases to be chargeable, and the proceedings would have to commence *de novo* if he became chargeable again. These results are sufficiently unsatisfactory, but do not exhaust the possibility of defeating the statute of Elizabeth.

"A case actually occurred during the past year where a man earning good wages, in the Isle of Purbeck, threw himself out of work for several days in the week, so that he might not earn enough to warrant an order of justices upon him to contribute to the support of his father. Although the man was of 'sufficient ability' to contribute, he defeated the order of the guardians by wilfully refusing to earn more than would suffice for his own keep; it being held that it was insufficient to prove that he could earn plenty of money if he chose, but that before an order could be made it was necessary to show that he actually had the money and refused to spend it in support of his father. This was doubtless an unusually unworthy instance, though not so uncommon as might be supposed. It does, in truth, seem a

---

[1] 19 L.G.B., p. 107.
[2] Maintenance of Destitute Parents Bill (Bill 250 of Session of 1891).

bad state of the law that, although children and parents are liable for their mutual support, and may be perfectly able to discharge that liability, they cannot be compelled to do so unless the needy person be pauperised and the law set in motion by the guardians; and further, that a subsequent order for support may be defeated by a wilful refusal to work.

"By this means many persons are made paupers who ought not to be destitute at all, and would not be so if the orders for maintenance could be made upon the plaint of the individual needing assistance, and could be enforced by punishment if disregarded."[1]

Mr. Knollys considers that the persistent neglect of sick or aged parents by "their children is one of the great evils of the age, requiring the strict attention of administrators of Poor Law relief."[2]

It is sad that army pensioners should so largely swell the numbers of paupers. The pensions are paid quarterly, and the money is often spent within a few hours after it is received. It would be an advantage if some better mode of paying these pensions should be established. It surely would not be difficult to pay them in weekly instalments through the Post-office. Mr. Baldwyn Fleming's remarks on the present system are as follows :—

"Another class which ought not to swell the numbers of paupers is that of pensioners. Pensioners are now only paid quarterly, and the result is that the provision which should ensure independence as the reward of brave service is frequently a ready inducement to the degradation of pauperism.

"A man who could have no reason for becoming a pauper if he had 7s. a week is in a totally different position if he receives nearly £5 in a lump sum at the end of the quarter. I am aware of the alleged difficulties and expense of altering the arrangements for the payment of pensions, but they fail to convince me that the alteration is not practicable and desirable.

"I think *every* effort should be made to keep pensioners above the shame of pauperism, and to prevent their names from appearing on the pauper list. It may be said that this is not a matter of much importance, as guardians can attach the pensions and prevent loss to the rates; but it is of the first importance to teach the lower classes of society the value of thrift and self-reliance, and the disgrace of coming upon the rates for their support.

---

[1] 18 L.G.B., pp. 115, 116.
[2] 19 L.G.B., p. 132.

"Parents and children who can be maintained by their children and parents, and pensioners whose pay is sufficient for their keep, ought not to be paupers, and any change in the present practice which would tend to save them from this disgrace would be advantageous to society, and would well repay whatever amount of trouble might be necessary to bring it about."[1]

It is possible that in some unions (especially urban ones) the application of the workhouse test might be assisted if some provision were made for the storage of the pauper's furniture while he is in the workhouse. Thus the alleged hardship—an imaginary one in our opinion—of "breaking up the home" might be obviated. This system was adopted by the Manchester Guardians, and worked successfully.[2]

In order to lead guardians to apply the workhouse test more frequently than they do, the following proposals mentioned by Mr. Courtenay Boyle have often been made:—

"1. A modification of chargeability throwing the cost of in-maintenance over a larger area, of out-relief over a smaller one, by making for instance the in-maintenance a county charge, leaving out-relief as now a union charge, or (less preferable) by making in-maintenance a union, and out-relief a parochial expense.

"2. An imperial grant per week per head for every pauper maintained in a properly certified workhouse, infirmary or school."[3]

He says that the first proposal has been adopted in the Metropolis with beneficial results, and would possibly have the good effect of making the county the managing authority of all Poor Law institutions; and that the second proposal has been described by several of the most experienced guardians and relieving officers in the district as the method which would do more than any other to check unnecessary out-relief; and to the objection that pauperism is a local and not an imperial matter it may be urged that Parliament has sanctioned a grant in respect of pauper lunatics, that from in-door pauperism it is scarcely possible for the country to be wholly free, and that such a scheme would bring under further contribution that

---

[1] 18 L.G.B., p. 116.   [2] 2 L.G.B., d. 8.   [3] 8 L.G.B., p. 110.

large proportion of property which, though paying no rates, derives much benefit from local prosperity.

Mr. Baldwyn Fleming has answered those who desire a greater stringency in the regulations regarding out-door relief, and his remarks have undoubtedly great force.[1] We have already quoted them (*supra*, p. 99). He says that all that is needed is the steady and intelligent application of the powers which guardians already possess.

It is indeed a dangerous thing to go in advance of public opinion, by laying down rules as to the advantages of which it is not convinced. Boards of guardians have been learning by experience how necessary it is to restrict the grant of out-door relief to its narrowest limits, and the statistics of pauperism are irrefutable evidence of the extraordinary progress which has been made during the last twenty-two years. It is something to reflect upon with pride that the pauperism of the country has fallen from 46·5 per 1000 in 1870 to 25·8 per 1000 in 1893;[2] and the small increase shown during the last two years is merely temporary, and entirely accounted for by the unfortunate and calamitous strikes and lock-outs which have taken place. As Mr. Davy says:—

> "The current administration must be improved to the highest point before any general policy of restriction could have any chance of even a temporary success; and as such a policy would be unpopular among certain classes—not probably the labouring classes—the guardians must, in self-defence, take care that there is nothing to be said against their machinery of relief. Then, apart from all question of general policy, as the administration approaches the highest standard, the proportion of out-door relief will diminish, for the simple reason that, not only will the cases who are not destitute be discovered and struck off the lists, but the guardians, as their knowledge of the circumstances of each case increases, will come to realise how impossible it is to adequately relieve a large proportion of them by any grant of out-relief."[3]

---

[1] 20 L.G.B., pp. 226, 227.      [2] See 22 L.G.B., p. 266.
[3] 22 L.G.B., pp. 71, 72. The full quotation from Mr. Davy's Report will be found *supra*, pp. 76-78.

## CHAPTER XVI.

### GENERAL REMARKS ON POOR LAW ADMINISTRATION, AND CONCLUSION.

WE have tried to show in the preceding chapters how absolutely necessary it is to administer out-door relief, in whatever form it may be given, very discriminately. The evidence is overwhelming that, all things being otherwise equal, those unions which make the getting of out-door relief most difficult have the least pauperism and the lowest poor rates. This was so before 1870, and it is the case now. But it is only since 1870 (as we have shown) that the principles of the report of 1834 have come to be more generally admitted. Few unions were working on those principles previously to 1870,[1] whereas a great many are doing so now, and their good example is being more and more followed.

"The true object of a sound administration of the Poor Law is to administer relief so as to offer the minimum of discouragement to the formation by the poor of provident and independent habits. The substitution of this system for the lax system which has too commonly prevailed, has been universally and uniformly followed, as a direct and obvious consequence, by a diminution of pauperism. This, which is the more tangible and immediate result of a recourse to sound principles of administration, and which is, indeed, a secondary and subordinate object of their application, is thus frequently assumed to be the exclusive aim, as it is the readiest test, of the success of the sounder system which is gradually, though slowly, gaining ground. It seems almost superfluous to prove that a system which, while it ensures adequate and full relief to the destitute, offers it in such a form as to discourage in-

---

[1] *E.g.* Atcham and Farringdon among others. (See 23 P.L.B., p. 100.)

dolence in the able-bodied, and improvidence in all classes of applicants, must tend directly, if it be not paralysed by a co-existing system of recognised mendicancy and indiscriminate almsgiving, not only to diminish pauperism, but to lead and stimulate the poor to independence."[1]

Mr. Longley is very cautious about relying implicitly on statistics, and especially at the time he was writing (1873), when the rebound in the labour market, the rise in wages, and the partial cessation of the previous immigration of the poorer classes from the country into London had materially contributed to the decline of its pauperism.

"The following statement, however, which has come to my notice during the preparation of this report, may be cited with some confidence as a definite and substantial proof of the success of a very abrupt change in the course of administration followed in a union in the east of London, in which the guardians have for the last few months applied the workhouse test to a large proportion of the applications made to them for relief. And this, not only because the change in question was so marked in point of time as to render it possible to connect it definitely with the consequent and equally marked decrease in the pauperism of the union, but also, because it has taken place within the last twelve months, and so long after the other causes which have contributed to the general decrease of pauperism in London had commenced to operate in the union in question, as to make it possible in a great measure to discriminate between their effects and those of the efforts which have been recently made by the guardians.

| | |
|---|---:|
| Number in the workhouse— | |
| 1st week August, 1872 | 720 |
| ,,           1873 | 808 |
| Increase | 88 |
| Number in receipt of out-relief— | |
| 1st week August, 1872 | 2584 |
| ,,           1873 | 1366 |
| Decrease | 1218 |
| Deduct increase of in-door | 88 |
| Net decrease of paupers | 1130 |

[1] 3 L.G.B., p. 198.

Cost of out-relief—

| | | | |
|---|---|---|---|
| 1st week August, 1872 ... ... ... | £164 | 13 | 10 |
| ,, 1873 ... ... ... | 90 | 16 | 0 |
| Decrease | 73 | 17 | 10 |
| Cost of 88 additional inmates of the workhouse at 4s. 2d. per week ... ... | 18 | 6 | 8 |
| Saving in one week's relief (*i.e.*, at the rate of £2889 per annum) ... ... ... | £55 | 11 | 2 |

He adds in a note that the progress thus made in this union has been maintained, as shown by the following statement for the week ended 4th April, 1874, which, like that in the text of his Report, gives the result of a comparison with the corresponding week in the previous year:

| | |
|---|---|
| Decrease of numbers in the workhouse ... ... ... | 61 |
| Decrease of out-door paupers ... ... ... ... | 1219 |
| Total decrease | 1280 |

The decrease in the total number of paupers chargeable is at the rate of 34 per cent.

| | | | |
|---|---|---|---|
| Decrease in the cost of out-relief given in the week (*i.e.*, at the rate of £3522 per annum) | £67 | 14 | 4 |

But now we have statistics covering a considerable number of years, and it is most satisfactory to find that the decrease of pauperism is general all over the country.

As regards *able-bodied pauperism*,[1] the great decrease has taken place since 1870, a decrease of no less than 43 per cent.; whereas, between 1850 and 1870, the decrease was only 6 per cent. This decrease since 1870 has been most marked in the case of *female* able-bodied paupers, and has actually been accompanied by a decrease in the numbers of this class relieved inside the workhouses.[2]

---

[1] See Appendix B, p. 226, for figures.
[2] 63,151 widows were receiving relief on the 1st January, 1871, as against 52,441 on the 1st January, 1849; but only 37,124 widows were

As regards *not-able-bodied pauperism*,[1] a considerable decrease is to be noticed since 1870. The numbers of them rose from 337,578 on the 1st January, 1849, to 451,810 on the 1st January, 1871; but they had sunk again to 355,078 on the 1st January, 1893 (a decrease of 21 per cent.). Improved administration has thus had the effect of reducing this class of pauperism, and while there was 1 not-able-bodied pauper to every 45 of population on the 1st January, 1849, the proportion was 1 in 83 on the 1st January, 1893. The large *absolute* decrease since 1870 leads us to hope that a continuance in our present policy of administering the Poor Law may in no very long time reduce not-able-bodied pauperism to a comparatively small amount.[2]

One of the happiest results attending the decrease of adult pauperism is the decrease in the number of pauper children by which it is naturally accompanied.[3] Since 1850 the number of them has decreased from 382,720 to 236,185 (nearly 40 per cent.). Still more satisfactory is the great reduction in the numbers of illegitimate children relieved, from 17,305 to 6470 (no less than 62 per cent.). There is a small *absolute* increase (though not a *relative* one if the increase of population be taken into account) in the numbers of orphan and deserted children; but the fact is indicative of improved administration, and of greater attention bestowed upon them.

If we turn now to the expenditure on poor relief, and consider the immense improvements which have been made for the comfort, care, and treatment of all classes of paupers, and especially of the infirm, the sick, and the insane, it is a subject for congratulation that although there had been an *absolute*

---

receiving relief on the 1st January, 1893. (See further, chapter xi., p. 138.)

[1] See Appendix C, p. 227, for figures.
[2] See Chapter XI., pp. 132-138.
[3] See Appendix D, p. 228, for the figures.

increase of expenditure, it has not kept pace with the increase of population. In other words, *the burden of taxation for poor relief purposes is less than it was forty years ago*, while the wealth of the country has greatly increased during the same period. The tables of expenditure set out in the Appendix [1] will be found to present many interesting features, and it will be noticed that the increase in expenditure since 1870 is almost entirely owing to the increase which has taken place in the Metropolis in consequence of the many improvements made for the treatment of its in-door poor. The Metropolis is, indeed, responsible for £716,585 of the total increase of £840,275, although the mean number of its paupers of all classes has actually decreased.[2] Excluding the Metropolis, the tables show that notwithstanding the increase of the population in the remainder of the country from 19,461,343 in 1871, to 24,790,782 in 1891, the expenditure on poor relief has only increased by £123,690; in other words, the burden per head of population has been reduced during that period from 6s. 5d. to 5s.[3]

These favourable results are entirely owing to the greater restriction now put upon the grant of out-door relief; the saving on out-door relief expenditure since 1870 having been £1,209,191 (or 33 per cent.) in the whole of the country, £193,330 (or 51 per cent.) in the Metropolis, and £1,015,861 (or 31 per cent.) for the remainder of the country.

We can now sum up the results of improved administration since 1870, excluding lunatics and vagrants, and taking into consideration the increase of population:

---

[1] See Appendix E, p. 229.

[2] From 150,827 in 1870 to 107,373 in 1893. (See 22 L.G.B., p. 266.) The mean number of out-door paupers decreased from 114,386 to 47,472 between the same dates.

[3] The figures of population are taken from the Census returns for 1871 and 1891.

(1) The general pauperism of the country is considerably less than half what it was.

(2) Able-bodied pauperism is considerably less than half what it was.

(3) Not-able-bodied pauperism is nearly half what it was.

(4) Child pauperism is less than half what it was.

And (5) Had the expenditure on poor relief increased in proportion to the increase of population, we should have paid during the year ending Lady Day, 1892, about $10\frac{1}{4}$ millions pounds sterling, and this without taking into account the expenses connected with the greater care and attention paid to the wants of the poor by the establishment of excellent infirmaries and asylums, and by the improvement of workhouses.

If individual unions are taken, the effect of a stringent administration of out-door relief is very marked, as we have shown in Chapter VII., and this connotes "good administration," which, as Mr. Baldwyn Fleming says,

"has invariably been wholly successful. It has been tried under every variety of circumstances and with the same result. Atcham Union was a purely rural one, and maintained its position even after the very trying experiment of amalgamation with Shrewsbury. Bradfield Union is a rural one, with part of the suburbs of the great town of Reading. Brixworth, Manchester, Bradford, and even Whitechapel, besides many others, afford absolutely conclusive evidence that a high rate of pauperism is caused by the bad administration of a good law. Where the necessary time is given, and right principles are worked by competent officers, the same end has always been attained. No instance of failure can be adduced. This fact it is which make it so grievous to reflect uoon the intolerable burden inflicted by pauperism upon the community."[1]

On the other hand, the lax administration of out-door relief increases, or, at most, does not diminish pauperism.

Too much importance may be made of an increase or decrease in expenditure. An increase by no means necessarily implies bad administration, and if it does occur in well-administered

---

[1] 18 L.G.B., p. 114.

unions, it is not caused by an increase in expenditure on out-door relief, but by improving the condition and treatment of the in-door poor. What we have to look at is the increase or decrease in the *number* of paupers,[1] and in comparing the pauperism of one union with that of another, we must uot neglect to inquire whether the conditions in both are similar or different.[2]

If a board of guardians sets to work to follow the methods found to answer so well in other unions, they will soon diminish the pauperism of their union, and will not have to wait long before they reap the fruits of their action. Mr. Baldwyn Fleming shows how they should set to work, (see *supra*, p. 101), and we have pointed to some essentials of good administration in Chapter IV. They have the experience of Atcham, Bradfield, Brixworth, etc. (if their union is a rural one), and of Whitechapel, St. George's-in-the-East, Oxford, Manchester, Liverpool, Reading, etc. (if it be an urban one), to guide them; and the late Mr. Bland Garland has described more than once how he carried out his reforms in the Bradfield Union.[3]

Reform must be gradual (see *supra*, pp. 46-49), for the proverb, "*Qui va piano, va sano,*" applies here as well as in other matters.

It is no use denying the fact that in most unions, especially in country unions, guardians are wedded to the system of out-door relief. It is so much more pleasant and easy to give than

---

[1] A rough test of good or bad administration is to notice the ratio which the number of in-door paupers bear to that of the out-door paupers, after deducting the number of lunatics and vagrants.

[2] As an instance of the way figures may be manipulated quite unconsciously, we will refer to the paper read by Mr. Mitchison on the Advantages of Out-Door Relief at the Central Poor Law Conference, 1891. When analysed, they proved the exact reverse of his intention. See *Charity Organisation Review*, May, 1892, p. 186.

[3] See for example "From Pauperism to Manliness," a pamphlet published by the Charity Organisation Society.

to refuse. They are apt to forget that they "are not the trustees of a benevolent fund, but the administrators of rates compulsorily levied, and which press most hardly upon those who are often sadly worse off than the paupers to whose support they have to contribute."[1] Thus,

"At Peterborough the guardians still continue to administer relief, as though the poor rate were a charitable fund out of which they are at liberty to grant small pensions, or sums to all applicants who came before them, representing themselves as worthy people in reduced circumstances, and, needless to say, the guardians are never at a loss for applicants. The proportion of out-door to in-door poor surpasses that of any other union in my district, being for the year at the rate of 19 to 2, and is at times as high as 11 to 1. There are three districts, and the relieving officer for the Peterborough district has over 600 out-door poor on his book, with an expenditure ranging from £70 to £80 per week.

"The administration of relief in this union is as demoralising to the poor as it is inequitable to the ratepayer."[2]

Mr. Longley, writing in 1873, thought that the struggle of principle was over, and the only difficulty which remained was to disabuse boards of guardians of the belief, too commonly entertained by many of their number, that the special circumstances, either of their own locality, or of the particular case before them, were such as to absolve them from the observance of the general principles to which, in the abstract, they did not refuse their assent. He says:—

"The principle, or rather the absence of principle, which characterises the administration of many of these boards cannot, indeed, be better described than by the hackneyed phrase:—

"Video meliora, proboque ;
Deteriora sequor,"

which has been distinctly paraphrased in my hearing, on several occasions, by the admissions made by individual guardians as to their own practice."[3]

---

[1] 17 L.G.B., p. 66. See also 22 L.G.B., p. 71.
[2] 20 L.G.B., p. 201. See also 23 L.G.B., p. 99.
[3] 3 L.G.B., pp. 199, 200.

The attacks which have been recently made on our Poor Law system seem to show that Mr. Longley was too sanguine, and that the time has come for the principles to which he refers to be restated and re-affirmed. This has been the object of this work. The statistics which have been given make it clear that our pauperism is gradually diminishing year by year. If all boards of guardians would only take and follow the path which a few boards have followed with such conspicuous success, illustrating how little difficulty there really is in applying the principles of the Reformers of 1834 to Poor Law administration, we should make faster progress towards attaining the goal for which all are striving, namely, the virtual abolition of preventible pauperism.

# APPENDIX A.

Four tables showing diminution of Pauperism since 1850; the first three tables excluding the number of Lunatics and Vagrants.

## TABLE I.

| Day and Year. | In-door Paupers. | Out-door Paupers. | Total Paupers. | Population, 1851, 1871, and in middle of 1892. | Proportion of Paupers per 1000 of Population. |
|---|---|---|---|---|---|
| 1st July, 1850 | 84,550 | 703,452 | 788,002 | 15,428,116 [1] | 51 |
| ,, 1870 | 127,749 | 806,889 | 934,638 | 22,701,137 [2] | 41·2 |
| ,, 1892 | 155,359 | 495,407 | 650,766 | 29,403,346 [3] | 22·1 |

## TABLE II.

| Day and Year. | In-door Paupers. | Out-door Paupers. | Total Paupers. | Population, 1851, 1871, and in middle of 1892. | Proportion of Paupers per 1000 of Population. |
|---|---|---|---|---|---|
| 1st Jan., 1851 | 99,452 | 716,173 | 815,625 | 15,428,116 [1] | 52·8 |
| ,, 1871 | 153,185 | 880,709 | 1,033,894 | 22,701,137 [2] | 45·5 |
| ,, 1893 | 182,951 | 515,490 | 698,441 | 29,403,346 [3] | 23·7 |

## TABLE III.
### Mean Pauperism.[4]

| Year ending Lady Day. | In-door Paupers. | Out-door Paupers. | Total Paupers. | Population, 1851, 1871, and in middle of 1892. | Proportion of Paupers per 1000 of Population. |
|---|---|---|---|---|---|
| 1851 | 92,001 | 709,813 | 801,814 | 15,428,116 [1] | 51·9 |
| 1871 | 140,467 | 843,799 | 984,266 | 22,701,137 [2] | 43·4 |
| 1893 | 169,155 | 505,449 | 674,604 | 29,403,346 [3] | 22·9 |

## TABLE IV.
### Mean Pauperism (inclusive of all Classes).[4]

| Year ending Lady Day. | In-door Paupers. | Out-door Paupers. | Total Paupers. | Population, 1851, 1871, and in middle of 1892. | Proportion of Paupers per 1000 of Population. |
|---|---|---|---|---|---|
| 1851 | 114,367 | 826,948 | 941,315 | 15,428,116 [1] | 61 |
| 1871 | 156,430 | 880,930 | 1,037,360 | 22,701,137 [2] | 45·6 |
| 1893 | 192,512 | 566,264 | 758,776 | 29,403,346 [3] | 25·8 |

[1] Population of 597 unions. (See 4 P.L.B., p. 113.) The total population of England and Wales, according to the census of 1851, was 17,927,609.

[2] Population of 647 unions. (See 1 L.G.B., p. 443.) The total population of England and Wales being 22,712,266 in 1871.

[3] Estimated population of 648 unions in the middle of 1892. The total population of England and Wales having been 29,002,525, according to the census of 1891.

[4] See 22 L.G.B., p. 264. It is important to note that the great decrease has taken place since 1870.

## APPENDIX B.

Table showing the reduction in able-bodied Male Pauperism.[1]

| Day and Year. | In-door Paupers. | Out-door Paupers. | Total Paupers. | Population, 1851, 1871, and in middle of 1892. | Proportion of Paupers per 1000 of Population. |
|---|---|---|---|---|---|
| 1st Jan., 1849 | 11,100 | 55,134 | 66,234 | 15,428,116 | 4·3 |
| ,,   1871 | 12,714 | 44,112 | 56,826 | 22,701,137 | 2·5 |
| ,,   1893 | 18,226 | 15,984 | 34,210 | 29,403,346 | 1·2 |

Table showing the reduction in able-bodied Female Pauperism.[1]

| Day and Year. | In-door Paupers. | Out-door Paupers. | Total Paupers. | Population, 1851, 1871, and in middle of 1892. | Proportion of Paupers per 1000 of Population. |
|---|---|---|---|---|---|
| 1st Jan., 1849 | 17,014 | 118,396 | 135,410 | 15,428,116 | 8·7 |
| ,,   1871 | 16,606 | 116,407 | 133,013 | 22,701,137 | 5·8 |
| ,,   1893 | 16,526 | 56,442 | 72,968 | 29,403,346 | 2·4 |

Table showing the reduction in the able-bodied Pauperism of both sexes.[1]

| Day and Year. | In-door Paupers. | Out-door Paupers. | Total Paupers. | Population, 1851, 1871, and in middle of 1892. | Proportion of Paupers per 1000 of Population. |
|---|---|---|---|---|---|
| 1st Jan., 1849 | 28,114 | 173,530 | 201,644 | 15,428,116 | 13 |
| ,,   1871 | 29,320 | 160,519 | 189,839 | 22,701,137 | 8·3 |
| ,,   1893 | 34,752 | 72,426 | 107,178 | 29,403,346 | 3·6 |

[1] Excluding lunatics and vagrants.

# APPENDIX C.

Table showing the reduction in not-able-bodied Male Pauperism (other than children).

| Day and Year. | In-door Paupers. | Out-door Paupers. | Total Paupers. | Population, 1851, 1871, and in middle of 1892. | Proportion of Paupers per 1000 of Population. |
|---|---|---|---|---|---|
| 1st Jan., 1849 | 20,731 | 98,845 | 119,576 | 15,428,116 | 7·7 |
| ,, 1871 | 41,579 | 117,681 | 159,260 | 22,701,137 | 7 |
| ,, 1893 | 58,210 | 73,306 | 131,516 | 29,403,346 | 4·4 |

Table showing the reduction in not-able-bodied Female Pauperism (excluding children).

| Day and Year. | In-door Paupers. | Out-door Paupers. | Total Paupers. | Population, 1851, 1871, and in middle of 1892. | Proportion of Paupers per 1000 of Population. |
|---|---|---|---|---|---|
| 1st Jan., 1849 | 15,302 | 202,700 | 218,002 | 15,428,116 | 14·1 |
| ,, 1871 | 26,912 | 265,638 | 292,550 | 22,701,137 | 12·9 |
| ,, 1893 | 37,987 | 185,575 | 223,562 | 29,403,346 | 7·6 |

Table showing the reduction in not-able-bodied Pauperism generally (other than children).

| Day and Year. | In-door Paupers. | Out-door Paupers. | Total Paupers. | Population, 1851, 1871, and in middle of 1892. | Proportion of Paupers per 1000 of Population. |
|---|---|---|---|---|---|
| 1st Jan., 1849 | 36,033 | 301,545 | 337,578 | 15,428,116 | 21·8 |
| ,, 1871 | 68,491 | 383,319 | 451,810 | 22,701,137 | 19·9 |
| ,, 1893 | 96,197 | 258,881 | 355,078 | 29,403,346 | 12 |

## APPENDIX D.

Table showing the reduction in Child Pauperism.

| Day and Year. | In-door Paupers. | | Out-door Paupers. | | Total Paupers. | | Grand Total. | Proportion of Paupers per 1000 of Population. |
|---|---|---|---|---|---|---|---|---|
| | Legitimate. | Illegitimate. | Legitimate. | Illegitimate. | Legitimate. | Illegitimate. | | |
| 1st Jan., 1849 | 41,193 | 9,292 | 324,222 | 8,013 | 365,415 | 17,305 | 382,720 [1] | 24·8 |
| ,, 1871 | 55,374 | | 333,879 | 2,992 | 392,245 | | 392,245 [2] | 17·2 |
| ,, 1893 | 46,041 | 5,961 | 183,674 | 509 | 229,715 | 6,470 | 236,185 [3] | 8 |

Orphan and Deserted Child Paupers (included in last table).

| Day and Year. | In-door Paupers. | Out-door Paupers. | Total Paupers. | Proportion to total number of Child Paupers. | Ratio of Paupers to Population. |
|---|---|---|---|---|---|
| 1st Jan., 1849 | 23,208 | 16,701 | 39,909 | 1 to 9 | 1 in 386 [1] |
| ,, 1871 | .. | 14,897 [2] | .. | .. | .. |
| ,, 1893 | 33,216 | 9,942 | 43,158 | 1 to 5 | 1 in 681 [3] |

[1] 3 P.L.B., p. 145.
[2] 23 P.L.B., pp. 374 and 377.
[3] 22 L.G.B., p. 251.

# APPENDIX E.

Table showing the Total Expenditure on the Relief of the Poor for every tenth year from 1844 to 1892.[1]

| Year ending Lady Day. | Population of England and Wales at each Decennial Census | Expenditure in Poor Relief. | Percentage of increase of Population from 1844. | Percentage of increase of Expenditure from 1844. | Rate per head of Estimated Population.[2] |
|---|---|---|---|---|---|
| | | £ | | £ | s. d. |
| 1844 | 15,914,148 | 4,976,093 | .. | .. | 6 1 |
| 1852 | 17,927,609 | 4,897,685 | 12 | [dec, 1·5] | 5 5¼ |
| 1862 | 20,066,224 | 6,077,525 | 26 | 22 | 6 0¾ |
| 1872 | 22,704,108 | 8,007,403 | 42 | 61 | 7 0¼ |
| 1882 | 25,974,439 | 8,232,472 | 63 | 65 | 6 3¾ |
| 1892 | 29,001,018 | 8,847,678 | 82 | 78 | 6 1 |

Table showing the items which make up the Expenditure in the preceding table for the years ending Lady Day, 1857,[3] 1872, and 1892.

| Year ending Lady Day. | In-Maintenance. | Out-relief. | Maintenance of Lunatics in Asylums and Licensed Houses. | Workhouse and other Loans repaid and Interest therein. | Salaries and Rations of Officers. | Other Expenses of or[4] immediately connected with Relief. | Total. | Adjusted total after allowing for sums received from, or paid to, the Metropolitan Common Poor Fund. |
|---|---|---|---|---|---|---|---|---|
| | £ | £ | £ | £ | £ | £ | £ | £ |
| 1857 | 1,088,558 | 3,152,278 | 377,659 | 217,196 | 637,629 | 425,437 | 5,898,757 | 5,898,757 |
| 1872 | 1,515,790 | 3,583,571 | 742,483 | 278,566 | 871,402 | 945,867 | 7,937,679 | 8,007,403 |
| 1892 | 2,044,062 | 2,374,380 | 1,331,733 | 644,709 | 1,496,340 | 1,194,009 | 9,085,233 | 8,847,678 |

[1] The expenditure on the relief of the poor for the year ending Lady Day, 1834 (the last parochial year previous to the passing of the Act of 1834) amounted to £6,317,255, being 8s. 9½d. per head of population.

[2] See 22 L.G.B., p. 328.

[3] We have been obliged to start with this year, because it was the first in which the item for maintenance of lunatics was separately returned. (See 10 P.L.B., p. 60.)

[4] "Other Expenses" include *(inter alia)* expenditure on furniture, building, and repairs; certain establishment charges; the expenses of the maintenance of paupers in institutions other than Poor Law institutions, *e.g.*, in institutions for the deaf and dumb, for blind, in hospitals and in certified schools; the cost of drugs and medical and surgical appliances, so far as it cannot be apportioned to "In-Maintenance" and "Out-relief"; rents and rates; the cost of printing, stationery, and advertisements; the cost of wood, oakum, stone, etc., used for the employment of paupers; and the expenses connected with the cultivation of workhouse gardens and farms, so far as they cannot be apportioned to "In-Maintenance," "Rations of Officers" etc.

## APPENDIX E—(*Continued*).

Table showing the Expenditure on Poor Relief in the Metropolis for the year ending Lady Day, 1857, 1872, and 1892.[1]

| Year ending Lady Day. | In-Maintenance. | Out-relief. | Maintenance of Lunatics in Asylums and Licensed Houses. | Workhouse and other Loans repaid and Interest therein. | Salaries and Rations of Officers. | Other Expenses of or immediately connected with Relief. | Total. | Adjusted total after allowing for sums received from, or paid to, the Metropolitan Common Poor Fund. |
|---|---|---|---|---|---|---|---|---|
| | £ | £ | £ | £ | £ | £ | £ | £ |
| 1857 | 302,235 | 242,803 | 87,990 | 45,312 | 82,450 | 106,545 | 867,335 | 867,335 |
| 1872 | 433,215 | 374,736 | 159,530 | 101,235 | 168,745 | 449,744 | 1,687,205 | 1,756,929 |
| 1892 | 757,361 | 181,406 | 288,438 | 341,181 | 528,386 | 614,297 | 2,711,069 | 2,473,514 |

Table showing the Expenditure on Poor Relief in England and Wales (excepting the Metropolis).

| Year ending Lady Day. | In-Maintenance. | Out-relief. | Maintenance of Lunatics in Asylums and Licensed Houses. | Workhouse and other Loans repaid and Interest therein. | Salaries and Rations of Officers. | Other Expenses of or immediately connected with Relief. | Total. |
|---|---|---|---|---|---|---|---|
| | £ | £ | £ | £ | £ | £ | £ |
| 1857 | 786,323 | 2,909,475 | 289,669 | 171,884 | 555,179 | 318,892 | 5,031,422 |
| 1872 | 1,082,575 | 3,208,835 | 582,953 | 177,331 | 702,657 | 496,123 | 6,250,474 |
| 1892 | 1,286,701 | 2,192,974 | 1,043,295 | 303,528 | 967,954 | 579,712 | 6,374,164 |

[1] See 10 P.L.B., p. 64; 2 L.G.B., p. 142; and 22 L.G.B., 308.

# APPENDIX F.

### *Article 215 of the General Order of 1847 relating to the Duties of a Relieving Officer.*

THE following shall be the duties of a Relieving Officer :—

No. 1. To attend all ordinary meetings of the Guardians, and to attend all other meetings when summoned by the Clerk.

No. 2. To receive all applications for relief made to him within his district, or relating to any parish situated within his district, and forthwith to examine into the circumstances of every case by visiting the house of the applicant (if situated within his district), and by making all necessary inquiries into the state of health, the ability to work, the condition and family, and the means of such applicant, and to report the result of such enquiries in the prescribed form to the Guardians at their next ordinary meeting; and also to visit from time to time, as requisite, all paupers receiving relief, and to report concerning the same as the Guardians may direct.

No. 3. In any case of sickness or accident requiring relief by medical attendance, to procure such attendance by giving an order on the District Medical Officer, in the Form (V.) hereunto annexed, or by such other means as the urgency of the case may require.

No. 4. To ascertain from time to time from the District Medical Officer, the names of any poor persons whom such Medical Officer may have attended or supplied with medicines, without having received an order from himself to that effect.

No. 5. In every case of a poor person receiving medical relief, as soon as may be, and from time to time afterwards, to visit the house of such person, and until the next ordinary meeting of the Guardians, to supply such relief (not being in money) as the case on his own view, or on the certificate of the District Medical Officer, may seem to require.

No. 6. In every case of sudden or urgent necessity, to afford such relief to the destitute person as may be requisite, either by giving such person an order of admission into the Workhouse, and conveying him thereto if necessary, or by affording him relief out of the Workhouse, provided that the same be not given in money, whether such destitute person be settled in any parish comprised in the Union or not.

No. 7. To report to the Guardians at their next ordinary meeting all cases reported to him by an Overseer, in conformity with Article 218, and to obey the directions of the Guardians with reference to the relief administered in such cases.

No. 8. To perform the duties with respect to pauper apprentices prescribed by Articles 60, 61, and 62.

No. 9. To give all reasonable aid and assistance at the request of any other Relieving Officer of the Union by examining into the case of any applicant for relief, or administering relief to any pauper whose name has been entered on the books of such other Relieving Officer, and who may be within his own district.

No. 10. Duly and punctually to supply the weekly allowances of all paupers belonging to his district, or being within the same, and to pay or administer the relief of all paupers within his district to the amount and in the manner in which he may have been lawfully ordered by the Guardians to pay or administer the same.

No. 11. To visit, relieve, and otherwise attend to non-settled poor, being within his district, according to the directions of the Guardians, whose officer he is, and in no other way, subject always to the obligation imposed on him in cases of sudden or urgent necessity.

No. 12. To set apart one or more pages in his out-door relief list, in which he shall duly and punctually enter up the payments made by authority of his own Board of Guardians to non-settled poor, and to take credit for such payments in his receipt and expenditure book.

No. 13. To present his weekly accounts to the Clerk for his inspection and authentication before every ordinary meeting of the Guardians, and to the Guardians, at such meeting, for their approval.

No. 14. To submit to the Auditor of the Union all his books, accounts, and vouchers, at the place of audit, and at such time, and in such manner, as may be required by the regulations of the Commissioners.

No. 15. To assist the Clerk in conducting and completing the annual or other election of Guardians, according to the regulation of the Commissioners.

No. 16. To observe and execute all lawful orders and directions of the Guardians applicable to his office.

## APPENDIX G.

*Relief to the Poor in the Metropolis: Minute of the Poor Law Board.*[1]

THE published statements of Metropolitan pauperism have for some weeks past shown a considerable increase in the number of the out-door poor, not only as compared with previous weeks, but as compared with the high totals of 1867 and 1868. At the same time it has come to the knowledge of the Board that many persons (especially in the East End of London), who two winters ago were most eager in soliciting charitable contributions, have now expressed the opinion that the large sums spent then in charity tended to attract pauperism to those districts where money flowed most freely, and that they deprecate a repetition of the system then pursued. Under these circumstances the Board consider it equally important to guard on the one hand against any alarm which might arise on the part of the public, and result in an indiscriminate distribution of charitable funds, and, on the other hand to take such precautions and make such preparations as may enable Boards of Guardians and charitable agencies to work with effect and rapidity if any emergency should arise. And indeed, without considering the question of an increase in the numbers of the out-door poor, and looking simply to the present expenditure on poor relief, it appears to be a matter of essential importance that an attempt should be made to bring the authorities administering the Poor Laws and those who administer charitable funds to as clear an understanding as possible, so as to avoid the double distribution of relief to the same persons, and at the same time to secure that the most effective use should be made of the large sums habitually contributed by the public towards relieving such cases as the Poor Law can scarcely reach.

The question arises, how far it is possible to mark out the separate limits of

---

[1] 22 P. L. B., p. 9.

the Poor Law and of charity respectively, and how it is possible to secure joint action between the two.

One of the most recognised principles in our Poor Law is that relief should be given only to the actually destitute, and not in aid of wages. In the case of widows with families, where it is often manifestly impossible that the earnings of the woman can support the family, the rule is frequently departed from, but, as a general principle, it lies at the root of the present system of relief. In innumerable cases its application appears to be harsh for the moment, and it might also be held to be an aggravation of an existing difficulty to insist that, so long as a person is in employment, and wages are earned, though such wages may be insufficient, the Poor Law authorities ought to hold aloof and refuse to supplement the receipts of the family, actually offering in preference to take upon themselves the entire cost of their maintenance. Still, it is certain that no system could be more dangerous, both to the working-classes and to the ratepayers, than to supplement insufficiency of wages by the expenditure of public money.

The fundamental doctrine of the English Poor Laws, in which they differ from those of most other countries, is that relief is given, not as a matter of charity but of legal obligation, and to extend this legal obligation beyond the class to which it now applies, namely, the actually destitute, to a further and much larger class, namely, those in receipt of insufficient wages, would be not only to increase to an unlimited extent the present enormous expenditure, but to allow the belief in a legal claim to public money in every emergency to supplant, in a further portion of the population, the full recognition of the necessity for self-reliance and thrift.

It is clear, therefore, that the Poor Law authorities could not be allowed without public danger to extend their operations beyond those persons who are actually destitute, and for whom they are at present legally bound to provide. It would seem to follow that charitable organisations, whose alms could in no case be claimed as a right, would find their most appropriate sphere in assisting those who have some, but insufficient means, and who, though on the verge of pauperism, are not actual paupers, leaving to the operation of the general law the provision for the totally destitute.

It is, however, important not to ignore the fact that, even in the case of the destitute, whose maintenance the Poor Law authorities avowedly take upon themselves, there is a great disposition on the part of charitable persons, in what may be known to be deserving cases, to add to the minimum relief granted as a matter of legal obligation. At the same time, so long as the almoners of charities know that the amount of any allowance made by them to a poor family will be considered by the Poor Law authorities in determining the scale of out-door relief, they are likely either to withhold the money altogether, as only given in alleviation of rates, or (what is more probable) to give it without the knowledge of the local authorities. The first course stops the flow of charity, the second is demoralising and opens the door to many abuses. The best means to meet the difficulty would seem to be, that in all those cases where the Board of Guardians are granting relief—and in all such cases the relief must, by law, be adequate—the almoners of charities should abstain from giving food or money, or supplying any such articles as the Guardians are themselves strictly bound to grant, and especially from giving their charity in such a manner as would constitute a regular increase of income. If the charitable agencies wish to interpose at all in such cases, they should confine their assistance to donations of bedding or clothing or any similar articles which the Guardians may not consider themselves bound to provide at a particular moment, and which can be easily distinguished from other relief. It may be well to add that Boards of Guardians cannot legally give relief—

1. In redeeming tools or clothes from pawn,
2. In purchasing tools,
3. In purchasing clothes (except in cases of urgent necessity),
4. In paying the cost of conveyance to any part of the United Kingdom,
5. In paying rent or lodging,

so that assistance rendered for any of these purposes will not interfere with the action of the Guardians.

The general principle to be borne in mind seems to be that the obligations of the Guardians should not be curtailed, and that where the charitable associations consider it within their province to deal at all with persons on the parish lists, they should do so not by affording additional means of income, but by supplying once for all such articles as do not clash with or overlap the relief administered by the Guardians. It should, however, be clearly understood that no invitation is suggested to the charities to come, even in an indirect way, to the assistance of those for whom the Guardians are bound "to provide adequate relief." What is suggested is, that where the charities, as a matter of fact, do come in contact with that class of poor, they should act on the principles indicated, and, as far as practicable, in concert with the Guardians.

A cordial understanding between the Poor Law authorities and the charitable organisations based upon arrangements of the kind suggested, does not appear to be hopeless. It remains to consider by what means such an understanding can be brought about.

The first point is, that there should be every opportunity for every agency, official or private, engaged in relieving the poor, to know fully and accurately the details of the work performed by all similarly engaged. The lists of the relieving officers would form the natural basis for the necessary information. No funds are at the disposal of the Poor Law Board with which they could appoint a staff and provide offices for organising a general registration of Metropolitan relief. Other means must, therefore, be sought for providing that a public registering office should be established in every large district, where registers should be kept of all persons in receipt of parochial relief, with such particulars attached as might guide others in their inquiries. The clergy of all denominations, and the representatives of all the charities in the neighbourhood, should be invited to send in their lists to such offices, and to make themselves acquainted with the other lists deposited there, by which means an accurate dictionary or reference book might be framed, which would supply the necessary information about almost every person who had once received relief, either parochial or charitable. In the absence of any sufficient legal power in the Poor Law Board to enforce an organisation of this kind, the working of the plan must mainly depend on the voluntary action of the Guardians and of the various charitable bodies, but the Poor Law Board will be happy to afford any aid that may be in their power, and to authorise such expenditure as may fall within legal limits. They would be prepared—

1. To authorise the Guardians to print weekly lists, containing the names and addresses of out-door paupers, and the sums given in relief in each case.
2. To authorise any reasonable remuneration for extra work to officers whom the Guardians may employ to carry out this arrangement.
3. To instruct their inspectors to facilitate the communication between the official and private agencies, where such interposition may be of any service, and to assist in systematising as far as possible relief operations in various parts of the Metropolis.

It is evident that the suggestion made may be acted upon in all those Unions where the Guardians may be prepared to adopt them, without waiting for the adhesion of any Union which may be less disposed to co-operate in the scheme. The successful working of the plan in even a few of the largest and most pauperised districts would in itself be of great value, and undoubtedly secure a similar organisation throughout the Metropolis.

When the means of communication are established, it might be possible to agree on certain regulations which the charities might, with much advantage, engage to observe, not indiscriminately, or as an inflexible rule, but as a general practice. They might undertake—

1. To abstain from giving money or food to those in receipt of parish relief.
2. To inform the relieving officers of any gifts of blankets or clothing, upon the understanding that these gifts should not be taken into account for the purpose of curtailing the ordinary relief.
3. They might apply to the relieving officer on behalf of all such totally destitute persons whom, in the course of their operations, they might find unrelieved, but who properly fall within the sphere of the relieving officer. On the other hand, when the relieving officers are applied to for relief, and are bound to refuse it because the applicants are not actually destitute in the strict sense of the term, they might pass on the names and addresses to the charitable agencies where they think that the cases are likely to fall within the class which the charity undertakes to assist.

It will, of course, be understood that the Poor Law Board have no power in this matter to act beyond granting the necessary authority for the expenditure incurred on a part of the organisation required as described above. They can only invite the various charitable agencies and the Boards of Guardians to consider the suggestions which they have made. In 1867 great advantage resulted in the East End of London from the understanding established between the Guardians on the one hand, and the representatives of the charities on the other, with the co-operation of Mr. Sclater-Booth, then Secretary of the Poor Law Board, and Mr. Corbett, Poor Law Inspector. At the time of the cotton famine the Poor Law authorities and the administrators of charities also worked together with great success. These precedents justify the belief that great benefit would result to the Metropolis if a cordial understanding could be arrived at, and arrangements made between all parties engaged in relieving the poor, based on practical and systematic rules, in conformity with the general plan sketched in this minute.

GEORGE J. GOSCHEN, *President*.

POOR LAW BOARD, *November 20, 1869.*

## APPENDIX H.

*Mr. Longley's Suggestions for Improvements in Administration.*[1]

THE improvements suggested are such as may be effected by the guardians themselves, and being based upon the existing practice of one or more boards

---

[1] 3 L.G.B., pp. 203-205.

of guardians in London, "have thus been submitted to the test of actual experience. Many of them are, in fact, the expression of the elementary rules which guide, almost unconsciously, the administration of relief by those boards of guardians whose administration is conducted with strictness. They are offered, it is scarcely necessary to say, as merely supplementary to the orders of the board, as well as to the resolutions of the conferences of guardians already referred to.

1. The guardians should provide for the weekly supervision, either by themselves or their clerk, of the entries in and the general mode of keeping the Application and Report Books. Errors and omissions in these books should be pointed out to, and corrected by, the relieving officers. Special care should be taken to see that all applications made to the officer are recorded in this book, and that full information is afforded to the guardians by the entries in it, specially as to the visits of the officer to the homes of the applicants, their means, and the names of relatives liable to contribute towards their maintenance.

2. Provision should be made for making inquiries as to the circumstances of paupers after the grant of relief, and especially when relief is given in the workhouse. A memorandum on this point, which has been prepared by the Clerk of the Whitechapel Board of Guardians, is annexed to this Report.[1]

3. An officer should be appointed in each union with the exclusive duty of making inquiries, beyond the limits of the relief district in which they reside, into the circumstances of paupers and their families; of enforcing the payment of money due to the guardians; of taking legal proceedings in the name of the guardians, and (so long as the law of removal remains unaltered) of assisting in conducting removals under the superintendence of the clerk. It is highly undesirable that relieving officers should leave their districts for these, or, indeed, for any other purposes.

4. The guardians should discourage by every means in their power, and should make special inquiries as to the grant of relief by the relieving officer, in any circumstances whatever, before visiting the homes of the applicants. Recourse should be had to an increase in the number of relieving officers if this practice can be checked in no other way.

5. Relief should be administered, as far as possible, by the whole board of guardians, whether at their ordinary or at special meetings. Where relief committees are necessary, arrangements should be made for the attendance of not less than five guardians, some of whom should, if possible, be residents in other parts of the union than that for which the committee acts. The clerk or his deputy should attend all relief committees.

6. Where relief is administered by the whole board, the applications for relief should be dealt with in the order, in respect to the rest of the business of the guardians, which is pointed out by Article 41 of the General Consolidated Order.

7. The attendance of the district medical officers should be required at all meetings of the guardians at which applications for relief are heard.

8. Relief should be given in no case for a longer period than three months, and to the able-bodied of both sexes for not more than one month. The relieving officers should be required to visit the homes of all paupers at least once a month, and of able-bodied paupers at least fortnightly.

9. Cases in which provisional relief has been given by the relieving officer should be brought before the guardians as distinct applications for relief.

10. Medical relief should be given for a period not exceeding one month, and the attendance before the guardians of the applicant, or of some person on his behalf, should be made a condition of relief.

---

[1] Appendix B to Mr. Longley's Report.

11. Cases of doubtful or temporary destitution, in which out-relief may be given, should be met by relief by way of loan.

12. No out-relief should be given to paupers on their discharge from the workhouse, except by the board or committee ordinarily charged with the hearing of applications for relief, before whom applications for this relief should be brought, in the regular manner by the relieving officer,

13. Each guardian, sitting to administer relief, should be furnished with a written or printed abstract of the entries in the Application and Report Book which relate to the applications for relief to be entertained at each meeting.

14. Care should be taken that the stamp of pauperism is plainly marked upon all relief given, in whatever form, by the guardians, *e.g.*, the words 'dispensary' and 'infirmary' should never be used in forms, advertisements, or addresses, without the prefix '*Pauper*,' or '*Poor Law*,' or '*Workhouse*,' which should, indeed, appear as far as possible in every document issued by the guardians to those relieved by them.

15. Out-relief should not be given to able-bodied widows with families (except during the first six months of widowhood):—
 (a) Where they are in receipt of regular weekly wages.
 (b) Where their earnings appear to be below the general market price of their labour.
 (c) Where there is reason to believe they have not truly stated their means.
 (d) Where they have either no home, or a home in which it is undesirable, on account of its condition or locality, that they should remain.
 (e) Where there is reason to believe that they are of drunken or immoral habits.
 (f) Where they have received out-relief for a specified period (*e.g.*, a year), without making any progress towards independence.
 (g) Where they have refused a definite offer of employment, whether made by the guardians or others.

16. No out-relief should be given to applicants of the disabled class (being capable of removal to the workhouse):—
 (a) Where their home is such that they cannot be properly cared for there.
 (b) Where they are of bad character.
 (c) Where it appears that they have relatives able or liable to contribute to their maintenance, who refrain from doing so.
 (d) Where they have made no provision for their future wants, having been previously in receipt of such wages as to enable them to do so.

17. A limit (*e.g.*, two or three weeks) should be fixed to the duration of relief in the form of nourishment or stimulants, recommended by the district medical officer for out-door paupers capable of removal to the workhouse, in which they should be required to receive all further relief of this nature which they may need.

18. District medical officers should be discouraged from treating as pauper patients, except in cases of urgent necessity, any persons in respect of whom they have not received some formal order for attendance.

19. Medical orders, and out-relief in the form of nourishment and stimulants, should in no case be given to out-patients of hospitals.

20. Care should be taken that all relief in the form of nourishment and stimulants should, as far as possible, be ordered by the guardians before it is issued by the relieving officer.

21. Immediately after each meeting of the guardians at which the grant of relief has been made or confirmed, a list, authenticated by the signature of the clerk, of the names and residences of the adult paupers or orphan children to whom out-relief has been given on an original application, should be published

'n one or more of the local papers now so commonly found in every part of London. And at least twice a year, a list containing the like particulars in respect of each person then in receipt of out-relief should be similarly published. I am confident that the cost, considerable as it might be, of carrying out this suggestion, would become, by the self-acting check upon pauperism which it would provide, a profitable investment. Ample information of the relief given by the guardians would be thus afforded, apart from personal communication, to all distributors of charity, and there is every reason to believe that much of the imposture now practised by applicants for relief would be checked. In some instances, too, the notoriety thus given to the receipt of relief would have, it is to be hoped, the effect of rendering the receipt of relief less eligible than it now is."

## APPENDIX I.

*Relief to Members of Benefit Societies: Letter from the Poor Law Board to R. H. Paget, Esq., M.P.*[1]

"Poor Law Board, Whitehall, S.W.,
"5th January, 1870.

"SIR,—I am directed by the Poor Law Board to acknowledge the receipt of your letter of the 14th ult., in which you ask them to give definite information on the following questions bearing upon the very important and difficult subject of the relations between workmen's clubs or benefit societies, and the Poor Law system of this country. You state the case of two widows, each having the same number of children, one of whom is in receipt of six shillings from a benefit society, while the other is totally without resources. The latter receives ten shillings a week poor relief, the former only four shillings; the aggregate income of each being ten shillings a week. You inquire 'whether the guardians of your union would be legally justified in granting any relief to the widow in receipt of the six shillings from the benefit society beyond the four shillings which they now give? And 'if so, to what extent?'

"In answer to these precise questions as to the legal bearings of the case, I am directed to state, that in the opinion of the board, the guardians would not be justified, according to the strict law applicable to such cases, in giving to the widow in question any further relief than such an amount as would, together with the sum she was receiving from the benefit society, render the amount of her weekly income equal, and no more than equal, to that amount which the guardians hold to be necessary to relieve the destitution of a person similarly circumstanced, but who has no other means of support.

"In your third question you ask, 'on what principles are amounts received from benefit societies to be dealt with by boards of guardians in granting relief?' The board, in answering your two previous questions, have treated the matter as one of law rather than policy, as they understand you require a precise answer for immediate use. With regard, however, to the general aspect of the case, I am directed to call your attention to a minute circulated by the Poor Law Commissioners in the year 1840, on the question of allowing medical relief to persons receiving sick pay from a benefit society. In this minute the Com-

[1] 22 P.L.B., p. 108.

missioners reviewed the relation between benefit societies and the Poor Law system of this country, and pointed out that 'when an application is made for relief by a person who possesses some means of supporting himself, whether from a friendly society or otherwise, the guardians will only have to consider what are the absolute wants of the applicant and his family, which cannot be supplied from these partial resources. If the applicant has the right to the attendance of a medical man and medicines, in respect of his belonging to a friendly society,' this will, of course, not be one of the wants to be provided by the guardians; if he has not this right, the guardians will give him medical relief in the same manner as it would be given to any other person unable to provide it for himself.

"'With regard to the money allowance granted by the friendly society, the guardians cannot but take into account this allowance in estimating the resources of the applicant and his family, and if they acted in consistency with universally admitted principles of Poor Law administration, the guardians would not grant further aid than would be sufficient, together with this allowance, to relieve the destitution of the applicant and his family to the same extent as they would relieve the destitution of any other applicant and his family not being a subscriber to a friendly society.

"'The Commissioners, however, believe that in practice the guardians have treated the friendly society allowance as in some degree more immediately destined for the restoration of the health and strength of the subscriber, and have, therefore, granted a larger allowance to the family than would have been given if no such consideration had presented itself. The Commissioners have not deemed it advisable for the present to interfere with this mode of proceeding, but they entertain no doubt, that it will, at no distant period, be found to be more in accordance with the interest of the labouring classes to carry out the principles adverted to at the commencement of these observations, and not to permit the contributors of friendly societies to receive relief at the same time from the funds of the contributors and the poor rates.'

"With these views of the Commissioners the board fully concur. They would further observe that the Commissioners state, in the same minute, that their views are corroborated by the practice of the working classes themselves. 'From the evidence received in this office, the Poor Law Commissioners have carefully considered the question, in what cases and to what extent a man who, as a member of a friendly society, is entitled to certain advantages in respect of it, ought to receive parochial relief? The chief principles of the Poor Law Amendment Act received their strongest corroboration from the examples set by the labouring classes themselves, in the administration of relief to the members of their own friendly societies. From the evidence received on this topic, especially from Mr. Tidd Pratt, the barrister charged with the revision of their rules, it appears that on no point was their opinion and practice more decided and unanimous than in the prohibition of partial relief. They constantly acted on the rule that, whatever were the apparent special circumstances of the particular case, entire and individual reliance on one source or other should be rigorously enforced. They were well aware that where, by any arrangement, more than one source of relief is opened to the same individual at the same time, the vigilance of the dispensers of relief is weakened, their means of protecting the funds under their charge are diminished, and an increased and undue reliance upon the divided and extended sources is created, which is, moreover, always attended by an influx of fraudulent claims. The labourers who act on the principles set forth in the best considered rules of the friendly societies would, no doubt, decide that it were better that benefit societies should not exist at all, than that they should exist as means to eke out the amounts of a pauper's allowance, and add to the inducements to obtain and rely on such an allowance.'

"The board regret to observe, from the communication now made to them, that some of the Somersetshire colliers look in a totally different light upon their claims to parish relief. In stating the special case of the two widows, they assume that, notwithstanding the annuity received by one of them, the two women are left in the same position. But that is far from being the fact. In the great majority of similar cases of able-bodied widows with families, either the widow herself or some of the children are able, by their own work, to add to the income of the family.

"The widow receiving 6s. a week from the benefit club would, so soon as she and her children earned the small sum of 4s., be beyond the line of pauperism, while the other would, in all probability, remain under the line.

"Again, so soon as the widow in the present case earned 5s. a week, she would be in receipt of a larger income than the other could ever hope to reach. The latter could never look to receive more than that minimum relief which the guardians are alone empowered to grant. It must be assumed throughout that the guardians do not grant more than minimum relief; that is to say, relief adequate, but not more than adequate, to meet the absolute necessities of the applicants. It must also be assumed that the guardians may, at any moment, apply the workhouse test. Minimum out-door relief or the workhouse are, therefore, the alternatives from which the widow, left totally destitute, cannot escape, unless she should be able to provide for the entire maintenance of herself and her family, while every contribution received from a benefit society makes it more probable that even with very limited earnings she may escape from these contingencies.

"The board cannot admit as a practical argument, that able-bodied widows and their children, in receipt of 6s. a week from a benefit society, would, as a matter of course, come upon the rates. And they would further point out the great difficulty in drawing distinctions between annuities from benefit societies and other kinds of property. If, instead of subscribing to the benefit society, the husband had invested in a savings bank, he would have shown himself equally prudent, and on the principle contended for, his widow might equally claim to have the property thus bequeathed to her left out of account if she asked for parish relief. Property left to a widow in cottages, or derived from a policy of insurance on the husband's life might be held to establish a similar claim.

"The result accordingly would be that a vast number of persons not destitute would be encouraged to become paupers. The principle of leaving property bequeathed to widows out of account in granting relief, would establish the principle that the rates were not the very last resource of the poorest class, but a collateral insurance fund, to which not destitution alone, but the receipt of annuities from other sources would establish a claim.

"In the opinion of the board, it would not be expedient to administer poor rates, which are levied from all classes down to those on the very verge of destitution, in such a manner as to cause them to be recognised by the working classes of the country as a provision substituted by the law of the land for that which, in the absence of such a system, they would be willing to provide for themselves and their families through the medium of benefit societies. The board regard the prosperity and extension of these benefit societies as a matter of extreme importance, and would be anxious to encourage their establishment by all legitimate means. But the board, as at present advised, believe that this encouragement could not safely be given by allowing the poor rates to be treated as a subsidiary fund. The board cannot shut their eyes to the fact, that the only safe basis on which the system of benefit societies can rest, under the present system of the legal right to relief, is, that they afford the means of providing, in times of distress or disability, a more eligible, respectable, and liberal maintenance than that supplied under the Poor Law, and that they should be still regarded as a mode for avoiding the degradation of parish support, rather than as conferring a title by which a claim to such support may be established even beyond the line of actual destitution.

"You will understand from the foregoing remarks, that the present state of the law is clear upon the point on which you ask for explanation, and that the wishes of the colliers, to which you allude, could not legally be complied with. But I am directed to add, that the attention of the board will continue to be most earnestly directed to this important subject, and that any representations made to them will receive their most careful consideration.—I am, &c.,

"H. FLEMING, *Secretary.*

"To R. H. Paget, Esq., M.P.,
"Cranmore Hall,
"Shepton Mallet."

## APPENDIX J.

*Pauperism and Distress: Circular Letter to Boards of Guardians.*[1]

"Local Government Board, Whitehall, S.W.,
"*15th March,* 1886.

"SIR,—The inquiries which have been recently undertaken by the Local Government Board unfortunately confirm the prevailing impression as to the existence of exceptional distress amongst the working classes. This distress is partial as to its locality, and is no doubt due in some measure to the long continued severity of the weather.

"The returns of pauperism show an increase, but it is not yet considerable; and the numbers of persons in receipt of relief are greatly below those of previous periods of exceptional distress.

"The Local Government Board have, however, thought it their duty to go beyond the returns of actual pauperism, which are all that come under their notice in ordinary times, and they have made some investigation into the condition of the working classes generally.

"They are convinced that in the ranks of those who do not ordinarily seek poor law relief there is evidence of much and increasing privation, and if the depression in trade continues it is to be feared that large numbers of persons usually in regular employment will be reduced to the greatest straits.

"Such a condition of things is a subject for deep regret and very serious consideration.

"The spirit of independence, which leads so many of the working classes to make great personal sacrifices, rather than incur the stigma of pauperism, is one which deserves the greatest sympathy and respect, and which it is the duty and interest of the community to maintain by all the means at its disposal.

"Any relaxation of the general rule at present obtaining, which requires, as

---

[1] 16 L.G.B., p. 5. See *supra* p 176.

a condition of relief to able-bodied male persons on the ground of their being out of employment, the acceptance of an order of admission to the workhouse, or the performance of an adequate task of work as a labour test, would be most disastrous, as tending directly to restore the condition of things which, before the reform of poor laws, destroyed the independence of the labouring classes, and increased the poor rate until it became an almost insupportable burden.

"It is not desirable that the working classes should be familiarised with poor law relief, and if once the honourable sentiment which now leads them to avoid it is broken down, it is probable that recourse will be had to this provision on the slightest occasion.

"The Local Government Board have no doubt that the powers which the guardians possess are fully sufficient to enable them to deal with ordinary pauperism, and to meet the demand for relief from the classes who usually seek it.

"When the workhouse is full, or when the circumstances are so exceptional that it is desirable to give out-door relief to the able-bodied poor on the ground of want of work, the guardians in the unions which are the great centres of population are authorised to provide a labour test, on the performance of which grants in money and kind may be made, according to the discretion of the guardians. In other unions, where the guardians have not already this power, the necessary order is issued whenever the circumstances appear to require it.

"But these provisions do not in all cases meet the emergency. The labour test is usually stone-breaking or oakum-picking. This work, which is selected as offering the least competition with other labour, presses hardly upon the skilled artisans, and, in some cases, their proficiency in their special trades may be prejudiced by such employment. Spade husbandry is less open to objection, and when facilities offer for adopting work of this character as a labour test, the Board will be glad to assist the guardians by authorising the hiring of land for the purpose, when this is necessary. In any case, however, the receipt of relief from the guardians, although accompanied by a task of work, entails the disqualification which by statute attaches to pauperism.

"What is required in the endeavour to relieve artisans and others who have hitherto avoided Poor Law assistance, and who are temporarily deprived of employment, is—

"1. Work which will not involve the stigma of pauperism.

"2. Work which all can perform, whatever may have been their previous avocations.

"3. Work which does not compete with that of other labourers at present in employment.

"And lastly, work which is not likely to interfere with the resumption of regular employment in their own trades by those who seek it.

"The Board have no power to enforce the adoption of any particular proposals, and the object of this circular is to bring the subject generally under the notice of boards of guardians and other local authorities.

"In districts in which exceptional distress prevails, the Board recommend that the guardians should confer with the local authorities, and endeavour to arrange with the latter for the execution of works on which unskilled labour may be immediately employed.

"These works may be of the following kinds, among others:—

"*(a)* Spade husbandry on sewage farms.

"*(b)* Laying out of open spaces, recreation grounds, new cemeteries, or disused burial grounds.

"*(c)* Cleansing of streets not usually undertaken by local authorities.

"*(d)* Laying out and paving of new streets, etc.
"*(e)* Paving of unpaved streets, and making of footpaths in country roads.
"*(f)* Providing or extending sewerage works and works of water supply.

"It may be observed that spade labour is a class of work which has special advantages in the case of able-bodied persons out of employment. Every able-bodied man can dig, although some can do more than others, and it is work which is in no way degrading, and need not interfere with existing employment.

"In all cases in which special works are undertaken to meet exceptional distress it would appear to be necessary, 1st, that the men employed should be engaged on the recommendation of the guardians as persons whom, owing to previous condition and circumstances, it is undesirable to send to the workhouse, or to treat as subjects for pauper relief; and 2nd, that the wages paid should be something less than the wages ordinarily paid for similar work, in order to prevent imposture, and to leave the strongest temptations to those who avail themselves of this opportunity to return as soon as possible to their previous occupations.

"When the works are of such a character that the expenses may properly be defrayed out of borrowed moneys, the local authorities may rely that there will be every desire on the part of the Board to deal promptly with the application for their sanction to a loan.

"I shall be much obliged if you will keep me informed of the state of affairs in your district, and if it should be found necessary to make any exceptional provision, I shall be glad to know at once the nature of such provision, and the extent to which those for whom it is intended avail themselves of it.—I am, &c.,

"(Signed)      J. CHAMBERLAIN.

"The Clerk to the Guardians."

## APPENDIX K.

*Workhouse Administration.*

LOCAL GOVERNMENT BOARD,
WHITEHALL, S.W., *29th January, 1895.*

SIR,—I am directed by the Local Government Board to state that in view of the important changes made in the system of the election of Poor Law Guardians by the Local Government Act of last session, and of the fact that many of those who have been elected as Guardians have had no previous experience in the administration of the Poor Law, the Board deem it desirable to bring under the special attention of the Guardians certain points connected with workhouse administration.

It is undoubtedly the case that since workhouses were established under the Poor Law Amendment Act, 1834, the circumstances connected with the administration of relief, and the character of those for whom accommodation in workhouses has to be provided, have so materially changed, that arrangements originally adequate, and in accordance with the spirit of the times, have ceased to be so. It may be pointed out that whilst workhouses were in the first instance provided chiefly for the relief of the able-bodied, and their administration was therefore intentionally deterrent, the sick, the aged, and the infirm now greatly preponderate, and this has led to a change in the spirit of the administration although it is still based on the General Consolidated Order of 1847. The Board feel sure that the Guardians will bear in mind this change in the character of the inmates who are under their charge.

The Board direct me to remind the Guardians that, subject to the rules and regulations of the Board, the guidance, government, and control of the workhouse, and of the officers and servants, and the inmates, are placed in the hands of the Guardians, and that the responsibility for the management of the workhouse and the welfare of the inmates rests with them and the officers under their control.

Under a General Order issued in January, 1893, authority was given to every member of a Board of Guardians to visit the workhouse at any reasonable time that he might think proper, but this does not affect the duty of the Guardians to appoint one or more visiting committees rom their own body, or the duty of the committees so appointed to carefully examine the workhouse, to inspect the reports of the Chaplain and Medical Officer, to examine the stores, to afford as far as practicable to the inmates an opportunity of making complaints, and to investigate any complaints which may be made to them, and from time to time to write such answers as the facts may warrant to certain questions in a book provided by the Guardians for the purpose. The manner in which these duties should be performed is very clearly set forth in a circular letter which was issued by the Poor Law Board on the 6th July, 1868,[1] which the Board trust will have the careful attention of the Guardians.

*Visiting Committees.*

There are, however, two points to which the Board would specially refer. The Committee should bear in mind that surprise visits are of great value to enable them to ascertain the real character of the administration of their workhouse, and if they ordinarily meet at fixed intervals they should be careful that visits of this nature are also made. It is also important that opportunities should be given to the inmates of the workhouse to make any communication they may wish to members of the Committee, without any officers being present at the time.

By the Order of January, 1893, above referred to, the Guardians were expressly empowered, from time to time, to appoint, in addition to the Workhouse Visiting Committee, a Committee or Committees of ladies, whose duty it should be to visit and examine those parts of the workhouse in which the female inmates and the children are maintained, and to report to the Guardians any matters which may appear to the Committee to need attention. The Board consider that the appointment of such Committees has been attended with great advantage.

As regards the classification of the inmates of workhouses, the regulations specify the classes to which separate wards or buildings and yards are to be assigned, but the Guardians are also directed, so far as circumstances will permit, to further sub-divide any of these classes, with reference to the moral character or behaviour, or to the previous habits of the inmates, or to such other grounds as may seem expedient. This is a matter to which Guardians should give careful consideration.

*Classification.*

It seems desirable once more to call attention to the arrangements that should be made for married couples, as misconception appears still to exist as to their separation in workhouses. The Poor Law Act of 1847 provides that where any two persons, being husband and wife, both of whom shall have attained the age of 60 years, shall be sent into any workhouse, such two persons

---

[1] See Appendix M.

shall not be compelled to live separate and apart from each other, and by the 39 and 40 Vict., c. 61, it is further provided that the Guardians may permit any married couples to live together, either of whom shall be infirm, sick, or disabled by any injury, or above the age of 60 years.

The altered character of the inmates of the workhouse in the present day, which has been previously referred to, has brought the question of the infirmary wards, and the arrangements that should be made for the care of the sick, into special prominence. **The Sick and Infirm.**

The due performance, by the Medical Officer of the Workhouse, of the duties attaching to his office, is, of course, of paramount importance in ensuring proper administration in the sick wards, and, amongst the principal of these duties is that of advising the Guardians, by written reports, upon the dietary of the inmates, the drainage, ventilation, warmth, and other arrangements of the workhouse, and as to every defect which he may observe in the arrangement of the infirmary and sick wards, and as to the performance of their duties by the nurses of the sick. The Guardians should be careful to see that the reports required from him by the General Consolidated Order, and by the General Orders of April 4th, 1868, and August 24th, 1869, are regularly laid before them. The half-yearly statement required by the last-named Order the Board consider of especial importance. Care should also be taken that the requirements of the General Consolidated Order, by which the dietaries of the sick and of the young children are placed entirely under the control of the Medical Officer, are complied with. The proper use of bed cards in every case the Board deem of much importance; it is a safeguard, both to the nurses and their patients, that all directions of the Medical Officer should be given in writing. It is desirable that these cards should, in a great measure, show the history and treatment of each case, and they should be carefully preserved.

It is, no doubt, the case that the majority of the Boards of Guardians have, under the advice of the Board, and at the instance of their Inspectors, improved the system of nursing in the workhouses, and that in many workhouses an adequate standard of efficiency has been attained. But, notwithstanding this, there are many workhouses where the present nursing arrangements have not been brought to the standard of modern requirements, and the Board must strongly urge on the Guardians that this matter should receive their most careful consideration.

The Board, in a circular letter issued some years since, referring to the nursing arrangements in workhouses, stated as follows:—

"The office of nurse is one of very serious responsibility and labour, and requires to be filled by a person of experience in the treatment of the sick, of great respectability of character, and of diligent and decorous habits. Such person cannot discharge the duties of the office singly, but must have the assistance of others of both sexes; and there is scarcely less need of the same qualities in the persons who are to be the assistants than of those required for the chief officer. Hence it is necessary that the nurses should be adequately remunerated, and that they should be appointed after a strict investigation of their qualifications for the office. But the Board consider it of the highest importance that the assistants to the nurse should also be paid officers. By appointing paid assistants the Guardians will have an opportunity of selecting persons whose qualifications for the office can be properly ascertained, and they will also be able to hold such officers responsible for negligence or misconduct, as in the case of the superior officers of the workhouse. Where pauper inmates are directed to act as assistant nurses, there is no stimulus to exertion, no test of capacity, and no responsibility for negligence. The Board therefore recommend that the Guardians will, as far as possible, discontinue the practice of appointing pauper inmates of the workhouse to act as assistant nurses in the infirmary or sick ward."

The difficulty of obtaining such nurses as those referred to has, in some instances, been assigned by Boards of Guardians as a sufficient reason for not complying with these recommendations. But whatever may have been the case in the past, in view of the general advance that has taken place in recent years in the provision for training nurses, no such difficulty should now arise, and the Board think it desirable to draw the attention of Guardians generally to the enclosed memorandum of the Board's Inspector, Dr. Downes, dated April, 1892,[1] with reference to the general question of nursing arrangements in workhouses, which has already been forwarded by the Board to the Board of Guardians of many unions, where the nursing arrangements have been insufficient.

The Guardians should be satisfied that the nursing staff by day and by night s in numbers fully equal to the proper nursing of the sick, and they should give their most careful consideration to any representations which may be made on the subject by the Medical Officer of the Workhouse in the discharge of his prescribed duty. They should also be careful when they make appointments of nurses that the persons appointed are, by training and experience, fully equal to the responsible duties which they have to discharge.

Whilst the Board are not prepared to lay it down as a rule that in no case should pauper inmates act as attendants in sick wards, as clearly distinguished from nurses, they consider that their services should only be used with the approval of the Medical Officer, and under the closest supervision at all times of paid officers.

In the larger workhouses the infirmaries have in many cases been placed under separate administration from the workhouse proper, with very beneficial results; but in cases where the buildings form part of the same establishment the Master and Matron necessarily remain the chief officers of the whole establishment, and primarily responsible for its administration and discipline. It seems to the Board important that this should be understood, as their experience shows that the improvement that is taking place in the character of workhouse nursing from the employment of trained nurses, occasionally leads to objections being raised to the legitimate exercise of the authority of the Master and Matron in the arrangements connected with the sick wards. The Board consider that so long as these establishments are constituted as at present, the nurses should be responsible to the Medical Officer for the treatment of the patients, but should clearly understand that in other matters they must defer to the authority of the Master and Matron.

The proper care of imbeciles retained in workhouses is a matter which should receive the special attention of the Guardians, It is important that they should,

**Imbeciles.** as far as practicable, have means of suitable employment, that adequate provision should be made for their exercise and recreation, that ample means should exist to ensure their personal cleanliness, that their food should be sufficient and properly served, and that the officers in charge of them should be careful and kindly, and the buildings and appliances be of such a character as to minimise the risks of injury.

With regard to the children in workhouses, the Board note with satisfaction to what a large extent those still maintained in workhouses are sent out for

**The Children.** education to public elementary schools, and they are clearly of opinion that, where it is practicable, Boards of Guardians should adopt this course. It may also often be possible for arrangements to

---

[1] See Appendix L

be made for the children to attend the Sunday Schools of their own denomination. The Board attach much importance to all children maintained in Poor Law institutions being given opportunities for mixing, as far as circumstances will admit, with other children.

Special care should be taken that a sufficient part of each day is set apart for recreation only, that the children should be allowed to take exercise frequently outside the workhouse premises, and that they should be encouraged in healthy games of all sorts.

The Board need hardly point out that all children in workhouses should be under the charge of officers, either industrial trainers or caretakers, and should not be left to the charge of adult paupers.

All children should be frequently and individually inspected by the Medical Officer.

There are questions connected with the boarding-out and emigration of orphan and deserted children which will doubtless receive the careful consideration of the Guardians. The Board do not propose to refer to them in detail on the present occasion; they would only urge upon Guardians the importance of always remembering that they stand *in loco parentis* to such children, and that whether they are retained in the workhouse or in a district or separate school or cottage homes, or are sent to a certified school, or are boarded-out or emigrated, it is on the Guardians that the responsibility for their welfare primarily rests.

As regards the hours to be observed by inmates of workhouses for getting up, meals, work, etc., the Board think it unnecessary to make any alteration in those prescribed in existing regulations. They attach much importance to uniformity in this matter, but they would draw attention to the point which appears to be frequently overlooked, that these hours do not apply to the infirm inmates or the young children. It rests with the Master and Matron, subject to the direction of the Guardians, to fix the hours of rising and going to bed for inmates infirm through age or from any other cause, and for children under seven years of age, and for these inmates the meals are to be provided at such times and in such manner as the Guardians may from time to time direct. *[Hours for getting up, Meals, etc.]*

It appears desirable to refer to the question of the clothes to be supplied by the Guardians to inmates of the workhouse. The clothing to be worn by the inmates is to be made of such materials as the Board of Guardians may determine, and in their instructional letter of February 5th, 1842, the Poor Law Commissioners called attention to the fact that this clothing need not be uniform either in colour or material. The Board would specially suggest that the clothing worn by inmates when absent on leave from the workhouse should not be in any way distinctive or conspicuous in character. *[Clothes.]*

As regards the power which Guardians possess of authorising the Master to allow an inmate to quit the workhouse and to return after a temporary absence only, it appears to the Board that in the case of the aged and infirm inmates, so long as they are well behaved and do not abuse the liberty given to them, it is desirable, so far as it can be done without undue interference with the discipline and management of the workhouse, that permission to leave the workhouse should be given within reasonable limits. Of course, should it be found in any particular instance that the permission was abused, exception should be made, but a careful record should be kept by the Master of the refusal of leave on this ground. *[Liberty.]*

With reference to the important question of dietaries, it is to be observed that whilst the Guardians are empowered, subject to the sanction of the Local Government Board, to fix the amount and nature of the food which shall be given to the inmates generally, it is the duty of the Medical Officer to order such food as he may consider requisite for the sick. With regard to the inmates in health, a memorandum was drawn up by the Board's Inspector, Dr. Downes, in 1893, setting forth the general principles which should guide Boards of Guardians in framing dietaries for this class, and in any case when the Guardians may be proposing to revise the dietaries, the Board will be happy to furnish them with copies. *[Dietaries.]*

The security of the inmates in case of fire is a matter which, whilst it applies with special force to the sick and helpless, should receive the careful consideration of the Guardians as regards all inmates of the establishment, and the Guardians should satisfy themselves that adequate means of escape from all wards are available, and that the means are ready to hand of extinguishing any fire at its first outbreak. *[Escape in case of Fire.]*

The Board must impress upon the Guardians the grave responsibility which rests upon them as regards the selection of the officers employed in workhouses. They cannot do better than refer to the letter of the Poor Law Commissioners of February 5th, 1842, in which they said:—" The Commissioners are satisfied that good temper joined to firmness and self-command will enable a skilful teacher to manage children with little or no corporal punishment. The frequent use of corporal correction is the common recourse of teachers, who, through idleness or other defect, are incompetent to acquire command over children by a knowledge of their characters and by gentle means. . . . The observations made above with reference to the management of children are equally applicable to the treatment of adults. Warmth of temper and passionate conduct generally betray a consciousness of want of firmness. The discipline of a workhouse has to be maintained by an undeviating adherence to rules and a steadiness which defies provocation while it deliberately enforces obedience to orders by legal and authorised means. The Master of a workhouse is answerable for the general order of the whole establishment, and minute personal attention on his part can alone detect and remedy defects in the discipline and cleanliness of the house. The temper and discretion required for the discharge of his duties, and the confidence necessarily placed in his integrity, make it essential that the greatest care should be exercised in the choice of that officer. The Master, too, is in some degree dependent on the aid afforded him by the other officers of the establishment . . . . and as want of harmony between the principal officers of the establishment cannot fail to impair their efficiency and disturb the general discipline of the house, the Commissioners are desirous of inculcating the necessity of the utmost forbearance and command of temper in their mutual relations." *[Appointment of Officers.]*

In conclusion, the Board desire to point out that all experience shows that whether a workhouse is well or ill administered depends to a large extent upon the personal interest which the Guardians take in the matter. The work is often arduous, and the constant attention to small details which is absolutely necessary for efficient administration may impose a heavy tax on the time and patience of the Guardians; but the Board feel sure that they may rely on those who take upon themselves the office of Guardian discharging their duties with a due sense of the responsibility which the position involves.

I am, sir, your obedient servant,

HUGH OWEN, *Secretary*.

The Clerk to the Guardians.

## APPENDIX L.

*Nursing in Workhouse Sick Wards.*

Extract from Memorandum of Dr. Downes, Inspector of the Local Government Board, dated April, 1892.

It may be well to draw the attention of the Guardians who have not as yet ceased to employ pauper assistants in the sick wards to the following considerations:—

There is great and increasing difficulty in finding among the inmates in health persons of good character sufficiently able of body or fit in mind to act as nurses. To commit the care of the sick to paupers is, therefore, frequently to intrust them to unsuitable persons, having little at stake, without interest in their work, and practically irresponsible. Skill is obviously not to be expected of such persons, but, beyond the sum of suffering which lack of knowledge implies in such matters, experience of pauper-nursing has unhappily not seldom exemplified the evils which indifference, cupidity, and want of forbearance may entail.

The employment of pauper-inmates in sick wards is in a variety of ways costly.

If fit for such employment, they should be fit to earn their own living, and a proof of this is often afforded by the discharges which are taken when the extras and indulgences of the sick wards are no longer forthcoming.

The removal of wardspeople usually sets free a number of sick beds having a money value which may be estimated on an average at £100 per bed.

The waste and misappropriation of food, which is commonly so large an item of infirmary expenditure, is largely dependent on the employment of pauper helps, whose interest is selfishly concerned in its continuance.

The want of proper care of appliances is no small item of cost. It is not unusual, for example, to find a costly water-bed spoiled through want of knowledge.

It may be observed also that Guardians will rarely obtain the full value of their paid nurses' service so long as there remains opportunity or excuse for these officers to delegate their duties to inmates.

Humanity and economy alike dictate that the sick poor in workhouse sick wards should receive nursing treatment not less efficient than that which is now afforded in general hospitals, and in well-administered cottage hospitals.

In workhouses where pauper nursing is dispensed with, it is usually found that the majority of paid nurses and assistant nurses to the average number of occupied sick-beds should be from about one to fifteen to one to ten, this allowance including night nurses and nurses off duty.

The actual provision must largely depend on the size of the infirmary and the character of the cases, but it should be remembered that, although the sick are mostly chronic, a large number are of such a kind as to require constant care and attention.

In some unions the practice of employing as paid "scrubbers" widows, who would otherwise be chargeable to the rates, has been successful.

In the larger workhouses the nurses should be under the direct control of a trained and experienced superintendent, or head nurse, subject to the directions of the medical officer in all matters of treatment, and of the master and matron, so far as the Orders of the Local Government Board may require, in regard to discipline. In workhouse infirmaries under separate administration the matron should herself be a trained nurse and have charge of the nursing staff.

It is very essential that due provision should be made for efficient nursing by night. This, above all, is a time when the sick wards should be watched by responsible officers; it is a period of much trial to the sick.

Attention to the warmth and ventilation of the wards, and to the administration of medicine, stimulants, or food, the application of poultices, management of the natural wants of the feeble and paralytic, and care for those in pain, or dying, are all duties which should be confided to none but responsible nurses. Want of proper assistance to "wet" cases at night-time not only greatly increases work for the day nurse, but is one great cause of bedsore and suffering.

When arrangements are duly made for paid night nursing, the day nurses ought to be enabled to obtain undisturbed rest away from the immediate vicinity of the sick wards.

In their Circular Letter, the Poor Law Board expressed their opinion "that where the arrangements of the workhouse will permit, it is very desirable that special accommodation should be provided for the nurse and the paid assistants, so that they may be always ready to attend upon the patients, and to be removed as much as possible from the distraction which the proceedings in a large workhouse are calculated to produce."

In some of the smaller workhouses this provision may be made on a separate floor of the infirmary, or frequently some other portion of the workhouse may be adapted for the purpose. In the largest workhouses it may be requisite to furnish a detached nurses' home. In either case the cost would be largely counterbalanced—in the former, probably, more than counterbalanced—by the value of increased sick-ward accommodation consequent on the removal of wardspeople.

Many advantages have been found to follow the establishment of nursing on the lines above indicated. Not nursing alone, but medical attendance is increased in efficiency, and experience shows that with improved treatment, speedier cure and lessened stay of curable cases may be looked for.

One of the chief duties of a skilled nurse is to watch the dietaries, and by her reports to enable the Medical Officer to prescribe for each patient such food as may be suitable and acceptable, so that waste shall sink to a minimum. Few, perhaps, realise how large an economy and how much increase of comfort to the sick may be thus effected.

It will be generally admitted that the sick poor can usually be better tended and nursed by skilled nurses in well-equipped sick wards than in their own homes; and the regularity, neatness, and order of the wards, tend to diminish the repugnance to entering the workhouse which is often evinced by the sick poor of the better class when reduced to want by failing health.

Frequently wards of indifferent construction may be much improved in wholesomeness by the care of a well-instructed nurse.

Nursing, while demanding special personal qualifications, must, like every business, be learned; and by establishing a well-considered system of nursing, the Guardians of a large workhouse may, in due course, train their own nurses, and assist in supplying a demand which is certain to increase.

In balance-sheet form, the financial side of the question would stand somewhat thus:—

| | |
|---|---|
| Salaries. | Efficiency. |
| Uniforms. | Saving in waste. |
| Rations. | Saving in wear of appliances. |
| Quarters. | Detection of malingering. |
| | Curable cases more quickly fit for discharge. |
| | Increased sick ward accommodation. |
| | Training of probationers. |

The diminution of suffering consequent on skilled nursing is a gain which cannot be expressed.

One important point remains. Much evil frequently results from the continuance in office of nurses long incapacitated by ill-health or advancing years.

It is obviously very desirable to guard against this, by enabling nurses to retire when they are no longer able to discharge their duties with efficiency.

The Guardians are aware of the powers which they possess as regards granting superannuation allowances, and attention may be especially directed to the facilities which are now afforded to nurses for making provision against sickness and old age.

ARTHUR DOWNES, M.D., *Inspector*.

Local Government Board,
*April*, 1892.

## APPENDIX M.

### *Visiting Committees.*

POOR LAW BOARD,
WHITEHALL, *6th July*, 1868.

SIR,—The attention of the Poor Law Board has been called by reports recently received from their Inspectors, with regard to certain unions, to the imperfect way in which Articles 148 and 149 of the General Consolidated Order are not unfrequently observed by Guardians throughout the country. Although, at the commencement of each parochial year, a Visiting Committee is almost always appointed in accordance with Article 148, the Board are led to believe that this Committee does not invariably, in the performance of its duty, " carefully examine the workhouse once in every week at the least, examine the stores, and afford, so far as is practicable, to the inmates an opportunity of making any complaints; " in still fewer unions does the Committee reply every week to the queries that are printed in " *The Visitor's Book.*" The Board attach the greatest importance to the careful and punctual discharge of the prescribed duties by the Visiting Committee, as it is upon their supervision that the efficient management of the workhouse must mainly depend. If the workhouse be carefully examined once, at least, in every week, the books of the medical officer and chaplain inspected, the stores examined, and if an opportunity of stating any complaint they may have to make be afforded to the inmates, no irregularity can long remain unnoticed; while if the queries in the *Visitor's Book* are answered—not as a matter of form, but after careful inquiry—the Guardians would have before them, from time to time, full information upon all material facts connected with the state of the workhouse and its management. In order to render this information of practical value to the Guardians, the attention of the Committee should be specially directed to the following matters :—

"*Query* 1.—Is the workhouse, with its wards, offices, yards, and appurtenances, clean and well ventilated in every part?—and is the bedding in proper order?—if not, state the defect or omission."

In reply to this query, the Committee should satisfy themselves whether there is any structural defect in any part of the house; whether painting or limewashing is required; whether the wards are clean and provided with such conveniences as lockers or shelves, so that they may be kept in proper order; whether there is any defect in the construction or drainage of privies, or in the general sewerage of the house; whether the yards are defective as airing courts for adults or places of recreation for children. The attention of the Visiting Committee should be carefully directed to the subject of ventilation, which should be effected by special means, apart from the usual means of doors, windows, and fireplaces, and should be so arranged that each ward may be brought into uninterrupted communication with the open air. Although it is the duty of the medical officer to report to the Guardians any defect that may exist in the means of ventilation, yet it is most desirable that the Visiting Committee should satisfy themselves by inspection that there is no defect under this head. The beds and bedding should always be inspected, so that the Committee may be satisfied that they are in proper order. The Board avail themselves of this opportunity of suggesting that, for ordinary dormitories, bedsteads should be not less than 2 feet 6 inches wide, made of iron, with flexible (galvanised) laths; that the beds, whether of feathers, cocoa fibre, carded flock, cut straw, or chaff, should be properly made, kept full, and in good condition. A piece of cocoa-fibre matting or other material, or a mattress should be placed between the bedstead and the bed. A sufficient supply of blankets, sheets, bedroom furniture and conveniences, should be provided.[1]

"*Query* 2.—Do the inmates of the workhouse, of all classes, appear clean in their persons, and decent and orderly in their behaviour, and is their clothing regularly changed?"

Before replying to this query, the Committee should satisfy themselves that sufficient means for ensuring personal cleanliness are provided; that a convenient lavatory, as well as a bath, with water laid on, and supplied with towels, soap, and combs, is accessible to each class; also that there is a sufficient supply of clothing to enable all the inmates to have the requisite change.

"*Query* 3.—Are the inmates of each sex employed and kept at work as directed by the Guardians, and is such work unobjectionable in its nature? If any improvement can be suggested in their employment, state the same."

Suitable occupation should be provided for all inmates who are capable of doing any work, and the Visiting Committee should satisfy themselves, by inquiry from the officers and the inmates, that the work is so provided, and that it is unobjectionable in its character.

"*Query* 4.—Are the infirm of each sex properly attended to according to their several conditions?"

The Visiting Committee cannot satisfactorily answer this question without personally communicating with the aged and infirm inmates in their several wards. As a general rule it will be desirable that the officers of the workhouse

---

[1] To facilitate inquiry, and to insure an accurate record being kept of the furniture, bedding, linen, crockery, books, etc., assigned to each ward, an inventory of these articles should be printed for each, and placed in a conspicuous position in the ward. This will be found especially desirable in the sick wards. The number of beds for which each ward is limited may be also conveniently recorded in the same manner. (See No. 14.)

should not be present at interviews between the Visiting Committee and the nmates.

"*Query* 5.—Are the boys and girls in the school properly instructed as required by the regulations of the Commissioners, and is their industrial training properly attended to?"

In visiting the schools, the Committee should examine the school attendance book and the chaplain's report, and should ascertain, not only whether the whole of the children who are of school age attend school, either for at least three hours every day, or for an aggregate of 18 hours in the week, but also whether provision is made for imparting to them some systematic industrial training. There are very few workhouses in which arrangements might not be made for employing boys in some suitable out-door work, and girls in sewing, knitting, and washing. The Guardians will, the Board feel convinced, see the advantage of making such arrangements, and the Visiting Committee should ascertain at each inspection that such arrangements are carried out.

"*Query* 6.—Are the young children properly nursed and taken care of, and do they appear in a clean and healthy state?"

In every workhouse in which there are several children too young to attend school, a separate nursery, dry, spacious, light, and well ventilated, should be provided, and should be suitably furnished. In no case should the care of young children be intrusted to infirm or weak-minded inmates. Unless young children are placed under responsible supervision they cannot be said to be "properly taken care of," and the Committee should never fail to make careful inquiry under this head.

"*Query* 7.—Is regular attendance given by the medical officer? Are the inmates of the sick wards properly tended? Are the nurses efficient? Is there any infectious disease in the workhouse?"

The Workhouse Medical Relief Book should always be inspected by the Committee, and every attendance which is given, otherwise than by the medical officer in person, should be noticed, in order that the Guardians may ask for an explanation. The Committee will generally be able to ascertain, by freely communicating with the inmates in the sick wards, and by inquiry from the medical officer and the master and matron, whether the sick are properly attended to and the nursing is sufficient. In the sick wards of larger workhouses provision should be made for night nursing, and in all workhouses means of communication should be established between the sick wards and the sleeping apartment of some one of the officers. In answering the question, Is there any infectious disease in the workhouse? the Committee should satisfy themselves as to whether efficient means exist for separating infectious from other cases, and every defect should be brought under the notice of the Guardians.

"*Query* 8.—Is there any dangerous lunatic or idiot in the workhouse?"

The Committee should never fail to bring under the notice of the Guardians any case of the detention of a dangerous lunatic in the workhouse for a longer period than is absolutely necessary to effect removal to an asylum.

"*Query* 9.—Is divine service regularly performed? Are prayers regularly read?"

The Committee should ascertain from the chaplain's book whether divine service is regularly performed. In those workhouses in which no chaplain is appointed, the Guardians would, of course, be desirous of affording to the inmates an opportunity of attending the place of worship of the religious persuasion to which they belong. The duty of reading prayers, according to Article 124, should be discharged either by the master or the schoolmaster.

"*Query* 10.—Is the established dietary duly observed, and are the prescribed hours of meals regularly adhered to?"

As there is no subject upon which complaints are more frequently made by inmates of workhouses than their dietary, careful inquiry should always be made from the inmates of the several classes before the Committee reply to this question, and the Committee should ascertain, not only whether there is any complaint as to the quantity and quality of the food, but as to the hours and mode of serving it. As the Committee would doubtless frequently visit the workhouse either during the hours of meals or while meals were being prepared, they would have an opportunity of ascertaining whether there was any ground of complaint, either as to the preparation of the food, or its mode of distribution. This should be especially noticed with reference to the sick.

"*Query* 11.—Are the provisions and other supplies of the qualities contracted for?"

The Committee should never fail to visit the store-rooms and inspect the stores, and ascertain whether the delivery of articles of consumption by contractors takes place at sufficiently short intervals.

"*Query* 12.—Is the classification properly observed according to Articles 98 and 99?"

In answering this question the Committee should not be satisfied with a formal reply, which is too frequently given, that the classification is observed "as far as possible," or "as far as the arrangements of the house allow," but should specify every deviation from articles 98 and 99.

"*Query* 13.—Is any complaint made by any pauper against any officer, or in respect of the provisions or accommodations? If so, state the name of the complainant, and the subject of the complaint."

The Board desire to repeat here the suggestion already made, that the fullest opportunity should be given to the inmates of all classes to state any complaint they may have to make, and for this purpose the Committee should communicate with them, not in the presence of the officers.

"*Query* 14.—Does the present number of inmates in the workhouse exceed that fixed by the Poor Law Commissioners?"

In replying to this question the Committee should ascertain not merely whether the total number for which the workhouse is certified has been exceeded, but whether the number of any one class exceeds the accommodation available for it.—I am, etc.,

H. FLEMING, *Secretary*.

The Clerk to the Guardians.

## APPENDIX N.

### Assistance from Charitable Sources.

Upon the question of charity-income to persons in receipt of relief the opinion of the Local Government Board was expressed in 1879 to a guardian of the Bangor and Beaumaris Union in the following terms:—

"With regard to your inquiry the Board direct me to state that they do not see that they can do more than state the general principle applicable to it, *viz.*, that it is the duty of the guardians to relieve persons according to their actual necessities, and that, in judging of the amount of relief required in any case, they should take into consideration all the means of subsistence possessed by the applicant, whether derived from charitable gifts or other sources."

[From information supplied to us by Mr. Baldwyn Fleming.]

# INDEX.

ABLE-BODIED, Workhouse test to be applied to, 160. See *Out-door Labour Test Unemployed, Widows.*
Able-bodied Pauper, definition of, 131, 132 (note), 135; difficulty of finding suitable work for, 168; work for, 169-171.
Able-bodied Pauperism, decrease of, 10, 174, 175, 217; practically got rid of, 135.
Abuses of Out-door Relief, 66-68.
Accommodation in Workhouse, effects of inadequate, 19. See *Classification of Paupers.*
Administration of Poor Law, conditions of good, 16, 28; Mr. Longley's suggestions for improvement in, 101; results of improved, 220.
Aged and Infirm, reasons for granting out-door relief to, 133, 134.
Aged Married Couples. See *Married Couples.*
Almshouse, Workhouse must not become an, 136.
Applicant for Relief, questions to be answered by . . . . . in St. Cuthbert's parish, Edinburgh, 28; should attend meetings of board of guardians, 121, 122; statements of . . . . . to be verified, 28.
Application and Report Book, heads of information, 25 (note); to be properly kept, 25-27; to be supervised weekly, 236.
Applications for Relief, how to deal with, 20-46.
Army Pensioners, pensions of . . . . . should be paid weekly, 212.
Assistant Relieving Officer, not recommended, 40.
Atcham Union, compared as to pauperism with England and Wales, 4; its pauperism and expenditure on relief, 81, 82, 84; reduction of its pauperism since 1836, 3; its rules as to out-door relief, 95; its system of inquiry, 30-33.

Benefit Societies, growth injured by out-door relief, 69, 70, 237.
Bethnal Green Union, its administration compared with that of the Whitechapel Union, 85 (note).
Birmingham Union, diagram showing decrease of pauperism, 197; pauperism and expenditure on relief in the, 81, 82-84.
Boarding out of pauper children, its advantages, 151.
Bradfield Union, compared with Hungerford Union, 112; good effects of change of policy, 87; pauperism and expenditure on relief, 80, 82, 84.
"Breaking up the Home," 73-75, 91.
Brixworth Union, compared with Daventry Union, 112; effects of reform in, 7, 90; pauperism and expenditure on relief, 80, 82, 84.
Bury, Rev. Canon, Report on administration of Poor Law in Brixworth, 7.
Bye-laws as to Out-door Relief, advantage of, 93, 97; forms of, 93-96; necessary for Relief Committees, 43-45; recommended by Local Government Board, 94; suggestion that they should have force of Orders, and objection to proposal, 202, 204. See *Rules.*

"Case-Fee" System, of medical relief, 123.
"Case-paper" System, 33-38; how worked, 38 (note); forms, 35-38.
"Case Work," neglect of, 21.
Central Authority, necessity for the interference of the, 6, 7.
Central Poor Law Conference, 1876, proposals for reform, 203.
Chamberlain's Circular of 1886, Mr., Mr. Murray Browne's suggestions for applying 177; cannot be acted on generally, and why, 176; text of, 241.
Change of Policy, how to be effected, 46-49; instances of Bradfield and Whitechapel, 47.
Charity, best form of, 91; co-operating with Poor Law, 49-51, 91; its function, 91, 233.
Child Pauperism, decrease of, 135, 138, 218.

Children, boarding out of, 151; care of them in workhouse, 246; compelling them to support their parents, 211; district school system, 150; modes of dealing with them, 147; village school system, 148-150; workhouse schools satisfactory, 148 (note). See *Boarding Out, District School, Village School.*
Children of Widows, answer to objection against taking them into the house, 144. See *Widows.*
Classification of Paupers, 17, 105, 106, 244; beneficial effects of, 106.
Classification by Workhouses, 105-108; difficult in country, 107; easy in towns, *ib.*
Clothing of Workhouse Inmates, 78, 136, 247.
Comparative Statistics, (*a*) As to general pauperism: Atcham and England, 4; Bethnal Green and Whitechapel, 85; Bradfield and Hungerford, 58, 112; Brixworth and Daventry, 58, 112; Farringdon, Wokingham, Eton, Buckingham, Bicester, and Henley, 61; Holbeach and Spilsby, 60; Mr. Lockwood's district, 62; Spalding and Brigg, 60. (*b*) As to old age pauperism, 134; Aylesbury and Thames, 133; Bradfield and Wallingford with Wantage and Henley, *ib.*; Hawarden and Holywell, *ib.*; Newtown and Llanidloes, *ib.*; Ruthin and Corwen, *ib.*
Control of Relief, how guardians can obtain the, 26.
Co-operation between Poor Law and Charity, 15, 48, 49-51, 232. See *Exceptional Distress.*
Co-operation between Poor Law and Public Authorities, 16, 51, 52.
Corn-grinding, as work for the able-bodied, 169.
Cross-visiting, 40, 95.

Decrease of Pauperism, reasons for, 26, 195, 199, 202; in certain unions, 80-82; in-door pauperism decreases with out-door pauperism, 79-82.
Depression of Trade, a cause of pauperism, 199.
Deserted Wives, how to deal with, 94, 152, 179; practice in Poplar Union, 153.
Destitution, what constitutes, 53; alone gives right to relief, 233.
Detention of Paupers, 210, 211.
Diary of Relieving Officer, 27.
Dietaries of Workhouse Inmates, 248.
Dispensary System, 128-130; not to be considered permanent, 130; open to abuse and demoralising, 129.
Distribution of Relief, 42.
District Medical Officers, attending meetings of guardians, 23, 236; advantages of the practice, 23, 24.
District School System, its advantages, 150.
Dole System, evils of, 62-66, 77.
Dorking and Dunmow Unions, rules for out-door relief, 96.

Earnings, effect of out-door relief on, 54-62.
Economy, the argument of, . . . . in favour of out-door relief, 78, 83-86.
Employer, reference to applicant's, 28.
England and Wales, diagram showing decrease of pauperism, 197.
English Poor Law, fundamental doctrine of, 233. See *Principles of English Poor Law.*
Evasion of Poor Law Orders, 171-173.
Exceptional Distress. Co-operation of Poor Law with charity, 180, 189, 190-192, 193. How dealt with in Aston, 189; in Birmingham, 183-185; in Bolton, 178-182; in St. George's-in-the-East, 193; in London, 185-188; in Northumberland, 182; in Norwich, 190; in Reading, 188; in Uxbridge, *ib.*; and in Whitechapel, 192. Lessons to be learnt from experience in dealing with, 193; Mr. Macdonald's recommendations for dealing with, *ib.*
Expenditure on Poor Relief does not increase so fast as population, 219; reasons for increase, 218. See also *Statistics.*
Expenditure per head of population no test of good or bad administration, 86.

Foresters, Ancient Order of, increase in membership since 1852, 202.
Forms used in Paddington in case-paper system, 35-38.
Friendly Societies, their growth, 202; injured by out-door relief, 69, 70, 87, 88, 238; how to deal with applications for relief from members of, 157-159; relief to members of 238.
Furniture of Paupers, storage of, 213.

General Order of 1847, Articles 98 and 99, 17.
St. George's-in-the-East Union, pauperism and expenditure, 80, 82, 84.
St. George's (Hanover Square) Union, pauperism and expenditure, 81, 82, 84.

Goschen's Circular of 1869, Mr., 5, 232.
Grandchildren to support grandparents, 203, 204.
Guardians, how they can reduce pauperism, 10 ; personal influence of, 21.
Guildford Union, rules regulating out-door relief, 96 (note).

Hair Teazing, objection to it as work for paupers, 169.
Hearts of Oak Friendly Society, its growth since 1852, 202.

Illegitimate Children, great decrease in number of pauper, 138 (note).
Imbeciles, care of them in workhouse, 246; but should be dealt with in a separate establishment, 108.
Improvidence a cause of pauperism, 201.
Increase of Pauperism, reasons for, 5, 21, 195, 199-201.
Index Books, "case-paper" system, 33.
In-door Pauperism, reasons for increase of, 196; statistics, 196 (note 2).
In-door Relief, advantages of, 20, 79-92; always adequate, 63, 77; arguments against, 72-78; causes relations to assist, 88-90; the difficult path, 76; economical, 83-86; encourages thrift and providence, 68, 87, 88; does not act harshly, 76-78; in cases of widows, 139-147.
Infirmaries, 18, 128.
Inquiry, methods of. Atcham, 30-33; Paddington, 33-38; Whitchurch, 38.
Inspectors of Out-door Relief, 95.
Interference of Central Authority, reasons for, 6.
Isolation Hospitals, importance of, 18.

Kind, advantages of relief in, 99, 100.

Labour-yards, advertisement for starving people, 162; their defects, 161, 164; their discontinuance does not crowd workhouse, 165; not economical, 163; effects of closing them in Nottingham, 165, and in West Bromwich, *ib.*; effects of opening them in Birmingham, 168, and in Kendal, 166; orders for them to be given week by week, 94; preferred to workhouse, 161, 162; should be only opened temporarily, 164. See *Out-door Labour Test.*
Leicester, effect of workhouse test in 1858 in, 14, 20.
Lists of Paupers, 46, 51, 234; might be published periodically in local paper, 237.
Loan, grant of relief on, 99, 122-124, 237; Bradfield system, 123; St. Neot's system, *ib.*
Longley, Mr., his suggestions for improvements in administration, 235.
Lunatics, reason for increase of, 2 (note 2).

Macdonald, Mr., his plan for dealing with exceptional distress, 193.
Magistrates, duty of, in prosecutions of a pauper, 51.
Manchester Union, diagram showing decrease of pauperism in, 197; pauperism and expenditure on relief of, 81, 82, 84; reasons for decrease of population, 81; rules as to out-door relief, 96.
Mansion-House Fund, history of the—a warning, 186-188.
Married Couples in Workhouse, 18, 155-157; instances of their objecting to live together, 156.
Meals of Workhouse Inmates, 247.
Mean Pauperism, meaning of, 9, 80.
Medical Extras, abuse of, 116, 119.
Medical Orders, not to be given to out-patients of hospitals, 237.
Medical Relief, abuse of, 116; Bradfield system, 123; careful inquiry before granting, 119; circular of 1869, 5; generally, 114-130; how to reduce it to a minimum, 119; how long it should be given, 236; Milton Union Medical Club, 125; objections to, 115; powers of overseers, 120; regarded as different from other out-door relief, 115; reports on, 6; St. Neot's system, 123; to be granted on loan if possible, 122, 123; value should be placed upon it and reason, 204; why it is given, 114, 115.
"Medical Relief Only," 115.
Medical Societies, 124-128; importance of, 127.
"Merits of the Case," 96, 97.
Middlesborough Union, rules as to out-door relief, 96 (note).
Milton Union Medical Club, 125-127.

Necessaries of Life, their cheapness tends to reduce pauperism, 202.

Neglect of parents by children, 88-90.
St. Neot's Union, pauperism and expenditure, 81, 82, 84.
Non-Resident Paupers, 157.
Norwich Union, rules as to out-door relief, 96 (note).
Not-able-bodied Pauperism, decrease in, 175, 218.
Nursing in Workhouses, 245.

Oddfellows (Manchester Unity), growth of the order since 1852, 202.
Officers of Workhouse, qualifications for, 248.
Old Age Pauperism, reasons for, 135; will eventually disappear, 136. See *Aged and Infirm, Comparative Statistics, Statistics.*
Orphan and Deserted Children. See *Children.*
Out-door Labour Test, causes discontent, 164; costly, 163; demoralising, 162, 166; does not deter, 162; encourages idea of State finding work, 162; how to apply it, 179; more eligible than in-door relief, 162; no substitute for workhouse test, 165; no test of destitution, 20; renders discipline impossible, 163; in cases of women, 179, 181. See *Labour-yards, Workhouse Test.*
Out-door Pauperism, decrease of, 195; statistics from 1861-1870, 5.
Out-door Relief, advantages of restricting, 49, 79-92, 220; affects wages and earnings, 54-62, 65; alleged to be economical, 78, 83-86; alleged to be humane, 73-78; cause of old age pauperism, 133; causes discontent, 68; cost of, 5; demoralises, 59, 65, 91, 181; destructive of thrift and providence, 68-71, 87, 88, 92; easy to give, 76, 221; evils attaching to, 52-71, 77, 91, 92; how to minimise the evils of, 93-103; how long to grant, 94, 204, 206; inadequate, 62-66, 77, 91; impossible to prohibit, 102, 203, 209, 214; in-door pauperism not increased by restriction of, 79-82, 198; liable to abuse, 66, 68; no charity, 49; not economical, 83-86; not harsh to restrict, 90-92; not to be granted to able-bodied women and deserted wives, 94; Paddington system as to, 33; reasons for giving, 72-78, 104, 105; relations prompted to help by restriction of, 88-90; reports on, 5, 6; rules as to grant of, 94, 95, 96; should be the exception and not the rule, 93, 181; unnecessary to have more stringent regulations as to, 101-103. See also *Medical Relief.*
Out-door Relief Prohibitory Order, 3, 54, 103, 160; Mr. Longley's suggestions, 209; objections to making the order universal, *ib.*; objection to proposed alterations in, 207-209.
Out-door Relief Regulation Order, 52, 160; evasion of, 171-173.
Out-door Relief to Widows, cases to which it should be limited, 237; causes husband not to insure, 140; concealment of means, 141; discourages providence, 139; instances of its abuse, 141; keeps down wages and earnings, 142, 233; makes them dependent, 140.
Overseer, his powers as to medical relief, 120; his duty, 121.

Paddington Union, case-paper system, 33-38; pauperism and expenditure on relief, 81, 82, 84.
"Parish Pay," 71.
Pay Stations, evils of, 42.
Pauperism, causes affecting increase and decrease of, 195-202; dependant on administration, 59-62, 79-82, 133, 134. 197; and not much affected by other causes, 183, 184, 195, 198, 199-201; not dependant on wages, 58-62; nor on population, 82; reduction of pauperism, 9, 10, 79, 174, 195; its repression not local but national, 7.
Pauper Taint, 110, 111.
Permanent List, 47, 66, 97; opposed to economical administration, 97.
Permanently Unemployed, class included in the description, 176; how to deal with, *ib.*
Personal Influence of Guardians, 21, 44.
Pocket-Book for Relieving Officer, Atcham Union, 31.
Poor Law, in 1834, 1, 11. See *Principles of English Poor Law.*
Poor Law Administration, in London, 1873, 6; its true object, 215; policy of, 199.
Poor Law Amendment Act, 1834, effect of, 2.
Poor Law Conferences, their effect, 8.
Poor Law Dispensaries. See *Dispensary System.*
Poplar Workhouse for the Able-bodied, 105.
Powers of Guardians, sufficient, 102.
Principles of English Poor Law, 11-15, 25, 49, 222, 233; reasons for not acting on, 221 222.

# INDEX.

Prohibition of Out-door Relief, impossible and impolitic, 101, 102, 214.
Prohibitory Order, 54, 103, 160, 171.
Provident Dispensaries, 124-128.
Public Authorities, co-operation between Poor Law and, 51
Public Relief Works. See *Relief Works*.

Questions to be answered by applicant for relief in St. Cuthbert's, Edinburgh, 28.

Reading Union, pauperism and expenditure on relief in, 81, 82, 84.
Record Book, Whitchurch Union, 38.
Reduction of Pauperism, Atcham Union, 3; since 1834, 2, 4; since 1849, 225-228; since 1870, 2, 3, 9, 10, 79.
Reforms in Administration, 203-214; in certain unions, 7, 90; must be gradual, 221.
Regulations as to Out-door Relief, 101-103.
Reigate Union, rules regulating grant of out-door relief in, 96 (note).
Relations, applicant for relief and, 88-90, 95, 137.
Relief, in aid of wages, 55, 58; distribution of, 42; how a board gets control of, 26; should be recoverable, 204; two ways only of granting, 54.
Relief Committees, not recommended, 42-45, 236; should change about, 45; should consist of at least three guardians, 43.
Relief Districts, size of, 39, 40.
Relief in Kind, advantages of, 99, 100.
Relief Lists, each case to be dealt with at ordinary meetings, 98; quarterly revisions not sufficient, 98, 99.
Relief Orders should be stamped as "Pauper Relief," 237.
Relief Order Book in Atcham Union, 31, 32.
Relief Works, evil effects of, 177; only a palliative, 178.
Relieving Officers, diary, 27; duties generally, 24-27, 41, 42, 231; in cases of medical relief, 120; and where house has been offered and refused, 109; number of, 39, 40; pocket-book, 31; visits to be frequent, 41, 42, 95.
Removal of Applicant for Relief to Workhouse, arguments in favour of making it compulsory in certain cases, 204, 205.
Repression of Pauperism, national and not local, 7.
Restriction of Out-door Relief, advantages of, 49, 79-92.
Revision of Relief Lists, 33, 98; quarterly revisions inefficient, 98, 99.
Rules as to Out-door Relief, 93-96; advantage of having, 93, 97; in Atcham Union, 95; in Manchester Union, 96; rules recommended by Local Government Board, 94. See *Bye-laws*.

Scales of Allowances, 65, 66.
Sick, treatment of the, 18, 128-130, 245.
Size of Relief Districts, 39, 40.
Starvation, the offer of the house does not endanger, 75, 76, 108-110.
Statistics, Atcham Union, 3; Brixworth Union, 7, 90; decrease of pauperism since 1870, 9, 10; decrease of able-bodied adult male pauperism since 1849, 226, and since 1870, 174; decrease of able-bodied adult female pauperism since 1849, 226; decrease of able-bodied and not-able-bodied adult pauperism since 1870, 175; decrease in child pauperism, 135, 138, 218, 228; decrease of not-able-bodied adult male paupers since 1849, 227; decrease of not-able-bodied adult female paupers since 1849, *ib.*; decrease of out-door pauperism, 195; decrease of pauperism in England and Wales since 1849, 197, 225; decrease of pauperism in Birmingham, Manchester, and Whitechapel since 1870, 197; decrease of pauperism and of expenditure on relief in certain "in-door" unions, 80-85; statistical effect of the application of workhouse test in a London Union, 216; increase of in-door pauperism, 196 (note 2); increase in membership of Friendly Societies, 201; expenditure on relief in England and Wales, and in the Metropolis, 229, 230; variations in old age pauperism, 133, 134; variation in pauperism and expenditure on relief from 1860 to 1870. See also *Comparative Statistics*.
Stepney Union, pauperism and expenditure on relief in, 80, 82, 84.
"Stigma of Pauperism," 78, 176, 247. See *Taint of Pauperism*.
Stone-yards. See *Labour-yards, Out-door Labour Test*.
Strikes, evil effects of, 180, 181, 182, 201; affect pauperism, 200.
Sunderland Union, rules as to out-door relief in, 96 (note).

Taint of Pauperism, 110, 111.
Temporarily Unemployed, The, Bolton strike, 178-182; cause of, 178; how Birmingham acted in 1879 and 1887, 183-185; how to deal with, 178-194, 188; Mansion-House experiment a failure, 186-188; Mr. Macdonald's suggestions, 193; Northumberland coal strike, 182.
"Test House," 161; effect of, 168; in Birmingham, 166-168.
Thrift and Providence, 68-71, 87, 88, 140.

Unemployed, The, easily assembled, 186; no statistics of their number, 174; a problem how to be dealt with, 163. See *Exceptional Distress, Permanently Unemployed, Temporarily Unemployed.*

Vagrants, how encouraged, 2 (note 2).
Village School System, advantages of, 148, 150; disadvantages of, 148-150 Norwich system, 149.
Visiting Committees, 244, 251-254.
Visits of Relieving Officers, to be frequent and systematic, 41, 95, 236.

Wages and Earnings, adversely affected by out-door relief, 53-63, 142-147; in Atcham, 57, 143; in Bradfield, 57; pauperism not dependent on, 58-62.
Wallingford Union, pauperism and expenditure on relief in, 81, 82, 84.
"Watching the Case," objections to this course, 110.
Whitechapel Union, compared with Bethnal Green Union as to effects of administration, 85 (note); decrease of pauperism and diagram showing this, 197; pauperism and expenditure on relief in, 80, 82, 84-86.
Whitchurch Union, system of inquiry, 38.
Widowhood, an ordinary contingency of life, 140.
Widows, Bradfield system of dealing with, 145; careful inquiry necessary in applications for relief by, 143; cases in which relief should be refused to, 146; decrease in number of paupers, 138; reasons for taking into workhouse children of, 143; time limit for relief to, 147; why in-door relief should be offered to, 139-147; why out-door relief is given to, 139. See *Out-door Relief to Widows.*
Wives of Army Reserve Men, etc., how to deal with, 154.
Wives of Prisoners, how to deal with, 153.
Women, how to deal with able-bodied, 94; with illegitimate children, 154. See also *Widows, Wives.*
Wood-chopping, objections to employing pauper labour on, 169.
Workhouse, accommodation must be sufficient in, 17, 20, 182; effects of inadequate accommodation, 19, 161, 179; its hardships exaggerated, 137; not an almshouse, 136.
Workhouse administration, Circular of Local Government Board as to, 243.
Workhouse Inmates, children, 246; classification, 244; clothes, 247; dietary, 248; imbeciles, 246; liberty, 247; meals, *ib.*; nursing, 245, 249-251.
Workhouse officers, their qualification, 248.
Workhouse System, founded on practical experience, 112; instance of Leicester, 1858, 15; its success, 12-15, 20, 48, 111; objections met, 13, 83-86, 108-111.
Workhouse Test, advantage of, 164-171; Mr. Courtenay Boyle's proposals, 213; how to apply, 104-113; its effect, 113. See *Out-door Labour Test.*

*Printed by Cowan & Co., Limited, Perth.*

# THE CHARITY ORGANISATION SERIES.

## CHARITY ORGANISATION SERIES.

*Edited by C. S. Loch, Secretary to the London Charity Organisation Society. Cr. 8vo.*

1. Insurance and Saving. With an Introduction on the Poor Law as an Obstacle to Thrift and Voluntary Insurance, 2s. 6d.
2. The Feeble-minded Child and Adult: a Report on an Investigation of the Physical Condition of 50,000 School Children. With Suggestions for the Better Education and Care of this Afflicted Class, 2s. 6d.
3. The Epileptic and Crippled Child and Adult: a Report on the Present Condition of these Classes of Afflicted Persons. With Suggestions for their Better Education and Employment, 2s. 6d.
4. The Better Way of Assisting School Children, 2s. 6d.
5. The Better Administration of the Poor Law, 6s.
6. *(Shortly)* Records of Charity Organisation.

SINCE the establishment of the Society, the Council have from time to time published Reports of Special Committees and other Books and Papers bearing on various branches of charitable work. Some of these have had a wide circulation, and would, it is thought, have become better known to the general public if they had been published as volumes of a series. Accordingly, this plan of publication has now been adopted.

The Reports already issued include the following, which can be obtained at the Offices of the Council, 15 Buckingham Street, Strand, W.C.:—

Night Refuges (1870), 4d.
The Homeless Poor of London (1891), 1s.
Soup Kitchens* (1871), 1s.
Soup Kitchens* (Second Report, 1877), 3d.
Charity and Cheap Food (1887), 1s.
Medical Charities, with Rules for Provident Dispensaries* (1871), 6d.
Memorandum on the Medical Charities of the Metropolis (1889), 1s.
Voting Charities (1872), 1d.
Dwellings of the Poor* (1873), 6d.
Dwellings of the Poor* (Second Report, 1881), 1s.
Education and Care of Idiots, Imbeciles, and Harmless Lunatics (1877), 1s.

* These Reports are out of print.

The Feeble-minded, Epileptic, &c. (Interim Report, 1891), 3s. 6d.

Employment of Italian Children for Mendicant Purposes, &c. (1877), 1s.

The Training of the Blind (1878), 1s.

Exceptional Distress (1886), 6d.

The Preparation and Audit of Accounts of Charitable Institutions (1890), 1s.

School Children in Want of Food (1891), 6d.

On the new Series the same care has been bestowed as on the Reports previously issued.

C. S. LOCH, *Secretary.*

CHARITY ORGANISATION SOCIETY,
15 BUCKINGHAM STREET,
STRAND, W.C.